Modern American Grotesque

Modern American Grotesque

LITERATURE AND PHOTOGRAPHY

James Goodwin

 THE OHIO STATE UNIVERSITY PRESS / COLUMBUS

Library of Congress Cataloging-in-Publication Data

Goodwin, James, 1945–
   Modern American grotesque : Literature and photography / James Goodwin.
      p. cm.
   Includes bibliographical references and index.
   ISBN-13 : 978-0-8142-1108-3 (cloth : alk. paper)
   ISBN-10 : 0-8142-1108-9 (cloth : alk. paper)
   ISBN-13 : 978-0-8142-9205-1 (cd-rom)

   1. American fiction—20th century—Histroy and criticism. 2. Grotesque in literature. 3. Grotesque in art. 4. Photography—United States—20th century. I. Title.

   PS374.G78G66 2009
   813.009'1—dc22

                                    2009004573

This book is available in the following editions:
Cloth (ISBN 978-0-8142-1108-3)
CD-ROM (ISBN 978-0-8142-9205-1)

Cover design by Dan O'Dair
Text design by Jennifer Shoffey Forsythe
Typeset in Adobe Palatino

∞ The paper used in this publication meets the minimum requirements of the
American National Standard for Information Sciences—Permanence of Paper for
Printed Library Materials. ANSI Z39.48–1992.

9 8 7 6 5 4 3 2 1

For my children Christopher and Kathleen,
who already possess a fine sense of irony
and for whom I wish in time stoic wisdom as well

CONTENTS

ILLUSTRATIONS

ILLUSTRATIONS

ACKNOWLEDGMENTS

The purpose of the present study is to restore full meaning to cultural categories of the grotesque and to demonstrate their prominence and influence within modern American literature and photography. Over the years of research and writing spent on this subject I have benefited from the support of several institutions and individuals. Research and travel grants were provided by the Council on Research of the Academic Senate at UCLA. A summer stipend from the National Endowment for the Humanities funded research at the Library of Congress. The librarians and staff at the following institutions assisted with many research inquiries and requests: the Prints and Photographs Division of the Library of Congress; the Young Research Library and its Special Collections at UCLA; the Getty Research Institute; the Huntington Library; the Museum of Modern Art in New York; the International Center of Photography in New York; the Manuscript, Archives, and Rare Book Library at Emory University; and the Ina Dillard Russell Library at Georgia College and State University in Milledgeville. Like many researchers in American culture, I am particularly appreciative of materials in public domain made available online by the Library of Congress.

I am grateful to colleagues who have provided advice and encouragement along the way, particularly the two anonymous readers at the Press, Miles Barth, Paul Boyer, Richard Cross, Ronald Gottesman, and Cécile Whiting. Matt Dubord provided technical expertise in assistance with the illustrations. Sandy Crooms, Jennifer Shoffey Forsythe, and Eugene O'Connor at the Press have greatly facilitated the editorial and production process. And, as always, I am thankful to my wife, Andrea, and our children, Christopher and Kathleen, for our lives together during my years of work.

The Grotesque

ASK PEOPLE WHAT THEY FIND GROTESQUE in American life and many will readily offer examples from popular culture and its venues of tabloid journalism, talk shows, celebrity gossip, network reality programs, Internet Websites, and extreme movie genres. What Flannery O'Connor said in the 1950s of American mass culture—that the problem for a serious writer of the grotesque is "one of finding something that is *not* grotesque"—is incalculably truer today.[1] In making her assessment O'Connor acknowledges a familiar idiomatic sense of the grotesque that touches only the surface of the long cultural tradition designated by the term. This conversational sense commonly refers to an event or appearance noteworthy only for its bizarre or perverse qualities and only for its effects of shock or scandal. As contemporary culture is increasingly given over to these superficial senses of the grotesque, it is an appropriate time to understand the deeper, modern meanings the grotesque has in American culture.

Over the course of the twentieth century, a powerful cultural lineage of the modern grotesque evolved in the fiction of American writers Sherwood Anderson, Nathanael West, and Flannery O'Connor and in the images of American photographers Weegee and Diane Arbus. In their work the grotesque deploys a willfully oblique, partial, deforming, and contentious perspective that yields a comprehension of society and culture not otherwise possible. Their work presents by way of the grotesque an attitude toward history, to adapt a concept from the social thinker and literary critic Kenneth Burke. For all the excesses in imagination and form manifest in the grotesque, at a latent level the mode can be profoundly reductive. The grotesque figure and its meanings are designed to be detected and understood in terms of pronounced, and often absolute, contrasts. Much modern American literature and photography of the grotesque depends upon iconographic processes that enlarge awareness of the social sphere through delimiting one's perspective on it to antitheses such as perception/obscurity and light/dark. Contrastive structure is not only a formal property but a persistent theme of the grotesque as well in modes of both literary description and graphic depiction. The reductiveness one can associate with the grotesque is not in the end a matter of oversimplification but rather a radical procedure intended to disclose meanings otherwise obscured from *apprehension* in the phenomenal senses of this word: presentiment, perception, and comprehension.

Writing in the mid-1930s, Kenneth Burke asserted that the grotesque had persisted at least since the Renaissance as a common strain within cultures of the West to the point where it presently functioned as one of the underlying "attitudes toward history" evident in contemporary life. Along with tragedy, comedy, the elegy, satire, and didacticism, the grotesque operates, in Burke's estimation, as a primary poetic and symbolic mode and configures "the mental equipment (meanings, attitudes, character) by which one handles the significant factors of his time."[2] While its categories reiterate canons of literature, Burke's discussion is as concerned with "ideological architecture" and questions of belief in matters of politics and religion as it is with poems or novels (*Attitudes*, 58). His account of specific attitudes toward history derives from a general principle that guides much in Burke's work, namely that mind, in being "formed by language, is formed by a *public grammar*" (*Attitudes*, 341). And thus linguistic and symbolic modes or "actions," no matter how seemingly individualized in their expression, are always to be understood within larger frames of shared consciousness.

The grotesque gains insight into the historical meaning of a current situation whether in politics or culture, according to Burke's definition, through a perspective animated by incongruity. As distinct from the genre of comedy, however, the grotesque is a "cult of incongruity *without* the laughter" (*Attitudes*, 58). In using this idea, the present study does not claim that the grotesque is without comedy. Indeed, sometimes the comedy is great, as with the fatuous and narcissistic Hollywood types that Nathanael West delineates in *The Day of the Locust* and with the encounters between preacher and wanton women that Flannery O'Connor renders in *Wise Blood*. And a viewer will find much deadpan humor in photographs by Weegee and Diane Arbus. The modern grotesque does not require, however, any of the staples of comedy. Pure comedy is the most convivial of genres. While the grotesque is no less significant as a social genre, it is not sociable in its cultural means. The current discussion does not treat comedy as a dominant strain of the modern grotesque.

To develop perspective, the grotesque often transposes a paradigm across logical boundaries even though such an application may seem at first irrelevant, incoherent, or anarchic. In the process the grotesque functions as a method ultimately for disclosing a deep, shared structure among political, spiritual, and aesthetic domains. As an attitude adopted toward history for such purposes, the grotesque is by definition icono-clastic. To characterize the symbolic function of the grotesque, Burke terms it a means of "seeing in the dark" conducted through a "mystical reversal of the customary meanings for dark and light" (*Attitudes*, 59). Modern conditions that provoke consciousness to resort to the grotesque result from confusion within mass society over cultural values and from fissures within traditional institutions of power. At the time of Burke's reflections on the grotesque the dominant causes of such conditions in the West obviously were pandemic economic depression and the rise of fascism. Preliminary to further consideration of the grotesque in modern American contexts, it is helpful to retrace some paths that the term's meanings have taken.

ORIGINS

From its origins in Renaissance Italy to its frequent associations with modern art and literature, the term *grotesque* reflects a far-ranging migra-tion in meaning. The Italian word *grottesco* was coined in the late fifteenth century in response to archaeological discoveries made at the time of an unfamiliar ornamental style that dated back to the classical era of Rome. Examples of this style were first found among underground rooms (*grotte* in Italian, *cryptae* in Latin) of excavated Roman palaces and villas. Painted on the wall and ceiling sections, pilasters, and other prominent archi-tectural features, these designs employed a variety of organic, ordinary, metamorphic, and purely imaginary forms, and the forms were brought together in irregular, unexpected combinations, unrelated in scale or sub-ject matter. The play of fantasy and the direct appeal to visual delight in the grotesque style, without apparent thematic import, seemed to belong to a cultural realm set against the formalism, symmetries, and solemnity of the classical architecture and design that were familiar up to the time of these Renaissance discoveries.

Figure 1.1. Detail from the Domus Aurea, Rome (later first century CE)

At the time of its origins, long before the word *grotesque* was available, the Roman engineer and architect Vitruvius of the first century BCE condemned the new fashion for fantastic compositions in wall decorations. Vitruvius was affronted by an "improper taste of the present" that disdains "definite representations taken from definite things" and that has displaced the "reasoned scheme" of realist architectural motifs traditional to such decor. His account of the style provides a detailed depiction of the early grotesque: "Instead of columns there rise up stalks; instead of gables, striped panels with curled leaves and volutes. Candelabra uphold pictured shrines and above the summits of these, clusters of thin stalks rise from their roots in tendrils with little figures seated upon them at random. Again, slender stalks with heads of men and of animals attached to half the body."[3] Particularly offensive to him are the style's free use of heterogeneous and hybrid forms and its casual animation and anthropomorphism. Irrespective of any such protestations, the style that would be named grotesque in the Renaissance gained great prominence in Imperial Rome.

The palace complex Domus Aurea (literally, "Golden House") designed in 64 CE for Emperor Nero, and located in the center of the ancient city, featured such decoration extensively (fig. 1.1). The Domus Aurea was one of the major ancient sites excavated and studied later in the fifteenth century.⁴ The main building far exceeded the dimensions of previous palaces, and its murals and painted vaults were rich with fanciful designs unmotivated by nature or reason. Roman craftsmen and artists were profligate with their powers of invention in producing motifs commonly associated with the early grotesque. These motifs often entail an impossible mixture of vegetal forms with real and imagined life figures. Thus, a vine can be entwined with an architectural feature that supports a human or divine figure that is decoratively linked with savage animals or nightmarish beasts. The linkage is often compressed to the point where a process of transmogrification is suggested. In a comparative treatment E. H. Gombrich has demonstrated the broad presence of such grotesque motifs within the world history of art, with examples dating from the second millennium before the Christian era and stretching regionally across Asia, the South Seas, Europe, and the Americas. Gombrich offers this vast reach of examples to confirm his general thesis that "there are invariant dispositions in the human mind which account for the development of certain common features in . . . art." To indicate the specific disposition involved, Gombrich has named his chapter on the grotesque "The Edge of Chaos," where he defines the mode as a "mixture of the sacred and the profane, the serious and the playful" and, following a remark by Albrecht Dürer, likens its heterogeneity to "dreamwork."⁵ Dürer's mixed use of the grotesque mode is quite apparent in the coat of arms he fashioned in 1500 for Emperor Maximilian (fig. 1.2).

Grotta is a linguistic adaptation in Italian of the earlier Latin term for a cave, cavern, underground vault, chamber, or passage, as is the Latin in relation to an earlier Greek word. Well before the erection and consecration of temples to gods in ancient Greece natural caves and grottoes were identified as sacred places. Naomi Miller attributes to such natural and man-made grottoes in antiquity, and well into the Enlightenment, a cultural dualism: "Contemplation and creation constitute the higher forces, the Apollonian side of the grotto. But in a world also connected with Pan, Dionysian agents may rule. Surely primal elements are present in the association of caves with preterhuman existence—with rites of birth and death, magic ceremonies, mantic powers, erotic bacchanalian orgies."⁶ To some degree, a misattribution of the root word *grotta* may be involved in the Renaissance derivation of *grottesco*. In ancient Greece the natural rock cavern had been considered to be an abode for nymphs and deities, and for the Muses in particular. While the cavern retained a traditional role as a sacred site, its distinctive topographical features were as often valued for the novel sensory and aesthetic experience they provided, and the term equally identified a picturesque, refreshing human retreat. This

Insignia Regie Maiestatis

Figure 1.2. Albrecht Dürer, Coat of Arms for Maximilian I as Roman King (1500). Courtesy of the Germanisches National Museum.

meaning was quickly extended to spaces either excavated or erected for the purpose of providing such repose. Though *discovered* underground near the end of the 1400s, some of the decorated Roman rooms called *grotta* probably stood above ground originally. Writing in the 1560s, Benvenuto Cellini thought that this was the case. Their subterranean location centuries later could be explained as the consequence of cycles of ruin and construction on the same site. Whether a misattibution has occurred or not, one root, literal meaning of the word *grotesque* retains the reference to a place of shade or semidarkness unearthed, brought to light.

To Renaissance artists and humanists the grotesque contradicted standards of representation, whose visual norms were defined by geometry in perspective and definitive categories of subject matter and genre. For all the associations of the grotesque in later centuries with repulsiveness, depravity, and terror, we do well to remember the grotto's original significance as an accommodating, hospitable, restorative place. In the contexts of classical aesthetics and Platonic metaphysics, Mark Dorrian has argued, the qualities of deformity and aberration attached to the grotesque are to be differentiated from monstrosity and the utterly terrifying. According to this distinction, the monstrous stands apart "as a sign of sin and transgression" and defies any prohibition or antidote that common culture can offer, while the disorder or defiance encountered within the grotesque is in the end contained and recuperated within a stronger sense of encompassing, even if at times contradictory, cultural values.[7] It takes the epic hero of classical tradition, who functions as a cynosure of society's idealized power and promise, to overcome the monster and its threat of annihilation. The vision of the modern age advanced by the Americans discussed here is, by comparison, certainly not epic or valorous, nor does it provide the reassurances possible when a worldview is aligned along an axis hero/monster. This circumstance remains true even for Flannery O'Connor, irrespective of her abiding interests in encounters with grace and in matters of the Devil.

In derivation, the grotesque refers explicitly to forms and themes that belong to the visual, decorative arts. Michel de Montaigne appears to be one of the first writers to effect a transfer in its meaning to include nonvisual expression, and literary style in particular. His essay "Of Friendship" from the 1570s opens with this reflection upon his creative process, quoted here in the Florio translation of 1603:

> Considering the proceeding of a painter's work [as] I have, a desire hath possessed me to imitate him. He maketh choice of the most convenient place and middle of every wall, there to place a picture labored with all his skill and sufficiency; and all void places about it he filleth up with antic boscage [foliage] or crotesko [grotesque] works, which are fantastical pictures having no grace but in the variety and strangeness of them. And what are these my compositions, in truth, other than antic works.[8]

The earliest meanings of *grotesque* in English, a word which appears in print by 1561, directly render the original Italian definitions and connotations, as evidenced by the variant above in Florio's translation. In stipulating "There are no *Grotesques* in nature; nor any thing framed to fill up empty cantons, and unnecessary spaces" some decades later, Sir Thomas Browne in *Religio Medici* (1643) dissociates the term from any purely natural feature and places it in the domain of artifice and human intentionality.[9] In early English usages, the effect of the grotesque upon an observer or reader is associated with fancy and the lightly humorous rather than with fear or the nightmarish, but by the end of the seventeenth century such connections are made.

A general idea of the sister arts that links verbal and visual expression has been active in Western thought since the classical period. The subject is of special interest to W. J. T. Mitchell, whose *Iconology: Image, Text, Ideology* examines the notions of complementarity between word and image among art theorists from Lessing and Edmund Burke to Nelson Goodman and E. H. Gombrich. In this study, as in his later collection of essays *Picture Theory: Essays on Verbal and Visual Representation,* Mitchell concludes that material and cultural differentials between the verbal and the visual predominate over all claims of reciprocity.[10] Nonetheless, when applied strictly to literature, the grotesque retains strong visual assumptions about its means and its impact. Within English and German Romantic literature, as Frederick Burwick has demonstrated, evocations of grotesque experience are typically correlated to disturbance or derangement in visual perception.[11] The two scholars to have conducted the most extensive surveys of the grotesque in Western art and literature, Wolfgang Kayser and Geoffrey Galt Harpham, offer divergent accounts of its development and of its presence in the modern period.

In Kayser's view, over its history the mode typically features the unnatural and monstrous products of the artist's imagination, and it often engages in a dissolution of reality with ominous and sinister effect. It creates an estranged world that remains finally incomprehensible to audiences. From his perspective in the 1950s, the contemporary fulfillment of the grotesque tradition is the theater of the absurd, and indeed Kayser's generalizations about aesthetic principles clearly have been made with this outcome in mind: "the unity of perspective in the grotesque consists in an unimpassioned view of life on earth as an empty, meaningless puppet play."[12] Where a satiric purpose was often ultimately served by the imagination's exploration of a fantastic, alienated, deformed world in previous centuries, the grotesque in the twentieth century, according to Kayser, traces an arbitrary course and it no longer signals a need for moral or social correctives.

To mount his inquiry, published in the early 1980s, Geoffrey Galt Harpham starts from premises of indeterminacy and of imaginary and intellectual free play, assumptions indebted to ideas in poststructuralism and deconstruction. For Harpham the grotesque has no narratable history as an artistic mode and thus it has no clear lines of cultural evolution. In the event, the grotesque marks a situation of the indefinable, "a condition of being just out of focus, just beyond the reach of language."[13] Fostered by conditions of paradox and parody, of language and aesthetic style turned against themselves, the grotesque in Harpham's account strongly inclines toward ambivalence and anomaly. Rather than social or historical understanding, it stimulates subconscious and mythopoeic responses. The grotesque does not mediate between the terms of its contradictions, and in not doing so it discloses the properties of contradiction essential to the artistic process itself. In his conclusions, Harpham associates the grotesque with the cultural origins of metaphor as two primal means of visual and literary figuration wherein "form itself resists the interpretation that it necessitates" (Harpham, 178).

In making correlations between the grotesque and the absurd Kayser presents the modern examples he has chosen as expressions of either a void condition or a chaotic fantasy state bordering on madness. While Kayser acknowledges a connection to tragicomedy, his idea of the absurd excludes any sense of tragic pathos or insight and any existential notion of individual fate. Harpham, through his own synchronic, nonhistorical approach, positions the grotesque among the farthest, aboriginal traces of human culture, in the earliest cave and burial sites and, equally, in the id, as well as alongside contemporary notions of an uncentered, endless process of signification in language and culture. By considering the grotesque to be in the final analysis a cultural mode that operates through "self-abolishing incongruity," Harpham situates it at a degree zero of representation and meaning (Harpham, 178). In these respects, the accounts by Kayser and Harpham prove unserviceable for my purposes in the present study, which aligns the modern grotesque with conventions of depiction and description in the arts and which recognizes its referential ground and its oppositional functions in regard to society's orthodoxies.

For a fuller sense of the grotesque as a visual tradition we should turn to John Ruskin's monumental study *The Stones of Venice* (1851–53). There Ruskin separates the grotesque into categories of the ignoble and the noble in accounting for the art and architecture of Venice in the medieval and Renaissance eras. In periodizing a decadent phase of Venetian life and culture that began in the 1420s, Ruskin designates it a "Grotesque Renaissance" that is characterized by "a delight in the contemplation of bestial vice, and the expression of low sarcasm, which is, I believe the most hopeless state into which the human mind can fall. This spirit of idiotic mockery is, as I have said, the most striking characteristic of the last period of the Renaissance."[14] For Ruskin, meaningful distinctions remain to be made between this false grotesque and a legacy of the true grotesque. The task is complicated, however, by the hybrid nature of the mode: "It seems to me that the grotesque is, in almost all cases, composed of two elements, one ludicrous, the other fearful; that, as one or other of these elements prevails, the grotesque falls into two branches, sportive grotesque and terrible grotesque; but that we cannot legitimately consider it under these two aspects, because there are hardly any examples which do not in some degree combine both elements; there are few grotesques so utterly playful as to be overcast with no shade of fearfulness, and few so fearful as absolutely to exclude all ideas of jest" (*Venice*, 3:115). The terms of conceptualization here point directly to the hybrid tragicomedy.

The basis for distinctions between the ignoble and the noble that Ruskin devised amounts to a differentiation of the unreflective craft of a mere artisan from the intentions and mastery of an artist. While a craftsman "can feel and understand nothing, and mocks at all things with the laughter of the idiot and the cretin," a "master of the noble grotesque knows the depth of all at which he seems to mock, and would feel it at another time, or feels it in a certain undercurrent of thought even while he jests with it" (*Venice*, 3:128). Pathos in response to human weakness and mortality ennobles the grotesque. With a master, "it is because the dreadfulness of the universe around him weighs upon his heart that his work is wild" (*Venice*, 3:130). Through the power of empathy a master's imagination is "narrowed and broken by the inconsistencies of the human capacity; and it would seem to be rare that any very exalted truth should be impressed on the imagination without some grotesqueness" (*Venice*, 3:139). The noble strain of the grotesque arises ultimately from thoughts of death, and the stress consequently falls upon the tragic within tragicomedy: "these [thoughts of death], partly degrading us by the instinctive and paralyzing terror with which they are attended, and partly ennobling us by leading our thoughts to dwell in the eternal world, fill the last and the most important circle in that great kingdom of dark and distorted power, of which we all must be in some sort the subjects" (*Venice*, 3:143). It is interesting to note here that Ruskin attributes a fundamental darkness to the powers of the grotesque.

With the third volume of *Modern Painters*, published in 1856, Ruskin returns to these considerations, now more broadly within art history.

While the artist's imagination in its most noble work obeys the laws of reason and historical objectivity, Ruskin argues, imagination also possesses inalienable capacities to function independently from natural appearances and social proprieties. In the latter instance there is "a strange connection between the reinless play of the imagination, and a sense of the presence of evil, which is usually more or less developed in those creations of the imagination to which we properly attach the word *Grotesque*."[15] For Ruskin, as for Flannery O'Connor in the next century, the terror and evil perceived through the grotesque abide as persistent, ungovernable forces.

In his own account of the grotesque, E. H. Gombrich subscribes to some of Ruskin's conclusions about the hybrid makeup of the mode. Gombrich's main interests, though, lie in the complex of perceptual responses stimulated by grotesque compositions. Such compositions contain uncodable visual information that "outrages both our 'sense of order' and our search for meaning," the two tendencies that dominate behaviors of perception. Where "normally, as we scan any configuration we have learned to 'extrapolate,' . . . [these] creatures defy our classifications. . . . There is nothing to hold on to, nothing fixed, the *deformitas* is hard to 'code'" (*Sense of Order*, 256). Uncertainty in a viewer's response carries over from the perceptual sphere to the emotional one. And as a visual means to otherwise unseen truths the grotesque is profoundly "self-contradictory" in seeming to offer "a pattern for 'dreamwork,' a guidebook to chaos" (*Sense of Order*, 281). Grotesque images, "which oscillate between decorative form and representational images," are vastly ambiguous in relation to everyday appearances (*Sense of Order*, 256).

In assessing the aesthetic revival of the grotesque in the course of the 1500s, Gombrich observes that these treatments, in contrast to the drollery and diablerie of the medieval period, tend to submit such motifs to formal principles of symmetry and balance and to thus temper its spirit of license. Nonetheless, even within structured patterns the grotesque retains tangible potential for contradiction and disruption: "The grotesque has moved from the margin to the centre and offers its inconsequential riddles to focussed vision. . . . They are not mere designs, but signs" (*Sense of Order*, 281). Leonardo da Vinci on occasion drew casual studies in deformed or distorted physiognomy, starting in the 1490s until his death in 1519. The real and imagined facial features in these drawings are obvious signs of human personality (fig. 1.3). The cultural energies released through such renderings would lead by the late 1500s to the establishment of caricature as a distinct visual genre.

Figure 1.3. Leonardo da Vinci, A Grotesque Head (c1504)

While mimicry and mockery were certainly present in early forms of social expression and are amply evident in ancient literature and theater, the reinvention of the grotesque and the related rise of caricature embody for Gombrich a profound advance in visual culture: "In many periods of the past the ornamental border had given most scope to the artist's free play of imagination. In the late sixteenth century, however, this free play itself becomes emancipated from its shadowy range on the margin of a book or under the seat of the choir stall. Series of engravings or wood-cuts proudly displayed the artist's power of creating grotesques."[16] The recodification of physical appearances through caricature marks a new cultural freedom.

By applying Gombrich's ideas to present contexts, we can understand how the modern visual grotesque often isolates and individuates the human figure to the point where there is no longer any ability to temper or recuperate the grotesque through inclusion in larger, balanced and aesthetically pleasing patterns. As noted, the art historian considers a epochal change to have occurred during the Renaissance when grotesque motifs shift in their compositional role from the decorative margins to become a central feature.

MODERN GROTESQUE

In explaining the attitude of modernity from his perspective in France during the 1850s, Charles Baudelaire specified as a definitive component the new inflections of the grotesque prominent in the fiction of Edgar Allan Poe. For Baudelaire, close visual counterparts to these modern literary inflections are found in the graphic work of Francisco Goya and Honoré Daumier. In Baudelaire's mind the grotesque aspects of modern sensibility are often associated with the individual's exceptional responses and with cruel turns in circumstances. One immediate aesthetic consequence is that the familiarly human is suppressed or negated. While this property accords with Kenneth Burke's definition of the grotesque as an attitude that cultivates incongruity, for Baudelaire the grotesque *does* evoke laughter, albeit laughter of a distinctive kind. The effect of the "absolute comic" that Baudelaire attributes to the grotesque differs fundamentally from what he calls the "significative" humor of conventional comedy.[17] Significative comedy, by providing a social corrective or a psychological discharge of tension, is integrative and compensatory in effect. For its part, absolute comedy is unnerving, dissociative, and antisocial. An expression of humanity's heritage of "physical and moral degradation," grotesque laughter has its closest emotional counterpart in grief (*Art and Artists,* 143). Baudelaire associates qualities of cruelty, solemnity, and primitivism with grotesque laughter as well, but with a flourish of paradox he generalizes that the most profound correlation of the grotesque is to "the life of innocence and to absolute joy" (*Art and Artists,* 152). Some aspects of Baudelaire's ideas here, as we shall see, have unexpected relevance to Flannery O'Connor's practices of the grotesque.

Baudelaire acclaimed Daumier as an early master in the grotesque vein of modernity. He had in mind not so much Daumier's topical, political caricatures as drawings in which everyday life of the city is overshadowed by conditions that prey on defenseless humanity. Caricature depends upon a degree of clarity to convey an incisive idea or judgment about the character or situation depicted, and the mode obviously belongs to significative comedy, whereas the grotesque suggests an inherent obscurity and mystery. A specific Daumier lithograph that Baudelaire considered at length is *Rue Transnonain, le 15 avril 1834* (fig. 1.4). It is a death scene in a small room where a murdered man lies stretched across the floor and a small child, also apparently dead, is crushed beneath the corpse. In the semidarkness two more slain adults lie sprawled on the floor. Visual

Figure 1.4. Honoré Daumier, *Rue Transnonain, le 15 avril 1834* (1834)

impact from this image operates in ways far removed from the sharply targeted invective that commands awareness in the same artist's political caricatures.

For Baudelaire the *Rue Transnonain* drawing, through an open and unblinking attention to "trivial and terrible" particulars, achieves an extraordinary impression of presence: "it is history, it is reality" (*Art and Artists*, 218). While Baudelaire normally rejected realism as the nemesis of inspiration and the intangible, in the case of such subject matter harsh, pitiless outward appearances can render in totality an aspect otherwise unimaginable. To be sure no joy attaches to the scene, but in its unsparing depiction of the aftermath of violence an absolute in human experience and an exact measure of destroyed innocence are portrayed. In commenting more than twenty years after the event that provoked Daumier to make the lithograph, Baudelaire focuses on the immediacy of the atrocity rather than on its specific causes. For the record, on that day in Paris many innocent civilians in a Rue Transnonain tenement were massacred by government troops who stormed the building.[18]

Given one guiding purpose of the present book, it must be acknowledged that Baudelaire deplored the inroads photography had made upon the arts, especially painting, over the first two decades of the new technology. But Baudelaire also recognized that the photographic sensibility is entirely modern and that the medium served some appreciable cultural purpose as a sign of the times in its startling and often "cruel" allure. In response specifically to the polished silver of a daguerreotype plate, Baudelaire attributes to photography the "cold clarity of a mirror" in its indiscriminate power of replication, content to simply reflect whatever passes by (*Art and Artists*, 225). Irrespective of the static, calculated composition required in order to secure clear daguerreotype pictures, in making this remark Baudelaire has in mind the increasingly arbitrary and ephemeral manner in which a city person encounters and regards the finished images. They possess an undeniable potential for visual frisson precisely because they contain only a surface of appearances taken in quickly by the eyes. Thus, in their shallow yet unsparing actuality photographic images are possessed of a characteristic that is generally true of modern experience.

Writing in the 1890s, Henry James also expressed admiration for Daumier's genius, and the American novelist considered the grotesque style of his lithographs to exert great psychological power and cultural influence. This fact is all the more noteworthy because the high value he placed upon Daumier's work marks one of the few areas where James is in agreement (though for different underlying reasons) with Baudelaire's

aesthetic judgments. In reaction against the aesthetic cultivation of corruption, Henry James held Baudelaire partly responsible for a modern
tendency to lower "the moral complexities of life . . . down into [a] very
turbid element . . . and there present them to us much besmirched and
bespattered." According to James this tendency, as proves equally true
for him with the example of Poe, serves only in the end to demonstrate
a "dulness [*sic*] and permanent immaturity of vision."[19]

In James's estimation, the most forceful images created by Daumier
are the product of a measured kind of extremism based in a technique
of "black sketchiness" and a tonality of "abnormal blackness" that both
freely mingle the strange with the real. While "coarse and formidable" in
the specifics of their depictions, for James these lithographs achieve "an
almost symbolic generality" of darkness that functions well beyond any
manifest content as satiric commentary on moral weakness or political
corruption.[20] For James, then, the essential modern ingredient in the grotesque is a pandemic blackness. For Baudelaire, it is an axiomatic, clari-
fying violence.

American Traditions of the Grotesque

IN NAME, THE GROTESQUE has been present in American writing at least since the 1730s, and over the course of the eighteenth century the term appears in a host of literary contexts. One of its earliest uses is in comedy of manners and social satire, where *grotesque* is indicative of ill-suited language and behavior, and, in a more generalized sense, it applies to garish pretensions and self-delusion, as reflected in the character Whim from the 1730 play by James Ralph, *The Fashionable Lady; or Harlequin's Opera.* Where it retains the primarily topographical designation "like a grotto," the term serves in the description of isolated, daunting natural settings, places that stimulate intense emotional experience and that are thus sought out by a restless or adventurous soul, as is the case in Francis Hopkinson's poem of the 1790s, "Il Penseroso."

LITERARY GROTESQUES

By the end of the eighteenth century the grotesque emerged within American writing as a feature of the gothic world, where it signals the extremes imaginable in the individual's mental life and social interactions. A striking instance of the latter extremes occurs in Charles Brockden Brown's novel *Ormond; or, The Secret Witness* (1799). The wealthy eccentric Mr. Ormond is a master of disguises that enable him to effect "the most entire and grotesque metamorphosis imaginable." A particularly favorite ruse with him is "to exchange his complexion and habiliments for those of a negro and a chimney-sweep" in order to gain access and a kind of invisibility within households in the highest rank of society.[1] From this demeaned position, Ormond can spy upon potential victims and gain for future purposes superiority over them. The unsuspecting remain secure in a trust that their world is anchored by black-and-white distinctions as matters of social orthodoxy and civil law, which are visibly maintained through divisions along outward signs of race and economic class. What proves most grotesque about Ormond's impersonation of a Negro chimney-sweep, a charcoal-sooted blackness done in reality in blackface, is that it redoubles an incommensurate position vis-à-vis respectable white authority. In its way the act is mystical, if not demonic, in a practice of a "black art" of imposture for the subversion of an order based on categorical surface discriminations. Social malformation, in this instance of an "inferior" in race and working caste, affords a vantage through which can be gained unique understanding of the powers that be. From such practices in gothic literature, the grotesque as a modern attitude toward history develops.

In the early decades of nineteenth-century American literature the grotesque is commonly invoked through the presence of strange, misshapen, or intimidating forms, and these in turn often reflect anxiety over an encounter with "foreign" or "alien" elements. The specific identity of such elements can vary from Native Americans, black slaves, Italians, the Dutch, and Turks to untracked nature, mysterious strangers, Catholic icons, masquerade disguises, and political spies. The canonical authors of the period who use the term with some frequency include James Fenimore Cooper, Washington Irving, Henry Wadsworth Longfellow, and, of course, Edgar Allan Poe. Among these writers, with the exception of Poe, the grotesque is for the most part circumscribed in application to isolated or extraordinary appearances and situations, and it does not function as an attitude within consciousness or a defining perspective on experience to give a literary identity to the work as a whole. Poe gathered together for book publication in 1840 the various short prose pieces he had finished over the last seven years. In titling the two-volume collection *Tales of the Grotesque and Arabesque* Poe distinctly claims "a certain unity of design" and of sensibility for it even with the many apparent irregularities in subject matter, tone, and literary type among the tales.[2]

In origin, the arabesque refers to a unique style of ornamentation in the visual arts and crafts. Most specifically, the term names the distinctive vegetal designs that flourished in Islamic art from the tenth to the fifteenth century and that are found as well in Moorish decoration.

The designs are elaborately geometric and intertwined, with manifold correspondences among their patterns. These early exemplars did not include animal forms nor, following Islamic law, any human representation. Though in a literal sense it means "Arabian," the term is European, and the style became part of a Western visual vocabulary somewhat later, during the Renaissance, when it was particularly favored in book design for page decoration and ornamental bindings. With Raphael, Western arabesque motifs freely introduced animal and human figures, rendered in both natural and grotesque styles.[3] In a consideration of the functions of the sublime, the picturesque, the grotesque, and the arabesque within Poe's work, Frederick Burwick finds strong interrelations among these four aesthetic categories, especially in their shared evocations of visual experience and their contributions to "the self-reflexivity of Poe's insistent textuality," which creates "an effective *mise en abyme,* replicating and compounding the verbal-visual strategies of his descriptive prose."[4]

Scholars have identified Sir Walter Scott's essay "On the Supernatural in Fictitious Composition" (1827) as a source that explains Poe's selection of terminology and its aptness for tales of obsession and horror. But only some of the tales are composed in the supernatural vein. Others are farces, hoaxes, parables, fables, satires. At a generic level, the title *Tales of the Grotesque and Arabesque* announces that the two volumes are distinctive foremost for their heterogeneous and disjunctive quality. A promise of variety and strangeness invites the reader into their contents. The collection assumes that imagination is responsive to novelty and juxtaposition and that it is drawn disparately to the fanciful, the beautiful, and the deformed. The title is indicative as well of a literary procedure of visualization. In tales of fixation ("Ligeia," for example), mystery ("William Wilson"), and imposture ("The Man That Was Used Up") alike, the process entails a gradual dual movement that by turns adumbrates/elucidates intricate, expansive, and often distorted layers of appearance and meaning.

Storylines in these tales often advance through an interplay between unfamiliar appearances and the confusing or contradictory disclosures that alternately complicate or clarify these appearances. In some, the admixture of visual motifs proceeds by way of differentials as elemental as that of black/white. "Shadow. A Fable" (retitled "Shadow—A Parable" in later publication) is a vivid case in point. Narrated by Oinos (One) from beyond the tomb by some centuries, the tale is a lesson in death's impositions upon the living. Identifying himself at the outset as one who has "long since gone my way into the region of shadows," Oinos is confident that readers will "find much to ponder upon in the characters here graven with a stylus of iron" (*Poetry and Tales*, 218). Two superimposed graphic referents are unmistakably present in this initial statement: the words Oinos once wrote upon a manuscript and the words now read from the printed page.

In "Shadow. A Fable" language itself is to be viewed as an intricate sequence of shaded shapes engraved upon a lighter surface.[5] For both substance and manner the parable depends upon an elaborate interaction of light and dark tonalities. The opening tableau is a study in degrees of darkness. The time is a plague year during the Dark Ages. The setting is a spacious chamber at nighttime, and black draperies have been drawn to shut out moonlight, the stars, and the "dim city" beyond the walls. The chamber's few lamps cast only a "gloomy" hue (*Poetry and Tales*, 218). In their faint light, the ebony surface of a table becomes a dark mirror. From the obscure reaches of the scene, a shadow emerges to join the persons gathered together that night in refuge from the plague. Though unnamed as such in the tale, one intelligible identity of this physically vague, formless figure is the Black Death. The people present dare not regard it directly. They experience this visitation instead with downcast eyes that "gazed continually into the depths of the mirror of ebony" (*Poetry and Tales*, 220).

In the end the figure announces itself as "SHADOW." Through its utterance, Oinos and his companions recognize the embodiment of countless untimely deaths. The "cadences from syllable to syllable fell duskily upon our ears" at that moment, as now the reader's eye encounters them upon the page (*Poetry and Tales*, 220). Medium and message are inseparable in the tale: man's fate is to be read in the darkest signs decipherable on the surface of the human scene. Exaggerated, multiplied obscurity in the end provides a kind of clarity. "Shadow. A Fable" is exemplary of the modern grotesque in the manner by which perspective and, finally, comprehension are gained through overdetermination and incongruity. An additional feature of the modern grotesque here, as often with Poe's writings, is a pronounced reflexivity in the descriptive visualizations and in the appearance of graphic and textual forms, not the least of which is the typographical presence of the text itself. An early enthusiast of the daguerreotype—he posed for eight portraits, more than any other major American writer at the time—Poe valued the reflective/reflexive properties of the image in the mirrored surface of the daguerreotype plate: "The closest scrutiny of the photogenic drawing discloses only a more absolute truth, a more perfect identity of aspect with the thing represented. The variations of shade, and the gradations of both linear and aerial perspective are those of truth itself in the supremeness of its perfection."[6]

The Poe tale "Von Jung" (retitled "Mystification" in later publication) treats the grotesque as a psychological property. In appearance and bearing the Baron Ritzner Von Jung is the picture of sobriety, decorum, and intellectual gravity. The "mystery which overshadowed his character" lies in the remarkable, adverse influence he has upon the behavior of others (*Poetry and Tales,* 254). Over his acquaintances Von Jung reigns as a lord of misrule and he remains all the while an unmoved mover. Without any apparent premeditation or obvious effort the Baron prompts them to ludicrous, foolhardy actions: "he contrived to shift the sense of the grotesque from the creator to the created" (*Poetry and Tales,* 255). The tale's conclusion reveals the secret of his power. It depends upon the principle of maintaining "all the outward signs of intelligibility, and even of profundity, while in fact not a shadow of meaning existed" (*Poetry and Tales,* 260–61). A measure of absurdism in the modern sense thus emerges from the story's sense of the grotesque.

What Poe admired in the tales of Nathaniel Hawthorne was an "extraordinary genius" for "dreamy *innuendo*" and their variations upon a tone of "melancholy and mysticism."[7] Hawthorne also possessed a keen awareness of the grotesque. In his fiction its effects are sometimes horrible (as in *The Scarlet Letter,* 1850), at other times capricious (as in "The Hall of Fantasy," 1846) and humorous ("The Toll-Gatherer's Day," 1842). A frightful grotto dominates the hellscape depicted in "The Celestial Railroad" (1843): "the dismal obscurity of the broad cavern-mouth, whence, ever and anon, darted huge tongues of dusky flame,— . . . strange, half-shaped monsters, and visions of faces."[8] In *The House of the Seven Gables* (1851) Hawthorne weighs the implications of a severely contrastive method of description and disclosure and draws a connection with an early phase of photography. While some townspeople in the story suppose daguerreotypes to be connected with the black arts, Holgrave values the medium as the embodiment of a "wonderful insight in heaven's broad and simple sunshine," however dark "the secret character" of the truths ultimately revealed.[9]

"Wakefield" (1835), a story in *Twice-Told Tales* that received Poe's special praise, considers how readily an individual can overstep the routines and boundaries of normal daily life. Hawthorne presents the tale as a meditation upon the possibility for profound eccentricity in behavior. Wakefield's aberration is not easily condemned, however, for it reflects a potential for the grotesque inherent in humanity. To recall the plot line in "Wakefield," a London man of middle age decides without much forethought to absent himself from wife and home. By dint of habit rather than through any original intention, Wakefield prolongs the separation for two decades. All the while he lives in a lodging house located only one street away. Then one day Wakefield returns to his wife, though the reunion scene remains untold. The tale is offered as an exemplum in "marital delinquency," one "as remarkable a freak as may be found in the whole list of human oddities" (*Hawthorne's Tales,* 75). Though Wakefield is imagined to have assumed a disguise consisting of a reddish wig and "sundry garments" for years, the tale's grotesqueness consists mainly in his prolonged, perverse choice of separation, "this long whim-wham" (*Hawthorne's Tales,* 79). Notwithstanding efforts to change his appearance, Wakefield bears "in his whole aspect, the hand-writing of no common fate, for such as have the skill to read it" (*Hawthorne's Tales,* 80). With a reflexive purpose traditional to such character studies, the tale equates the unusual features of Wakefield's situation to a rhetorical figure of irregularity.

In the introductory section of *Mosses from an Old Manse* (1846), Hawthorne suggests one explanation for the power of the grotesque upon our imaginations by way of analogy to a time-worn apple orchard: "An orchard has a relation to mankind, and readily connects itself with matters of the heart. . . . There is so much individuality of character, too, among apple trees, that it gives them an additional claim to be objects of human interest. One is harsh and crabbed in its manifestations; another gives us fruit as mild as charity. One is churlish and illiberal, evidently grudging the few apples that it bears; another exhausts itself in free-hearted benevolence."[10] The sketch "The Old Apple Dealer" advises readers that "the lover of the moral picturesque may sometimes find what he seeks in a character which is nevertheless of too negative a description" for colorful treatment (*Mosses,* 495). Such is the case with a "faded and featureless" vendor, whose face and clothing consist of indistinct grays and browns (*Mosses,* 495). Upon close attention, however, one oddity emerges to give definition to his personality: "there is a continual unrest within him, which somewhat resembles the fluttering action of the nerves in a corpse from which life has recently departed" (*Mosses,* 497). To a remarkable extent, as shall become clear, these passages prefigure tropes essential to Sherwood Anderson's concept of the grotesque.

The early novels of Herman Melville utilize the grotesque in limited senses. The characteristic is associated in *Typee* (1846), *Omoo* (1847), and *Mardi* (1849) with unusual visual aspects in the landscape or in human appearances, as in cases of the elaborate pattern of tattoos on island warriors, which cause in the narrators a startled first reaction and a subsequently more informed understanding. In *Redburn* (1849) the term is associated with the narrator's overactive thought processes, which are "mixed with a thousand strange forms, the centaurs of fancy; half real and human, half wild and grotesque. Divine imaginings, like gods, come down . . . and there, in the embrace of wild, dryad reminiscences, beget the beings that astonish the world."[11] Many of the sublime effects in *Moby-Dick* (1851) involve grotesque extremes in appearances and situations, as with the appalling whiteness of the whale, the cosmic desolation of the black cabin boy Pip, and the unholy alliance of officers and crew in Ahab's obsessive quest. In *Pierre; or, The Ambiguities* (1852) Melville renders the absolute passions that overcome Pierre, Isabel, and Lucy—and that lead to an incestuous relationship, murder, and double suicide—through overdetermined and tortured psychological conflicts.

In the mature phase of Melville's literary career the presence of the grotesque, as conveyed descriptively through profound tonal contrasts, extends to the textuality of the books themselves. A primary conceit in the "Whiteness of the Whale" section of *Moby-Dick* is that whiteness "shadows forth the heartless voids and immensities of the universe," an image that confounds the norms of object/shadow relationships within a figure-ground context. The section additionally refers to itself as "this white-lead chapter about whiteness" in an allusion to the whitening pigment used in paper but also tangentially to the metal used for movable type, a material origin of the black printface we read.[12] Such conceits are further elaborated in *Pierre* where one "book," as its textual divisions are named, is dedicated to the topic "More Light, and the Gloom of that Light; More Gloom, and the Light of that Gloom." In that novel as a whole, truth is dark and forbidding and it is inscribed upon light-hued, vulnerable surfaces, both actual and metaphorical. Pierre's father, for instance, is idealized in the son's memories "without blemish, unclouded, snow-white, and serene." Over against memory, however, stands a painted portrait of his father that Pierre owns and that obsesses the son as a "shadowy testification" that opens onto depths of darkness.[13]

Melville's most elaborate and original use of the grotesque is to be found in *The Confidence-Man: His Masquerade* (1857). The Mississippi river steamer that provides the book's setting is, by virtue of the intricacy of its design and the complexity of characters and events aboard, a "daedal boat."[14] It transports a full complement of outright grotesques, like the soldier of fortune, the wizened and sickly miser, the Missouri backwoodsman in bearskin, and the cosmopolitan attired in parti-color. The novel deploys outsized and reflexive effects to create even greater incongruities. In the case of the mute stranger of the book's first scene, attributes of whiteness and gentleness are emphasized to an "extremist sense" (*Confidence-Man*, 1). With his flaxen hair, white fur hat, cream-colored suit, and "lamb-like" demeanor, the stranger is as pale and pure as "sugar-snow in March" (*Confidence-Man*, 4). When this stranger figure vanishes an avatar as suddenly appears, one diametrically opposite in appearance and manner. The new stranger is a Negro crippled beggar who gives his name as Black Guinea. A garrulous minstrel figure, he is eager to engage passengers in banter and he moves among them like a "black sheep nudging itself a cozy berth in the heart of the white flock" (*Confidence-Man*, 8). From the outset, Melville's novel indicates that only through such extreme contrasts can the fate of humankind be read.

Many aspects of the grotesque within *The Confidence-Man* involve the very textuality of what we read. Assorted cabins, alcoves, and passages on the riverboat *Fidèle* serve as stages for the novel's puzzling human encounters, and they are likened to "secret drawers in an escritoire" (*Confidence-Man*, 5). One early encounter takes the form of competing inscriptions when the mute white stranger writes on a small slate a succession of appeals, each beginning "Charity." In short time a riposte is made by the boat's cynical barber, who when he opens for business hangs in front of the shop a placard warning bluntly "No Trust" (*Confidence-Man*, 3). By comparison to the motley host of tricksters that Melville has rendered, the confidence man Mark Twain created to engineer the plot of "The Man That Corrupted Hadleyburg" (1900) is not in the least a grotesque shape-shifter.

Writers of the American Renaissance like Hawthorne and Melville thoroughly complicated and intensified contrasts between light and dark that once seemed univocal in their moral senses. Hawthorne, for example, writes in his preface to *Mosses from an Old Manse* of a clergyman whose life was enveloped within "a veil woven of intermingled gloom and brightness" (*Mosses*, 12). Harry Levin in his influential study *The Power of Blackness: Hawthorne, Poe, Melville* proposes a graphic equivalent in order to explain literary themes of blackness, which he compares to "a set of photographic negatives. . . . We stand in slight danger of forgetting that black is merely one side—the less popular side—of a famous polarity. The union of opposites, after all, is the very basis of the American outlook."[15] Levin's interpretative analogy fails, however, since in the technology of the photograph it is polarity and reversal—not union—that are the basis for the black and white image in forms of both the film negative and the positive print.

As one consequence of the histories of exploration, conquest, and slavery in the West, differences in skin color were inescapably incorporated into structures of cultural value founded upon moralized contrasts of light and dark.[16] In North American colonies local Puritan theocracies codified such differences into spiritual doctrine. In matters of categorical racial judgment, Melville's "Benito Cereno" (1856) provides an excruciating exploration into the antinomies of white and black, master and slave. At the end of the century Stephen Crane in his novel *The Monster* (1898) imagines through the fate of Henry Johnson, a Negro stableman, the redoubled social isolation and victimization of black Americans after Emancipation. The savior of a white boy from a terrible house fire, Johnson is mistakenly reported as dead by the local newspaper and he is eulogized in the community as a great hero. But Henry survives. Horribly disfigured and traumatized, he as quickly becomes a pariah. Henry continues to live in town but he is shunned by white and black society alike. He survives as a charred ruin of humanity, his head swathed in heavy, black crêpe to protect society from his horrible appearance. To convey this social condition Crane, American literature's foremost colorist, reduces his descriptive palette to intense darks and a few light hues, much as he had done in *Maggie: A Girl of the Streets* (1893) to depict the fate of a prostitute.

Matters of race have strongly inflected attitudes of the grotesque within American culture. The approach to the racial grotesque in a study by Leonard Cassuto explains it as a psychological dynamic of confusion and potential horror for whites in situations that jeopardize racial hierarchy and transgress categories of race identity. To defend itself against such uncertainties, dominant culture constructs an ideology of "the inhuman race," and this ethnic imperative is evidenced in textual designations of the racial Other.[17] The scope of Cassuto's discussion extends from colonial times through part of the nineteenth century, with attention directed mainly toward captivity and slave narratives, abolitionist fiction, works by Melville, and the Sambo type as an ideological crux within the system of slavery.

In the modern period Ralph Ellison has proven masterful in the critique of such discourse. To take a telling example from *Invisible Man* (1952), the pride of the Liberty Paint Company's product line is advertised through the slogan "If It's Optic White, It's the Right White," which capitalizes upon the common saying within segregated society "If you're white, you're right."[18] The unspoken truth of the special formula for this cover-all white paint, however, is the secret addition of a few drops of a "dead black" pigment (*Invisible Man*, 200). The book's black narrator has rigged up more than one thousand electric bulbs to illuminate his cellar retreat, an urban grotto if you will, and he claims with pride: "I doubt if there is a brighter spot in all New York than this hole of mine, and I do not exclude Broadway. Or the Empire State Building on a photographer's dream night" (*Invisible Man*, 6). This black refugee from American racism has come to understand the paradoxes of white and black: "I now can see the darkness of lightness. And I love light, . . . maybe it is exactly because I *am* invisible. Light confirms my reality, gives birth to my form" (*Invisible Man*, 6).

The literary grotesque in the modern instance has origins in the thought and creative work of Poe, Baudelaire, Daumier, Hawthorne, and Melville. The modern grotesque evinces qualities of violence and darkness that are overdetermined and that are not circumscribed by an author's intentions of moral judgment or satiric commentary. On a formal level, the modern grotesque relies more often upon a set of appearances than upon a series of events. In modern literary and graphic modes alike, the grotesque is predominantly visual and descriptive rather than ideational or narrative. Not confined to expository or explanatory functions, the modern grotesque stands at a threshold to alluring, intimidating obscurity. Such modern traits are contradistinctive to attributes Mikhail Bakhtin identifies in giving an account of the grotesque within medieval and Renaissance forms of the carnivalesque. There, the grotesque functions as a principal force within a demotic metanarrative that promises cultural revitalization. Operating from deep-rooted folk humor and collective wisdom about humanity's material experience, the grotesque in a carnivalesque tradition is "a triumphant, festive principle" that is "gay and gracious" in spirit.[19] In its forms and purposes, carnival is always to be understood at a collective, politically progressive level. Bakhtin maintains that contemporary understandings of the grotesque (and here he cites Wolfgang Kayser's study at some length) are imbalanced by Romantic preoccupations with alienated and irrational states of mind and with thoroughly individualized dimensions of human experience.

AMERICAN PHOTOGRAPHY AND THE GROTESQUE

Though photography became fully a part of American life during the 1840s, the grotesque did not enter its visual thematics prominently until well into the twentieth century. To be sure, subject matter typically associated with the grotesque was part of American photography of the nineteenth century. While working in San Francisco during the 1860s Eadweard Muybridge photographed an Asian man over eight feet tall on

Figure 2.1. Eadweard Muybridge, *The Heathen Chinese Giant* (c1869). From the Lone Mountain Collection of Stereographs by Eadweard Muybridge. Courtesy of the Bancroft Library, University of California, Berkeley.

exhibition as "The Heathen Chinese Giant" at Woodward's Gardens, an amusement park. The stereoscope images present the subject as elegant in his embroidered traditional costume and quite at ease in the company of park visitors as he poses for group portraits (fig. 2.1). The composition has posed and framed him as an exotic incongruity without asserting any grotesque dimension to the scene.

An archive of speciality portraits made by New York photographer Charles Eisenmann, whose studio was located in the Bowery, is available for comparison to the Muybridge approach. From the mid-1870s until he quit business in 1892, Eisenmann produced many *cartes de visite* of the performers and attractions in dime museums and traveling shows for sale as souvenirs. Most of these human attractions—midgets, giants, "wild" men and women, people born with physical anomalies—are pictured with the same backgrounds, furnishings, and poses that befitted middle-class patrons.[20] Grotesque incongruity in the Eisenmann images involves visual discrepancies between the utter uniqueness of each human attraction and the utter familiarity of the other compositional elements in the mass-style photograph portrait of the day.

In the 1880s Muybridge compiled an extensive, systematic photographic record of the movements of different human body types, a few of which could have been rendered easily as grotesques through other compositional approaches. Muybridge's central purposes in documenting animal and human biomechanics, however, steered clear of any such intentions. In 1885, as he conducted the project at the University of Pennsylvania, Muybridge stated a general preference in models: "Artists' models, as a rule, are ignorant and not well bred. As a consequence their movements are not graceful, and it is essential for the thorough execution of my work to have my models of a graceful bearing."[21] Yet at the same time, with the assistance of Dr. Francis Dercum, Muybridge selected patients from the University and Philadelphia hospitals as photographic subjects. Dr. Dercum was a pathologist on the medical faculty at the University of Pennsylvania, where he also lectured on nervous diseases. Muybridge's motion studies had the sanction of the university's prominent physiologists, anatomists, and neurologists, and they fit within the medical discourses of the time.[22]

When Muybridge published *Animal Locomotion: An Electro-Photographic Investigation of Consecutive Phases of Animal Movements, 1872–1885* in 1887, its limited edition of eleven volumes—eight on human subjects, three on animals—contained a total of 781 plates of series photographs. One volume with twenty-nine plates documents *Abnormal Movements* of male and female subjects, both nude and seminude. The physical conditions and disorders among these patients identified in captions to the plates include locomotor ataxia, lateral sclerosis, epilepsy, spastic paralysis, partial paraplegia, muscular atrophy, infantile paralysis, orthopedic malformation, a single amputee, a double amputee, and curvature of the spine. There is also one identified case of stuporous melancholia and one of convulsive seizures. Not a single one of these conditions constitutes in and of itself a visual grotesque, and Muybridge's principal interest in biomechanics meant that normal and abnormal movements alike are recorded through strict and consistent protocols of camera position and background grid. In published form a series in this volume can contain as many as forty-eight separate photograph images of the individual on a single plate; the majority of the plates consist of either twenty-four or thirty-six images. Such a serial presentation, even where a pronounced malformation is evident, helps prevent the individual from being arrested or essentialized into a singularly grotesque subject. In being presented strictly as physiometric studies the images effectively avoid overtones of the grotesque, which typically involve distorted, reflexive appearances. Muybridge also clearly intended to study a normative range of physical activity; abnormal human movements receive less than four percent of coverage in the project overall.

A severe case among the studies in *Abnormal Movements* involves a boy stricken with infantile paralysis, who walks on all fours. Most frames in the sequence of twelve photographs depicting his movement, however, capture a wide, winning smile on the boy's face. In this, the plate departs from the publication's general emphasis on physique and motor move-ment rather than on physiognomy. While physiognomy is often a promi-nent aspect of the human grotesque, here the boy's expression undoes the likelihood of any such association. The sole case of identified mental impairment in the volume *Abnormal Movements* is that of an adult male with "Stuporous melancholia, walking." This series leaves the subject's face indistinct in twelve profile photographs and out of view entirely in the twelve taken from a rear perspective. In its attention to body move-ment, the series contributes a new dimension to clinical efforts of the time to establish by means of photography a visual record of mental illness. Unlike this Muybridge series, the clinical interests of medical photography of the day fell almost exclusively upon facial portraits of the emotionally or mentally disturbed patient, with the intention to establish a physiognomy of insanity.

In his study *The Grotesque in Photography* (1977), A. D. Coleman includes institutional imagery made for medical, anthropological, forensic, and military purposes on grounds that an identification of a particular image as grotesque is as much a function of the viewer's response as it is one of image content or structure. Following this rationale, his book contains photographs of war casualties, from the Civil War to Vietnam, and of executions, among them two frames from Alexander Gardner's series on the Lincoln assassination conspirators. It also contains postmortem daguerreotype portraits of children and the Muybridge series on the paralyzed boy. Yet in none of these instances are the compositions inten-tionally grotesque, as Coleman comes to acknowledge in conceding that the images were produced by "photographers who, by their own lights, were not creating grotesqueries or even addressing the theme."[23] Nor can the visual effect in these examples be termed manifestly grotesque by the traditions of the mode within the graphic arts. For my purposes,

Coleman's admission demonstrates the general point that the visual and literary grotesque do not propose clinical or journalistic objectivity and that instead they engage at obvious levels in a manipulation of perspective and forms to deepen one's recognition of incongruity and/or to intensify one's psychological response.

The main argument of *The Grotesque in Photography* builds upon propositions, particularly those with "metaphysical implications," first set forth by Wolfgang Kayser. In the specific application to photography, Coleman identifies three principal modalities of the grotesque: 1) documented realities; 2) staged and directed realities, or "false photographic documents"; and 3) outright irrealities. Images in the first two categories violate cultural norms and psychological expectations; in the third they violate one's sense of natural order. It is in the last category, further explained as "descriptions of inner states rather than external phenomena," that for Coleman photographs "come closest to the traditional meaning of *the grotesque* in art-historical terms: non- or antiliteral evocations of dreams, fantasies, visions, and hallucinations."[24] The present study argues, to the contrary, that the strongest visual diacritics in grotesque photography are marked by adumbrations and disclosures about the often anomalous quality of shared reality rather than by utter departures from reality.

Humorous effects on a scale that reaches from whimsy to slapstick and caricature seem to be readily achieved in photography, especially in informal street portraiture done in a straight style. The nonstudio, straight style of camera portrait taken with minimal preparation became fully possible by the start of the twentieth century through the availability of hand-held equipment and rapid film exposure.[25] The sheer density of human life on city streets once excerpted by the camera into static postures and expressions can convey an unanticipated comedy of the everyday. Moreover, the often insistently graphic textures of the urban scene—from advertisements to graffiti—offer in visual form a vulgate expressive of experience in mass, man-made consumer society, one that contains rich veins of urban vernacular humor. Such comic possibilities are widely explored in the American street photography of Paul Strand, Helen Levitt, William Klein, Roy DeCarava, Garry Winogrand, and Lee Friedlander. In general, to return to the distinction made by Baudelaire, most of their candid street portraits serve the ends of significative social comedy, not the absolutes of the grotesque.

To begin to understand the comic effects possible through straight and candid camera portraiture, *as distinct from* grotesque effects, we can turn to Henri Bergson's monograph *Laughter,* published in 1900. While his study does not refer specifically to photography—it turns to literature, popular entertainments, and comic theater for examples—Bergson's concepts remain relevant in the present context. According to Bergson, laughter is based chiefly in the perception of human beings as inanimate and conversely, in a minor key, in the perception of inanimate things as alive. A deflection of human animation into the mechanical, into automatism of thought or action, and into a fixed expression or mind-set are all circumstances that provoke laughter. Comic circumstances, then, are in the main ones of "*mechanical inelasticity,* just where one would expect to find the wideawake adaptability and the living pliableness of a human being." Human vitality that would otherwise be mobile and fluid is suddenly exposed as arrested and rigid. Bergson considers this eventuality to be a condition of mental *and* physical "absentmindedness."[26] Undeniably, situations in candid street photography where an animated action or expression are stopped short and made to appear awkward are a ready source of humor. Though Bergson had yet to formulate fully his ideas on *élan vital,* in the study on laughter he portrays the soul that animates humanity as a force "infinitely supple and perpetually in motion" and he explains that "the immateriality which thus passes into matter is what is called gracefulness" (*Laughter,* 78). But the material world, to which the human body largely belongs, is resistant and recalcitrant. It easily thwarts the purposes of soul and the results are comic.

Comedy, to summarize Bergson, arises within the circumstances of everyday life when humans stray from the innate purposes of creative evolution, neglect to follow the inherently progressive ingenuity of life, and lapse into mechanical patterns of repetition, inversion, and interference in behavior and language. Bergson's idea of comedy is based in larger concepts of emotion, behavior, thought, and soul and upon an analytical induction from affect to genre. For him, where there is laughter there is comedy and laughter is categorically intellectual: the comic "appeals to the intelligence pure and simple; laughter is incompatible with emotion. Depict some fault, however trifling, in such a way as to arouse sympathy, fear or pity; the mischief is done, it is impossible for us to laugh" (*Laughter,* 150). Laughter, furthermore, is the instrument of a social, corrective process. Society is "suspicious of all *inelasticity* of character, of mind and even of body, because it is the possible sign of a slumbering activity as well as of an activity with separatist tendencies, that inclines to swerve from the common center round which society gravitates: in short, because it is the sign of an eccentricity" (*Laughter,* 73). Laughter is a "*social gesture*" that "restrains eccentricity" and serves utilitarian purposes of collective amelioration (*Laughter,* 73). And through laughter "society avenges itself for the liberties taken with it" (*Laughter,*

187). Thus, the comic can be viewed as a diagnostic mode that has identified offending instances of rigidity and eccentricity and laughter as a
therapeutic process that purges these conditions in order to restore elas-
ticity and sociability. Bergson's ideas are thus categorically antithetical to
the grotesque. Instead, they approximate in substantial ways Baudelaire's
thinking on significative comedy, and in terms of Kenneth Burke's distinctions they explain comedy as a genre of incongruity *dependent upon*
laughter.

That there was a mass audience for the visual grotesque in America
by the 1920s is demonstrated by the movie box office success of Lon
Chaney for more than a decade, up to his unexpected death in 1930 at
the height of his screen career. Prominently among the many feature
roles taken by this acclaimed "man of a thousand faces," Chaney played
a contortionist who fakes the miraculous faith healing of a disabled man,
a legless criminal mastermind, a grossly stereotyped Fagin, an ape-man,
Quasimodo, a crazed inmate who takes over the asylum, a thief who
disguises himself as an old woman, the Phantom of the Opera, a crook
masquerading as a benevolent cripple, a circus performer who poses as
an armless knife thrower and who is in the end actually dismembered,
a vampire, a paralyzed English magician who becomes a local tyrant in
Africa, and a heavily scarred animal trapper. Among Hollywood movies
this trend of the grotesque continued until enforcement of a new Motion
Picture Production Code in 1934.

Irrespective of Chaney's screen success in such roles, aberrant appearances and behaviors received little attention in the extensive documentary project in photographs organized by the federal government first
under the Resettlement Administration (1935–1937), then the Farm Security Administration (1937–1942), and finally the Office of War Information
(1942–1943).[27] The roster of men and women who worked at one point or
another in the division of visual information for these agencies includes
John Collier, Jr., Jack Delano, Walker Evans, Dorothea Lange, Russell
Lee, Carl Mydans, Gordon Parks, Edwin Rosskam, Arthur Rothstein, Ben
Shahn, John Vachon, and Marion Post Wolcott, each of whom would later
be ranked among the most important photographers of the time. In the
course of these years the agency information services printed and put
on file for a host of public uses some 88,000 photographs. Among these
tens of thousands of images, however, only a tiny, fractional minimum
can be related in subject matter to material commonly associated with the
grotesque. And with few exceptions, some to be noted below, the visual
treatment of such subject matter is not in any obviously intentional way
associated with the traditions of a grotesque style.

A number of agency photographers submitted picture stories on side-show attractions, but the attention among them falls almost exclusively upon the exterior to the tent, the area of advertising banners, and the barker's platform. Two posters in a Marion Post Wolcott photograph, for example, occupy half the frame and announce to a nearly empty midway: "Double Sex Person! Exposed Flesh" and "World's Fair Oddities. Alive Freaks." A tent front area fills another Wolcott image with its playbill cartoons of "Dolly Dimples: Personality Fat Girl," one of them a low comic dialogue scene (fig. 2.2). The mundane inconsequentiality of the scene is generally typical of the tone of most photographs on the subject of side-shows in the government file. Ben Shahn also documented an exterior view of the "Dolly Dimples" tent attraction, taken a year earlier than the Wolcott photograph and in a different part of the country, but with the same prosaic attitude. The compositional approach in such images treats the freak attraction as an open and familiar amusement, documented exclusively in the form of publicity rather than in the flesh. The only suggestion of a forbidden side to the scene is usually verbal, not visual, and at that the rhetoric is so hyperbolic or clichéd as to be merely comic.

A few photographs in the agency files do qualify as grotesque images by virtue of their reflexive engagement with the social or psychological incongruities involved. On field assignment in the South in October 1935, Ben Shahn, an activist artist before becoming a Resettlement Administration staff photographer, stopped in the town of Huntingdon, Tennessee to document the sidewalk pitch delivered by a traveling medicine man to a small crowd.[28] There are nine Shahn photographs on the event, and they vary the context and the perspective in order to provide sufficient reportorial coverage. The most immediate and interpersonal images among them involve the show's Negro assistant. This man appears in blackface, a feature not uncommon in minstrelsy performed by African Americans, with a portion of his face further darkened so as to accentuate the wide swath of white greasepaint around his mouth.

In one photograph the Negro assistant shares the same portrait frame with a large, costumed wooden figure that serves as the show's puppet or ventriloquist dummy (fig. 2.3). The foreground and centered position of the stereotype effigy organizes the portrait composition. It bespeaks the fate for a black man cast in the Sambo mold, as articulated through the guarded or at least noncommittal reaction of the man's face to the camera, his person otherwise turned away, and the permanent symbolism and battered condition of the manikin, which is positioned completely frontward. In the historical and cultural senses of a phrase coined by Flannery O'Connor, each figure in the Shahn photograph amounts to an

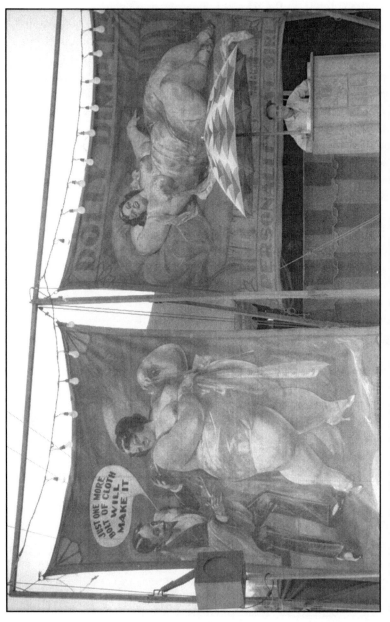

Figure 2.2. Marion Post Wolcott, *Dolly Dimples: Personality Fat Girl* (1939). Library of Congress, Prints and Photographs Division, FSA/OWI Collection [LC–DIG–fsa–8a40648 DLC].

Figure 2.3. Ben Shahn, *Medicine Show, Huntingdon, Tennessee* (1935). Library of Congress, Prints and Photographs Division, FSA/OWI Collection [LC-USF331-006167-M4 DLC].

"artificial nigger." While maintaining distinctions between the human and the artificial, in respect to the public fate of race the portrait delineates equivalences between the two figures. With this image Shahn compassionately decodes aspects of the racial grotesque in American social relations. Shahn's double portrait registers aspects of the racial grotesque while it preserves the underlying humanity of the object of such stereotypes.[29]

During his travels through the South under contract with the Resettlement Administration in 1936, Walker Evans turned his camera several times on circus and minstrel posters. The context for his images of this material was not the fairground or carnival but the streets and business districts in town. By the nature of its function, to publicize a limited or touring attraction, the material is ephemeral. To emphasize this feature Evans chose examples in varying stages of deterioration from time and the elements. With a graphic exactitude possible through the large format of his 8 × 10-inch view camera, these photographs partially expose the undersurface of earlier posters and the supporting wall. Effects of incongruity are particularly telling with the minstrel imagery.

The poster Evans documented while in Alabama of "J. C. Lincoln's Sunny South Minstrels" is dense in the visual discourse of grotesque racialization (fig. 2.4). The image offers practically a catalogue raisonné of stereotype elements: thickened and animalized facial features, watermelon and chicken thieving, a handkerchief-headed mammy, a razor-wielding youth, a dandified musician, domestic turbulence, and violence. As a repository of current, active stereotypes the poster may materially wither away in the short run but the social structure underlying such images, the photograph's iconography suggests, is as solid and long-lived as the brick wall that supports this kind of visual text. For its publication in *American Photographs* (1938) Evans cropped the image down to the borders of the poster illustration, thus emphasizing all the more its internal figure-ground relationships. With the exception of a few such images, the federal documentary project was disinclined to assert a grotesque attitude toward subject matter. In the 1930s it would be left to the press photographer known as Weegee to develop a definitively American grotesque style in photography.

Figure 2.4. Walker Evans, *Minstrel Poster, Alabama* (1936). Library of Congress, Prints and Photographs Division, FSA/OWI Collection [LC–USF342–T01–008243–A–A DLC].

The Modern

Depiction and Description

*F*OR VISUAL AND LITERARY MEDIA alike the modern grotesque is primarily depictive, descriptive, and reflexive rather than narrative in its strategies and reception. In favoring description over narration, the visible over the recounted, and self-reference over objective perspective, modes of the grotesque since Edgar Allan Poe participate centrally in the modernist movement. Reactions against modernism, in their turn, commonly censure the movement's reliance on just such descriptive, objectivist, and inwardly focused techniques. Condemnation from the Left attributes many of the aesthetic and political failures of modernism specifically to its grotesque and "camera eye" features. To better understand the grotesque, a consideration of modernism and photographic properties is in order at this stage. An effective place to begin is with these political condemnations.

A speaker at the Soviet Writers' Conference of 1934 condemned James Joyce's *Ulysses* as "a heap of dung, crawling with worms, photographed by a cinema apparatus through a microscope."[1] The rejection of literary modernism by Marxist critic Georg Lukács, while expressed in a more sophisticated tone and reasoned in learned ways, is based upon similar analogies and it is no less severe in its conclusions. Lukács posed a choice between the rich, progressive culture of epic tradition or reactionary cultural emphases upon impermanent, surface actuality, a choice he phrased "Narrate or Describe?" in one essay. Lukács's critique of modernism resonates through social analyses of photography put forward by Bertolt Brecht, Walter Benjamin, Susan Sontag, John Berger, and several others in the course of the twentieth century.

Lukács judges the writings of T. S. Eliot, Franz Kafka, William Faulkner, and Samuel Beckett to be alike in a dependence upon "descriptive detail . . . of extraordinary immediacy and authenticity" and alike in a consequent attenuation of reality and loss of meaning.[2] A hypertrophy of such details in literature is for Lukács symptomatic: "Description is the writer's substitute for the epic significance that has been lost."[3] And modernist description is indiscriminate in its acceptance of mundane details as fully representative of human existence, whereas epic subordinates and integrates description through an aesthetic totality of story content and plot. With the exception of epic novelists like Balzac, Tolstoi, and Thomas Mann, fiction in the nineteenth and twentieth centuries in this critic's view became largely the domain of literary specialists who authored works restricted and distorted by emphases on stylistic techniques, subjective perspectives, and surface appearances in the social world. Lukács singles out Poe as an early exponent of such stylistic specialization. With Poe and those he influenced, like Baudelaire, the style consists entirely in "lyric impressionism" expressive of "their own subjectivity, their own personal impressions and purely individual problems of creative expression with profound conviction and paradoxical bravado."[4] Such concentration on psychological sensations and heightened rhetorical effects produces a deformed worldview.

The medium of photography has contributed greatly to modernist aesthetics, and the critiques of photography and modernism serve to place in sharp outline properties important to a discussion of the modern grotesque.[5] The issues raised in these critiques are directly relevant since the present study argues that in visual art and literature alike the grotesque *is*, by far, more a way of describing than it is a way of telling.

NARRATE OR DESCRIBE?

Lukács expounds the main ideas of "Narrate or Describe?" (1936) through cognate terms in his essays "Healthy or Sick Art?" (1930s) and "Franz Kafka or Thomas Mann?" (1957), in which the polarity narration/description echoes through a host of cultural alternatives and value judgments. Here, it will suffice to enumerate the most prominent correlations:

NARRATION	DESCRIPTION
recounts	contemporizes
change	stasis
epic	formalism
epic concentration	surface depiction
related events	chance incidents
the fateful	the mundane
primacy of action	illusion of neutral objectivity
inquiry into ideology	schematic positivism

Lukács identifies a cultural crisis within modern Western literature—even within the socialist sphere—that results when description, originally one of several subordinate modes within the epic, predominates in literary form and thus destroys any opportunity to represent the deep social structures to human experience, which only epic narration can render. Formalist description reduces everything within fiction's purview—society, characters, and objects alike—to the pictorial, to still lives, while an epic account is genealogical in its disclosures about social and material interrelations. During the 1920s the German dramatist Bertolt Brecht, in developing the concept of an epic theater, had delivered a similar indictment against photography as a whole on charges that the medium was in its essence descriptive and nonnarrative: "Less than at any time does a simple *reproduction of reality* tell us anything about reality. A photograph of the Krupp works or GEC yields almost nothing about these institutions. Reality proper has slipped into the functional. The reification of human relationships, the factory, let's say, no longer reveals these relationships. Therefore something has actually to be *constructed*, something artificial, something set up."[6]

Walter Benjamin, whose "A Short History of Photography" (1931) contains and warrants the Brecht statement, counsels that "the caption must step in, thereby creating a photography which literalizes the relationships of life and without which photographic construction would remain stuck in the proximate." To a substantial degree, though, Benjamin's Marxism remains receptive to the medium of photography and to impressionist and modernist literary modes such as surrealism. He considers the work of photographer Eugène Atget, which was embraced by French surrealists, to mark a new phase in the history of visual perception, one that aligns the photograph image with "a scene of action," and thus with narrative considerations.[7] Benjamin reiterates this idea in "The Work of Art in the Age of Mechanical Reproduction" (1936), where he adds: "With Atget photographs become standard evidence for historical occurrences and acquire hidden political significance."[8]

Over the century the dichotomy narrate/describe has had several counterparts in linguistics, the human sciences, and art criticism. In work from the 1950s linguist Roman Jakobson conceptualizes language use in terms of two primary aspects or "gravitational poles." One aspect is that of combination and contexture, based on properties of contiguity; the other is selection and substitution, based on features of similarity. In elaborating this bipolar model, which derives in part from differentials posited originally by Ferdinand de Saussure in his general linguistics, Jakobson assigns to the aspect of combination the functions of metonymy and the predicative and to the aspect of selection the functions of metaphor and the substitutive. The first aspect or axis of language is structured by syntagmatic and diachronic relationships, the second by paradigmatic and synchronic ones. The correlations respectively to narration and to description, though not named as such, are clear. In an application of the model to literary history, Jakobson attributes to the realist movement in fiction a high development along the axis of combination and contexture and to the lyric and symbolist traditions in poetry development along the axis of selection and substitution. In Jakobson's final estimation, the potential for meaningful communication is greater through the first axis than through the second, for it is only by combination that "a higher degree of complexity" is achieved.[9]

Though no connection with the literary judgments of Lukács seems intended, to demonstrate high achievement through functions of combination and contexture, the syntagmatic axis, Jakobson offers examples of epic realism in Tolstoi's fiction. The structuralist analysis of literature generally favors narrative over description. In commentary on "the reality effect" in literary realism, however, Roland Barthes has remarked "the enigmatic character of all description" when it borders on "insignificant notation . . . apparently detached from the narrative's semiotic structure." Such description stands largely on its own in the text, serving no predictive or predicative function, yet it is indicative of an elaborately evolved language system. In Barthes's estimation "description appears as a kind of characteristic of the so-called higher languages, to the apparently paradoxical degree that it is justified by no finality of action or of communication."[10]

Within the critique of photography as essentially a descriptive, non-narrative medium, and thus inherently limited in its truth-value, the most influential voices have been those of Susan Sontag and John Berger. In Sontag's *On Photography* (1977), which will come under full discussion in the chapter on Diane Arbus, the critic judges the medium to exert harmful consequences upon humanity's capacity for ethical judgments and action: "Through photographs the world becomes a series of unrelated, freestanding particles; and history, past and present, a set of anecdotes and *faits divers*. The camera makes reality atomic, manageable, and opaque. It is a view of the world which denies interconnectedness, continuity."[11]

For John Berger photography, to its discredit, reflects a temporality of the instantaneous exposure. By arresting time in a still image, the medium falsifies one's experience of the world: "A photograph isolates the appearances of a disconnected instant. And in life, meaning is not instantaneous. Meaning is discovered in what connects, and cannot exist without development. Without a story, without an unfolding, there is no meaning."[12] This statement appears in *Another Way of Telling* (1982), a book created in collaboration with the Swiss photographer Jean Mohr with the purpose of opening the medium to new narrative possibilities. For Berger writing is the customary way through which to provide a narrative for the photograph and endow it with duration and a continuity that connects its moment from the past with the viewer's present and with his or her sense of a future.

In other commentary, however, Berger has credited images by rare "witnessing masters" and "descriptive masters" like Paul Strand, Walker Evans, and August Sander for fulfilling the promise of photography as a democratic medium with meaningful uses and with narrative powers. To Berger's mind some Strand photographs so deeply penetrate their subject matter that they reveal "the stream of a culture or a history which is flowing through that particular subject like blood. . . . The photographic moment for Strand is a biographical or historic moment, whose duration is ideally measured not by seconds but by its relation to a lifetime. Strand does not pursue an instant, but encourages a moment to arise as one might encourage a story to be told. . . . He turns his subjects into narrators."[13]

What a photograph also can provide intrinsically without words and without narrative, Berger further acknowledges, is a profound capacity at the depictive level to convey visual correspondences in the physical world and the human sphere that can achieve conceptual insight: "A photograph which achieves expressiveness . . . works dialectically: it preserves the particularity of the event recorded, and it chooses an instant when the correspondences of those particular appearances articulate a general idea" (*Telling*, 122). While his political convictions lead Berger as a critic to argue for a narrative recuperation of photography's expressivity, his passions as a creative writer nonetheless incline him toward its immediate, denotative qualities.

SEEING AND PHOTOGRAPHY

Properly speaking, it is not the human eye in itself that sees. Rather it is the whole human being, in whom the eye is an organ, who sees. A similar conclusion, though in a different vocabulary, was reached centuries ago by Johannes Kepler, the astronomer and a founder of the modern science of optics, when he postulated that the human eye is directed by reason. Visual perception is a combined activity of eye, brain, and body; it is not the result of a mechanical act of copying or recording, as is possible through a camera and in a photograph.[14] James Gibson, a contemporary scientist of sense perception, has warned: "It is misleading enough to compare the eye with a camera, but it is even worse to compare the retina with a photographic film."[15] Early and late, nonetheless, mechanistic correlations of eye to camera and retina to film have persisted in cultural commentary on photography as a medium. Little more than two decades after its invention Oliver Wendell Holmes celebrated photography's faithful reproduction and preservation of human vision in a series of articles where he designated the plate film surface located behind the camera lens an "unfading artificial retina."[16] Even a critical mind as sophisticated as that of Arthur Danto can lapse into the lens-eye fallacy: "It is widely appreciated that the camera is a sort of detached eye, the mechanisms of which are analogous to the mechanisms of the human eye. And it is a natural extension of the language of the eye as a mechanical system that photographic images should be thought of as analogous to optical images, images that impose themselves on the retina, which cannot help but register what is seen."[17]

According to broadly accepted scientific findings, however, the retina should be considered to be a light-sensitive extension of the brain that at an early stage in human development became physically separated from the brain itself. It has been demonstrated in the laboratory that the retina contains typical brain cells as well as specialized light- and color- sensitive receptor cells.[18] As further demonstration of integral connections between eye and brain, it is known that significant cognitive processing of perceptual information first takes place within the eye.

The reception of visual information in the retina entails neural mapping. In the retina there are two specialized kinds of light-receptor cells, *rods* and *cones*, named after the physical shape of their appearance under a microscope. Rods provide vision only in shades of gray, and they function mainly in conditions of low illumination. Cones, which enable color vision, function in daylight conditions. Near the edges of the retina there are very few cones and there is no color vision, only the detection of forms in shadow. The impressions formed by light on the retina through rods and cones are not equivalent, however, to what we see. A retinal impression is just one stage in a succession of events that make up the process of seeing. As Maurice Pirenne explains: "The eye is the only optical instrument which forms an image which has never been intended to be seen. This is the great difference between the eye and the photographic camera."[19] That is to say, visual perception is not mechanical, the organs of vision are not equivalent to simple optical devices.

Elaborate analogies of the eye to a camera mechanism are even more ill-founded. The human eye does not "take" instantaneous still exposures, it does not contain a shutter. Vision is a kinetic process instead of a receptive or retentive reflex based in biomechanics. Vision is guided by brain and physiology and conducted through a complex of neural functions and a set of simplifying rules of cognition. The eye is never in fact static, it never arrests one image nor rests upon a single point of focus. The eye constantly scans in order to bring sights to the fovea and activate the receptors that convert that information into neuroelectric signals. Vision does not function as a storehouse for discrete, framed, solitary images.

Of course, under normal circumstances the eye does not function alone; it has a companion and vision is binocular. In the waking state the eyes continuously make small movements known as *saccades*, a French term that means literally "jerk" or "twitch." The activity of saccades was discovered in the 1870s by Emile Javal. These darting movements of the eyes occur in fractions of a second; the period of rest between saccades is less than a second. In addition to larger movements intended to direct one's gaze, saccades serve to sweep optical impressions over the retina's photoreceptors. While the eyes constantly scan a field of vision, for the purposes of discernment they must be selective in their range of attention and focus in terms of both panoramic extent and depth of field. In practice, whole contexts of background, foreground, or periphery are left out of meaningful view as the eye draws into attention its objects of interest. The camera lens by itself, on the other hand, is not particularly discerning or selective. Up to its optical capacities, which in contemporary technology are great indeed, the lens admits all the available light reflected from the surfaces of everything within its field of view. The range of perspective and focus in a camera lens is determined by its design, and it is fixed in relation to other camera settings.

E. H. Gombrich has adopted findings from the science of visual perception to account for "the beholder's share" in responding to a still image. Gombrich proceeds from a general principle that there is no natural, given correlation between the world received or recorded optically and the world of a person's visual experience. Perception is an activity of the eyes *and* consciousness; it is an active looking for something of interest and meaning in the visual field. The movement of vision and consciousness across a sight "always assists in confirming or refuting our provisional interpretations and anticipations." Photography makes particularly evident one aspect of the process crucial for the artist: "Though the snapshot has transformed the portrait it has also made us see the problem of likeness more clearly than past centuries were able to formulate it. It has drawn attention to the paradox of capturing life in a still, of freezing the play of features in an arrested moment of which we may never be aware in the flux of events."[20] The portrait artist strives to activate the audience's habits of vision so that the artwork may give an animated impression of its still subject.

To say that photography is a visual medium really goes without saying. What needs to be said nonetheless is that photography is a medium of the *visible* consolidated within a frame and within a moment. Vision is the human being's most complex sense faculty. The wit of Oscar Wilde puts the matter concisely: "It is only shallow people who do not judge by appearances. The true mystery of the world is the visible, not the invisible."[21] Scientists estimate that a normally sighted person can perceive up to ten million shades and intensities of color. A black and white medium thus involves a great reduction in the capacities of visual perception. In color or not, a photograph provides a second order of the visible. A photograph's frame and composition filters and reduces much of the world's ordinary, distracting multiplicity. Such reductions enable consciousness, on the part of the beholder, to expand upon a few of the world's particulars by way of visual perception. A product of the instantaneous, the photograph achieves duration each time a person views that particular photograph image. Viewing is an act of seeing that has its own temporality and its own mental scene.

In another respect, photographs are now so fully and inseparably a part of lived reality that they are phenomena in their own right, irrespective of any particular content. What we can see specifically in a photograph, in addition to its objective content, is a purposeful, motivated act of looking or construction of a sight on the photographer's part. And since we are engaged in an analogous act, the process is never delimited

[45]

by the photographer's intentionality. Photography has fostered activities and habits of looking that possess their own norms. The medium influences as well one's senses of significance within fields of vision beyond those contained within photographs themselves. At this stage in cultural history, photography has the power to help shape one's general frame of reference, both visually and conceptually.

DEPICTION, DESCRIPTION

In the course of everyday experience amidst all the visual stimuli and media material that permeates the contemporary social environment, it remains for most of us uncommon in a given day to hold one's attention steadfastly upon and face fully a select portion of the world, or even to do so with a portion that has been made fast, depicted, framed, and made available through a photograph. The photograph that arrests one's attention, that induces one to stop and reflect upon it singularly, amidst the incessant passing show of sights and images in everyday life, has activated not only one's faculties of perception and consciousness but one's potential for imaginative connection in the world. Irrespective of specific subject matter, in looking at a photograph one also beholds a unique set of optical properties—fixed focus, unvaried depth of field, picture borders, and the transcription of atmospheric appearances through color or black and white processing. In a consideration of "thinking through photography" Patrick Maynard suggests that we approach the medium as one of the modern age's "depictive technologies." Rather than offering a direct view of its contents, "photography provides methods of marking surfaces that entice imagining."[22]

Photography holds a moment still. The momentary, nonnarrative quality of a photograph should be welcomed, I think, for the unique perceptual advantage its gives over the multitudinous rush of everyday reality, which of course includes its own flux of images. The French documentarian and portraitist Marc Riboud has said of photographers: "We aren't creators, we're interpreters."[23] And it is in this role that mastery has been achieved by many photographers whose work can be understood as a practice of "thick description," to adopt a concept fundamental to the work of anthropologist Clifford Geertz. Through the mode of thick description, according to Geertz, an ethnographic account interjoins observations of the strata and hierarchies of meaning within a culture with indications of the "structures of inference and implication" on the observer's own part. In other words, the activities of gathering information and making observations in the field are compounded with the activities of organizing and constructing this material into an ethnographic study. Interpretation is not held in reserve until all fieldwork is done, rather interpretation is all along an inseparable part of the process of observation. As one consequence the ethnographer relinquishes any pretensions to complete objectivity or comprehensive knowledge of another culture. The fitting scale for the findings in an ethnography is rather on the order of "local truths" in all their "complex specificness [and] their circumstantiality." Such a procedure gives full measure to paradigmatic and descriptive considerations in the human sciences and defers any promise of syntagmatic or narrative totality. At a terminological and methodological level, it should be acknowledged, Geertz denigrates the "I-am-a-camera, 'phenomenalistic'" approach to field observation and cautions that symbolic action is often "unphotographable."[24] Nonetheless, it still can be said that a photograph that arrests a viewer's attention possesses a quality of descriptive thickness. And such a photograph can function as a kind of ethnographic datum from the viewer's own culture, from that of others, and from the encounter of the two.

A descriptive rationale is prominent within modern American photography, from the work of Paul Strand early in the twentieth century through that of Diane Arbus in the 1960s. The snapshot camera vision of Robert Frank, Garry Winogrand, Tod Papageorge, and others is a related approach, but one that makes no explicit demonstrations of mastery in composition or darkroom technique. In a statement from the 1970s on the medium, Winogrand generalized: "Literal description, or the illusion of literal description, is what . . . still photography do[es] better than any other graphic medium." Additionally Winogrand explained, now famously, "I photograph to see what things look like photographed."[25] On another occasion he defined the essence of photography as a process of "Perception (seeing) and Description (operating the camera to make a record) of the seeing."[26] In pointed contradiction to Henri Cartier-Bresson's ideal of the decisive moment and its inherent story structure, Winogrand contended that "No one moment is most important. Any moment can be something."[27] Starting from shared premises yet reaching energetic conclusions instead of Winogrand's often rather deadpan ones, Tod Papageorge believes that "photography investigates no deeper relief than surfaces. It is superficial, in the first sense of the word; it studies the shape and skin of things, that which can be seen. By a passionate extension of this, its most profound meanings have to do with immanence, the indwelling grace of what Zen calls our ten thousand facts."[28]

A photograph depiction is an opportune ground for phenomenological description. To take a small liberty without I think taking great license, a photograph depiction can be likened to the bracketing (*epoché*) of the world important to procedures in phenomenology for a description of the interactions of consciousness and external reality, and through such description comes knowledge. Phenomenological contexts for a consideration of photography first gained prominence in the area of film theory and interpretation, most notably in the writings of André Bazin and Stanley Cavell. Bazin, for one, starts from a premise of complete phenomenal equivalence: "The photographic image is the object itself. . . . The photograph as such and the object in itself share a common being."[29] Cavell initially utilizes a similar premise in stating "A photograph is *of* reality or nature." His "ontology" of the image also registers, however, a property of exclusion within a photograph's framed *portion* of reality: "The implied presence of the rest of the world, and its explicit rejection, are as essential in the experience of a photograph as what it explicitly presents."[30] For both Bazin and Cavell the still image is of interest principally as a technical basis for motion picture photography, and their main concern is with film shots along axes of syntagmatic relations. Their commentary leaves unexplored the paradigmatic and descriptive potentials of the single photograph image.

Siegfried Kracauer has also made claims for the presence of physical reality within photograph images when the images are sequenced into motion pictures.[31] In early commentary on still photography, from the 1920s, Kracauer assesses the appearance of reality offered by the mode to be "mere surface coherence" limited to a depictive function: "In photography the spatial appearance of an object is its meaning." Kracauer places cultural priority instead on "historicism," which depends upon a "complete mirroring of a temporal sequence" and whose ideal medium would be "a giant film depicting the temporally interconnected events from every vantage point."[32] For Kracauer stillness in the photograph image is an impediment.

A practice of phenomenology for inquiry into still photography has been most seriously pursued by Norton Batkin and by Roland Barthes. Batkin's expository method is that of ordinary language philosophy, largely under the influence of Stanley Cavell and specifically through the kinds of questions viewing a photograph raises and the kinds of discourse that suggest possible answers or at least, where no answers are forthcoming, possible responses. Batkin maintains that the photographs that matter to an individual are limited to those that each of us regards through *intentionality*. In this, he applies the principle fundamental to phenomenology that the relationship of consciousness to reality is *intentional*, that acts of consciousness point beyond themselves to the external world, that experience involves perceptions of reality, outside consciousness. Every mental act is "about" or "of" an object. The object need not be actual; it can be irreal, such as a dream image. By function, consciousness always apprehends some*thing*, it is directed *else*where. In turn, the outside world is structured in ways receptive to consciousness; it points reciprocally to acts of consciousness intended toward the outside world.[33] On matters of temporality, Batkin insists that the "moment" of a photograph is marked by an absence of anything preceding or following: "One way to note the fact of stillness, the fact that photographs are still, is to note that photographs have no before and after." Though Batkin does not use the terminology, his account of the experience of viewing a photograph operates as a phenomenological description that sets aside any issues of duration and narrativity. Where photography has to do with philosophy is in questions and qualities of stillness. And these can lead to an apprehension of the unity of consciousness and world: "The fact of a photograph's stillness . . . [is] the fact of sight, the fact of a world altogether."[34] His study's s concluding section discusses the work of Paul Strand largely in such terms.

The book on photography, *La chambre claire* (1980) by Roland Barthes, translated as *Camera Lucida,* has been broadly influential. Its methods appropriate aspects of the project and language of phenomenology albeit, Barthes advises, "it was a vague, casual, even cynical phenomenology, so readily did it agree to distort or to evade its principles according to the whim of my analysis."[35] While Barthes's ideas warrant consideration here on the basis of their prominence within the study of photography, as an application of phenomenology they do not serve the purposes of the present study for reasons that become quickly apparent. The appropriation is also "cynical" in that Barthes knowingly violates fundamentals of "classical phenomenology, the kind I had known in adolescence (and there has not been any other since)" (*Camera Lucida,* 21). The specific tradition at issue here is the transcendental idealism of Edmund Husserl.

Camera Lucida is dedicated to Jean-Paul Sartre's 1940 study *L'imaginaire: psychologie-phénoménologique de l'imagination* (translated into English as *The Psychology of Imagination*). There, Sartre breaks from Husserl's construct of a transcendental Ego. The most important influence upon

Barthes from the Sartre book comes through its investigations into the existential problem of the image. Basic to understanding imagination as an act of consciousness, Sartre maintains, is the premise that perception is a greater faculty than vision: "I always *perceive more and otherwise* than I *see.*"[36] Intentionality supplies perception with a fullness and heterogeneity that vision alone does not possess. Through actions of consciousness an "image is built up by the intention, which compensates for its [i.e. the image's] shortcomings as a perception" (*Imagination*, 41). At an initial level of vision, Sartre explains, "the photograph is but a paper rectangle of a special quality and color, with shadows and white spots distributed in a certain fashion" (*Imagination*, 24). To apprehend the photograph consciousness mobilizes "a certain intention, the one that turns it [i.e., the photograph] into an image," into an object grasped by one's imaginative faculty (*Imagination*, 25).

Not all photographs enter the consciousness of a beholder fully as an *image*. Most photographs in fact do not, and Barthes designates their limited level of interest to imagination to be the *studium* of photography, "that very wide field of unconcerned desire, of various interest, of inconsequential taste" (*Camera Lucida*, 27). Another break from transcendental principle by Barthes results from an unwillingness to submit his feelings in relation to certain photographs to the *epoché* or phenomenological reduction. Barthes prefers instead to indulge in narcissistic intentionality in relation to his chosen images. The chief affect involved in such intentionality, as Barthes soon makes plain, constellates desire and grief. It is a desire for consciousness borne of mourning, specifically over the loss of his mother.

Seeing a photograph phenomenologically is for Barthes a matter of agonized, romantic recognition of loss. For him, the medium's capacity to evoke pathos arises from its lack of any real depth in space or time: "With the Photograph, we enter into *flat Death.* . . . The Photograph is a certain but fugitive testimony; so that everything, today, prepares our race for this impotence: to be no longer able to conceive *duration*, affectively or symbolically" (*Camera Lucida*, 92–93). This assertion identifies the modality of the photograph as depictive, with a corollary loss to any narrative meaning. Barthes's understanding of photographic depiction does not entail the deeply structured integration of consciousness and world through perception that the process of *description* in classical phenomenology seeks. In another interview Barthes explained: "Each perception and reading of a photo is implicitly, in a repressed manner, a contact with what has ceased to exist, a contact with death. I think that this is the way to approach the photographic enigma, at least that is how I experience photography: as a fascinating and funereal enigma."[37] Barthes elaborates the enigma in *Camera Lucida* by contemplating photographs that seem to invite his aggrieved intentionality and that thus can be classified by the quality he designates as *punctum*—"this wound, this prick, this mark" that "rises from the scene, shoots out of it like an arrow, and pierces me" (*Camera Lucida*, 26). The underlying power of its poignancy is experienced by Barthes consistently as the sensation that its subject seems already dead, apart from any consideration of that person's continued existence, and in this Barthes encounters being in an "anterior future" imperative mode, as the "imperious sign of . . . future death" (*Camera Lucida*, 96, 97).

In the transcendental phenomenology of Husserl consciousness is able to engage the world directly only after exercising the *epoché*, a suspension or bracketing of cultural assumptions, personal values, and empirical knowledge about phenomena. Barthes's practices are anything but dispassionate or transcendent. Yet, with ironic impertinence he explains them as a kind of *epoché*: "I am a primitive, a child—or a maniac; I dismiss all knowledge, all culture, I refuse to inherit anything from another eye than my own" (*Camera Lucida*, 51). *Camera Lucida* is a work of mourning, and its ideas on the temporality of photography are shaped to serve that intention. The *punctum* of a photograph involves a "lacerating emphasis" upon "Time," whose "pure representation" is in the conjugation "that-has-been" ("*ça-a-été*" in the original French) (*Camera Lucida*, 96). A beholder's perception of the photographed subject is bound within this tense form and an immutable calculus of time: "By giving me the absolute past of the pose . . . the photograph tells me death in the future" (*Camera Lucida*, 96). The study's perspective on its subject is that of a traumatized consciousness. In closing, Barthes reconstructs his motivation for writing it as a scene of romantic anguish and mania: "I entered crazily into the spectacle, into the image, taking into my arms what is dead, what is going to die" (*Camera Lucida*, 117). The duration of exposition in *Camera Lucida* is thus marked by submission to a belief that all that is meaningful has been, is, or will be past. In these circumstances Barthes is left external, extraneous, to the present and bereft of any future, even an immediate one, other than that marked by mortality, a prospect that is already past. The master narrative of *Camera Lucida*, and of photography itself in Barthes's view, is death. Phenomenology in its own right, on the other hand, generally operates elsewhere, amidst the living.

A DESCRIPTIVE APPROACH

Despite a near consensus in contemporary academic discourse against suggestions of any lasting or reliable truth in the matter, I think each of us will admit personally to the unique perceptual and contemplative effect some photographs have in the course of our lives.[38] And phenomenology can offer explanations for the power an image can have within consciousness. To the question "What is phenomenology?" that inaugurates his *Phenomenology of Perception*, Maurice Merleau-Ponty begins to answer with the explanation that it is a philosophy that "tries to give a direct description of our experience as it is, without taking account of its psychological origin and the causal explanations which the scientist, the historian or the sociologist may be able to provide."[39] Description thus stands at the forefront of the phenomenological project, as Merleau-Ponty reiterates: "It is a matter of describing, not of explaining or analyzing" (*Phenomenology*, viii). Perception and description, as acts of consciousness, are humanity's primary means of "access to truth" (*Phenomenology*, xvi). In a perceptual approach, a person's experience of the world is inseparable from the person's description of the world, and thus a phenomenological description has in view both the *entities and phenomena* as one experiences them and one's *experience* of entities and phenomena. This approach answers a fundamental challenge to knowledge, for "nothing is more difficult to know than precisely *what we see*" (*Phenomenology*, 58).

For Merleau-Ponty an unprejudiced description of one's perception and experience of the world reveals the basis of human existence. A person's experience of the world is of necessity perspectival. Moreover, perception and consciousness *embody* experience for a person. In other writings Merleau-Ponty explains that the role of phenomenology "consists not in stringing concepts together but in describing the mingling of consciousness with the world, its involvement in a body, and its coexistence with others." Moreover, "phenomenological or existential philosophy is largely an expression of surprise at [the] inherence of the self in the world and in others, a description of this paradox and permeation, and an attempt to make us *see* the bond between subject and world, between subject and others, rather than to *explain* it as the classical philosophies did by resorting to absolute spirit."[40] It is not a purpose here to reconcile or overcome differences between the practices of phenomenology identified as transcendental and associated with Husserl versus those identified as existential and associated with Merleau-Ponty. An operation of the *epoché* or reduction posited by Husserl is accepted by

Merleau-Ponty insofar as it is necessary to free consciousness from attitudes that presume truths about the world prior to one's experience of the world. Merleau-Ponty does not incorporate into his phenomenology, however, the eidectic *epoché* that became paramount to Husserl, who explained the transcendental project as follows: consciousness "can be purged of every empirical and psycho-physical element, but, being so purged, it cannot deal with 'matters of fact.' Any closed field may be considered as regards its 'essence' . . . and we may disregard the factual side of our phenomena, and use them as 'examples' merely. We shall ignore individual souls and societies, to learn their a priori, their 'possible' forms."[41] Phenomenology for Merleau-Ponty, to the contrary, "does not expect to arrive at an understanding of man and the world from any starting point other than that of their 'facticity'" (*Phenomenology*, vii). The process does not remain, however, at a level of facticity: "The phenomenological world is not the bringing to explicit expression of a pre-existent being, but a laying down of being. . . . [It is] like art, the act of bringing truth into being" (*Phenomenology*, xx).

To make the argument that embodied consciousness synthesizes sense perceptions like sound, touch, and sight into an experience of the totality of an object or a phenomenon, Merleau-Ponty elaborates an analogy to the complex coordination involved in binocular vision and the perception of a single image that results. Of all the senses, he posits the one most "capable of objectivity and accessible to intentionality" to be vision, and it predominates in our perceptual involvement with the world. Merleau-Ponty accepts "the taking over of sensory experiences in general in visual experience" as a general truth (*Phenomenology*, 234 n1). While it is true that Merleau-Ponty's published commentary gives precedence to vision over other modes of perceptual and cognitive activity and that his exposition of visual experience is conveyed exclusively through writing, his philosophy gives every indication that language is adequate to the responsibilities of phenomenological description.[42]

To Merleau-Ponty's way of thinking expressive modes, regardless of the specific medium, have much in common as phenomena: "A novel, poem, picture or musical work are individuals, that is, beings in which the expression is indistinguishable from the thing expressed, their meaning accessible only through direct contact, being radiated with no change of their temporal and spatial situation. It is in this sense that our body is comparable to a work of art. It is a nexus of living meanings" (*Phenomenology*, 151). In his concept of "the prose of the world," language "contains its own ebbing, it own rule of usage and vision of the world," and great literature "introduces us to new experiences and to perspectives that can never be ours, so that in the end language destroys our prejudices."[43] Reading is an activity that involves vision, yet it transports the reader into realms of the invisible: "The wonderful thing about language is that it promotes its own oblivion: my eyes follow the lines on the paper, and from the moment I am caught up in their meaning I lose sight of them. The paper, the letters on it, my eyes and body are there only as the minimum setting of some invisible operation" (*Phenomenology*, 401). With an echo of Oscar Wilde that would surprise the both of them, Merleau-Ponty explains the experience of invisibility evoked within consciousness by means of the visible as an "invisible *of* this world, that which inhabits this world, sustains it, renders it visible, its own and interior possibility, the Being of this being."[44] It is in this connection that he cites the image, devised by Paul Valéry, of a secret blackness of milk detectable only through its whiteness.

The application of phenomenology is far more developed in the study of literature than it is in the study of photography. The range of specific approaches to literature varies widely.[45] Rather than rehearse some of the philosophical varieties, however, it will be more effective to conclude with two examples of phenomenology possible in literature articulated from within literature itself, one by Wallace Stevens, a poet laureate of the imaginative faculties, the second by Joseph Conrad, a master of the novel of consciousness. In "Note on Moonlight" Stevens contemplates prospects simplified into darks and lights:

> The one moonlight, in the simple-colored night,
> Like a plain poet revolving in his mind
> The sameness of his various universe,
> Shines on the mere objectiveness of things.

Stevens draws a necessary connection among the world, human beings, and the visible:

> It is as if being was to be observed,
> As if, among the possible purposes
> Of what one sees, the purpose that comes first,
> The surface, is the purpose to be seen.

The connection embodies an intentionality that is appropriately considered existential *and* phenomenological:

The one moonlight, the various universe, intended
So much just to be seen—a purpose, empty
Perhaps, absurd perhaps, but at least a purpose,
Certain and ever more fresh.[46]

Visibility or its depiction alone, either will suffice, is sufficient to constitute being.

In the preface to one of his tales, Conrad says of literary art in general that "it may be defined as a single-minded attempt to render the
highest kind of justice to the visible universe, by bringing to light the
truth, manifold and one, underlying its every aspect."[47] And such truth
extends into domains not visible in themselves: its "appeal is made to
our less obvious capacities: to that part of our nature which, because of
the warlike conditions of existence, is necessarily kept out of sight within
the more resisting and hard qualities." Moreover, "such an appeal, to
be effective, must be an impression conveyed through the senses; and,
in fact, it cannot be made in any other way." While Conrad created
indelible grotesque characterizations, as with the young Russian clad in
motley and Mr. Kurtz of *Heart of Darkness* (1902) and the revolutionists
Mr. Verloc and Michaelis of *The Secret Agent* (1907), more importantly,
his explanation of the novelist's art is suggestive of the processes of
adumbration and elucidation essential to visual and literary traditions of
the grotesque. Conrad reaches a conclusion that has become canonical:
"My task which I am trying to achieve is, by the power of the written
word, to make you hear, to make you feel—it is, before all, to make you
see. That—and no more, and it is everything." His amplification of the
credo also warrants quotation: "The task approached in tenderness and
faith is to hold up unquestioningly, without choice and without fear, the
rescued fragment before all eyes" and to "disclose its inspiring secret:
the stress and passion, within the core of each convincing moment."
If achieved "the presented vision of regret or pity, of terror or mirth,
shall awaken in the hearts of the beholders that feeling of unavoidable
solidarity, . . . which binds men to each other and all mankind to the
visible world."

The ideas on perception, the visible, invisibility, intentionality, and
the complete moment that Stevens and Conrad express are all consonant
with the practices of description crucial in a phenomenological response
to the world. And, to reiterate, the modern grotesque is often graphic
and descriptive—as against conceptual or narrative—in its means. Modernist impulses complicate the grotesque through compound reflexive

uses of visualized description. A descriptive approach thus seems particularly well suited to an analysis of the grotesque in both literary and pictorial forms as an expression of modern culture. The present study undertakes the project in the spirit of phenomenology. Our daily experiences as readers and observers, free from any master narrative or dominant ideology within us or within our world, offer powerful vantages upon being.

Grotesques in Modern America

Sherwood Anderson

*E*ARLY IN THE TWENTIETH CENTURY William Carlos Williams associated the modern grain of American culture closely with the grotesque. He explained its most prominent tendencies as tropisms toward darkness and toward the socially marginal or subcultural. A short Williams poem of the time, "Sub Terra" (1915), defines a truly contemporary and American imaginative life in terms of newly rediscovered muses, a rebel band of "grotesque fellows." The poem literalizes the word's senses of "grotto-like" and of a shaded or subterranean place brought to light in explaining the impetus for poetic composition as an appetite for "the guts of shadows." Driven by "earthy tastes" and a "burrowing pride," the poet satisfies his curiosity and imagination in a kind of "half light," attracted variously by the "gloom and smell" of a black ghetto and by a scene of children "leaping around a dead dog." Brought into light from subterranean social realms, the poem's images are meant to convey a symbolic degree of violence (they "leap and snap . . . as with a million lashes!") in order to reveal their full nature. Elsewhere, in the brief verse "Grotesque" (1914), Williams likens this force to "blunt stub-horns" that "crack skulls / And spill brains."[1]

Williams credits photography with a significant role in the making of a uniquely modern culture in America at the start of the twentieth century: "the photographic camera and what it could do were peculiarly well suited to a place where the immediate and the actual were under official neglect." The new culture of immediacy is best portrayed and comprehended by means of "authentic crudeness," which for both verbal and visual media is far less a matter of stylistic manipulation than one of direct treatment of everyday urban subject matter. He further notes that under such circumstances when "something for a moment shows true" it appears "grotesque perhaps also" in the process.[2] In photography such truth is realized through close attention to society's vernacular of persons, objects, and ready-made sights.

In the writing life of Sherwood Anderson biographical and manuscript evidence indicates that the inception of *Winesburg, Ohio* (1919) came in fall 1915 when he drafted "The Book of the Grotesque." Over the next few years Anderson had in mind the title *The Book of the Grotesque* for a volume containing his recent stories, the majority of which he wrote that fall and during winter 1915–16. His new publisher Ben Huebsch, however, urged and gained the change in title for the book's ultimate release in May 1919.[3]

Constance Rourke, in her influential study *American Humor,* first published in 1931, classifies the American grotesque in the company of the tall-tale, the hoax, and other popular, comic oral forms. While Rourke acknowledges that the grotesque sometimes entails violent and nightmarish effects, she maintains that its cultural roots reach deepest into folk comedy. In her view, the comic power of folk traditions, adapted in literary forms, reawakens for society in the present some of the formative energies of American culture.[4] Although the term is not used, clearly Rourke's conclusion accords with ideas of the carnivalesque. By her account the species of grotesque fashioned by Poe in his tales casts aside social humor in favor of a private realm of mystery and terror. As a consequence, Poe's grotesque effects provoke a superficial reaction and neglect the possibilities for deeper, comic recognition. With Twain, Rourke finds, the American grotesque regains its ritual and mythic roles in the revitalization of culture. While *Winesburg, Ohio* with its introductory "The Book of the Grotesque" had appeared more than a decade before, Sherwood Anderson's fiction receives only passing mention in Rourke's study and, at that, only as a recent example of the comic monologue tradition. Though Anderson as a practitioner of the grotesque remained a prominent figure through much of the 1920s, Rourke largely confines American cultural achievements in this mode to the nineteenth century.

Positioned as the first tale in *Winesburg, Ohio,* "The Book of the Grotesque" was also the first of the future volume's sections to appear in print, in one of the small magazines of the era (the February 1916 issue of *The Masses*). "The Book of the Grotesque," which is notable in part simply for its abbreviated length, promises an explanation of the grotesque by way of a narrative account about an old writer lying in bed alone with his thoughts. From the outset, however, the account meets obstacles and meanders from its single purpose. In the course of the prose both the story and the pledged explanation border upon non sequitur at several places. The following analogies in description of the writer's state of mind, for example, are offered then abandoned: "Perfectly still he lay and his body was old and not of much use any more, but something inside him was altogether young. He was like a pregnant woman, only that the thing inside him was not a baby but a youth. No, it wasn't a youth, it was a woman, young, and wearing a coat of mail like a knight. It is absurd, you see, to try to tell what was inside the old writer."[5] What is conveyed here instead is failure in the efforts to contrive story syllogisms.

In terms of the account Roman Jakobson has given of the two aspects or "gravitational poles" of language, much of the syntax in Anderson's prose clearly belongs with the paradigmatic functions of selection, substitution, similarity, and metaphor. Syntagmatic functions, at the opposite pole as indicated earlier, involve combination, contextualization, contiguity, and metonymy. Within literary history by Jakobson's account, we recall, the richest examples of paradigmatic uses are to be found in Romantic lyricism and Symbolist poetry, while those of the syntagmatic are in realist prose epic. The polarity Jakobson has defined accords with the one between description and narrative. Description relies upon substitutive procedures and Anderson persists in their use even when they malfunction, as in the *Winesburg* example just cited. As against the procedures of analogy and word choice fundamental to description, narrative relies upon predicative functions and a construction of syntactic complements. Anderson often adopts a posture of uncertainty over his skill with narrative, leaving for someone more gifted the challenge to tell the story more eloquently.

When it finally does start, the explanation of the grotesque opens as a genesis story: "In the beginning when the world was young there were a great many thoughts but no such thing as a truth" (*Winesburg*, 6). In the next phase of creation, "Man made the truths himself and each truth was a composite of a great many vague thoughts. All about the world were the truths and they were all beautiful" (*Winesburg*, 6). This multitude of truths constitutes an aboriginal human endowment of unbounded experience, free from predeterminations and social strictures. At this stage, truth consists of notions and inclinations rather than definite ideas or values. What follows in the tale's digest treatment of events is a fall and devolution: "And then the people came along. Each as he appeared snatched up one of the truths and some who were quite strong snatched up a dozen of them. It was the truths that made the people grotesques" (*Winesburg*, 6). More specifically, a person's stubborn allegiance to a single truth, or to a fused set of truths, transforms that person into a grotesque and converts truth into falsehood. This imagined devolution of humanity into the people, and of the people into confusion and antagonism, recalls the Tower of Babel story and its purpose in explaining the origin of separate languages and the spread of disparate societies.

Some wording in "The Book of the Grotesque" seems to echo phrases from *The Declaration of Independence* that there stand as propositions of self-evident truths and of a new body politic, stated clearly in the affirmative syntax within its preamble: "When in the Course of human events it becomes necessary for one people . . . to assume among the powers of the earth the separate and equal station to which the Laws of Nature and of Nature's God entitle them." Contrary to any foundational claims made in the Declaration, however, "The Book of the Grotesque" assumes that the present condition of American society is one of inequality and disunity. In place of "one people" and of a collective purpose in securing life, liberty, or the pursuit of happiness, America is here conceived in terms of a "long procession" of grotesques, many of them horrible to be sure, but some are "almost beautiful," while others are simply amusing (*Winesburg*, 5). Whatever the particular form of its manifestation the grotesque expresses both the potential uniqueness of personality and an antisocial undercurrent. It preserves within the individual an intensity of life that is his or her private heritage from a larger, shared humanity, no matter how remote or warped the connection may appear. From the perspective of *Winesburg, Ohio* modern America outwardly marks "the most materialistic age in the history of the world" (*Winesburg*, 68), yet within individual Americans—and the majority of them are by no means fulfilled in the pursuits of happiness or prosperity—lies a compulsion to liberate a suppressed truth about humanity, if only momentarily.

The occasion for commentary upon the grotesque in "The Book," it will be remembered, is the portrait of an old man musing upon this subject. Off and on he stirs himself from bed to write down some thoughts and impressions. Over time he turns out "hundreds of pages concerning this matter" and these pages constitute in the end "a book which he called 'The Book of the Grotesque,'" a work that is never published. This last fact helps in good part to explain why the old writer, who is "in danger of becoming a grotesque," does not finally become one (*Winesburg*, 6). The integrity and originality of his efforts are not compromised by their textual codification into truths, an outcome that would transpire had they, as it were, been brought to the light of print. Instead of The Book of the Grotesque itself we get a brief tale of The Book which in its own right is less a proper story than an incomplete description and explanation of The Book of the Grotesque and its abiding notions. The dimensions of internal referentiality are redoubled when we remember Anderson's long-held intention to title his book *The Book of the Grotesque*. Reflexivity in this case, however, serves altogether different functions from those we observed in Poe's "Shadow—A Fable" with its elaborate wordplay and ingenious devices of *mise en abyme* in description and narration.

Reflexivity serves in "The Book" to convey an ultimately fortunate, estimable futility in circumstances. The principal medium through which "The Book," and Anderson's book as a whole, offers itself is oral, irrespective of the obvious fact that an audience encounters it in typographical form, a situation acknowledged in the very title. Among the grotesques of Winesburg are manic and frustrated writers, prone to verbal outburst on paper, as in the case of Dr. Reefy's compulsive scraps of thought and Louise Bentley's neurotic, lustful message to John Hardy. Some of the tales claim to remain, at least in part, in a condition of being unfinished and unwritten, alive with the full-blooded but still crude qualities of a first telling. The desired effect is declared early on: "Perhaps our talking . . . will arouse the poet who will tell the hidden wonder story" (*Winesburg*, 13). The simulated situation of their prematurity in print intensifies the note of vulnerability and the halting quality of confession already prominent in the book's accounts of individual grotesques. For all the stress on storytelling, in many respects *Winesburg*'s contents are given over more to description and attempts at explanation than to narration per se.[6]

Wing Biddlebaum, the book's first named grotesque and the subject of the second tale, "Hands," occupies a small house perched near the edge of a ravine. Associations in setting and character description to physical properties of the grotto are clearly intentional. He is said to often regard the world anxiously from within the shadows of the home's veranda. The man himself is possessed of a "shadowy personality, submerged in a sea of doubts" (*Winesburg*, 12). His tale is introduced on a note of inadequacy at the level of representation, a situation established in "The Book" as one reflexive trait of the grotesque and as an inversely proportioned sign of importance: "The story of Wing Biddlebaum's hands is worth a book in itself. Sympathetically set forth it would tap many strange, beautiful qualities in obscure men. It is a job for a poet" (*Winesburg*, 11). Anderson's grotesques are a poetic alternative to the brutes and bestialized humans of naturalist fiction and Social Darwinism. They are also an alternative to the freak show attractions popular through the nineteenth century and for much of the twentieth. The most common generic designations for such attractions were "Living Curiosity," "Human Curiosity," and plainly "What Is It?" As an integral part of such exhibitions "true life" pamphlets were sold from the show platform. Often extravagantly contrived, these published accounts gave biographical information, details of the person's physical condition, and statements purportedly from medical doctors or other natural scientists vouching for the authenticity and clinical significance of the abnormality and for the social value of the exhibition itself. When the person exhibited was claimed to have come from some faraway place, a pseudoethnography was included.[7]

It is of course the very ambition of *Winesburg, Ohio* itself to disclose the strange intensity hidden within men and women of no social consequence. When Wing Biddlebaum himself begins to tell it, the secret history of his hands opens as a genesis story, one that begins "in a kind of pastoral golden age" (*Winesburg,* 12) when he was known by his given name Adolph Myers rather than by the assumed name that now brands him as one of the accursed. In the inspiration of the moment the man raises his hands to caress his listener George Willard, the young reporter for the town newspaper the *Winesburg Eagle* and a surrogate narrator and writer figure for *Winesburg, Ohio* as a whole. Wing Biddlebaum's impassioned gesture reawakens within himself, however, the circumstances of his catastrophic fall from this state of grace. Upon that instant he breaks off the account and flees the company of George.

For the brief spell that the episode of his downfall remains unremembered, the man is whole with the truth and beauty of existence, in a privileged state before the confusion of languages. Indeed, he relates this past to George in the form of a dreamlike picture rather than one of verbal narrative. The wordless, untold condition in which he leaves the tale is itself a mark of authenticity, given the fallen state of both humanity and language. When the story is resumed in the literary voice of *Winesburg's* unnamed author source, there is within a few sentences another admission of shortcoming that registers an inability to embody its originality: "And yet that is but crudely stated. It needs the poet there" (*Winesburg,* 14). Hands are the poetic figure expressive of Adolph Myer's gifts early in adult life as a teacher of the young. Presently, for a brief interval they move in accompaniment to a "bold" and "inspired" harmony regained in Wing's voice (*Winesburg,* 13). These are the organs through which he sought some twenty years earlier to cultivate innocence and instill knowledge. At the same time, hands figure Adolph Myers' condemnation by townspeople in Pennsylvania after a half-witted schoolchild made accusations of sexual mistreatment against him. In their constant, compulsive movements, which he tries unsuccessfully to conceal and sup-press, Wing Biddlebaum's hands are at once a sign of the soul's truth and testimony to his social undoing.

Standards of authenticity and human worth for a tale of the grotesque are set forth in "Paper Pills," the third chapter in *Winesburg, Ohio*. The story title refers to the thoughts, half-thoughts truly, Doctor Reefy has scribbled on scraps of paper that he carelessly stuffs into his pockets. With time each scrap of writing becomes a hardened little ball of paper and when his pockets become crowded with these balls he discards the lot of them, only to begin the process again. The tale divulges that long ago the doctor acted as an abortionist for the young woman he would marry; she died under other circumstances less than a year after their wedding. In development of the book's genesis motif at a point after the human fall into a mortal state of knowledge, Anderson likens the paper balls to "the twisted little apples" left behind in the orchards around Winesburg after harvest time (*Winesburg*, 19). Hawthorne's tribute to the unique individuality of trees in the apple orchard, particularly to the gnarled and crabbed ones, will be remembered here.

The uniform, marketable apples have been shipped to cities, where they will be "eaten in apartments that are filled with books, magazines, furniture, and people" (*Winesburg*, 19). This comment brings to mind Walt Whitman's allusion in "Song of Myself" (1855) to literary traditions, made in his testament of independence from such canons: "Houses and rooms are full of perfumes—the shelves are crowded with perfumes."[8] With his statement Anderson directs attention toward distinctions between the imaginative worth of the grotesque and the market for popular writing. Though twisted and unappetizing in outward appearance the neglected apples possess a distinct sweetness and provide unique gratification. Indeed, for those who have tasted of this fruit, its visible attributes can be taken as a sure sign of remarkable inner qualities. Following the logic of the image's analogy to literature, it is through anomaly and unpresent-able externals that abiding human truths are to be transmitted. By com-parison, prose devised for the mass market and prevalent tastes proves barren of any distinctive style or knowledge.

George Willard's interactions with the grotesques of Winesburg have a nocturnal quality about them. Whether or not they actually take place at night, the encounters possess a dreamlike rush and compression of language and event. They reflect qualities of experience removed from the waking, practical preoccupations of business, family, and social life. While George is shown often to pass along Main Street, the usual desti-nations in his encounters with the town's grotesques are darkened alleyways or side streets, outlying and vacant fields or farm buildings, or the empty railroad tracks and country roads leading out of Winesburg. When the scene does not take place at nighttime, sometimes an element of darkness is conveyed by the grime of a grotesque's surroundings, as in the case of the rented office Doctor Parcival uses as his living quarters and which is described as "unspeakably dirty" in "The Philosopher" (*Winesburg*, 36). In other instances, darkness marks the physical appearance of a grotesque, as with the black smudge along the side of Louise Trunnion's nose in "Nobody Knows" or with the forbidding cast in the facial expressions of Wash Williams in "Respectability." The moment of revelation in the Wash Williams story does occur at night. In the pitch of darkness, however, the man's face is entirely obscured from George's view. It is through the low, filth-ridden, terrible tone in Williams' voice alone that George imagines the look in this grotesque's "black shining eyes," alight with his hatred of women (*Winesburg*, 117).

In general, the *Winesburg* tales involve an exposure of the unsuspected depths of futility and suffering contained within an individual's personality. Ofttimes George is a witness or an involuntary confessor to a grotesque as he or she lunges into an excavation of the secret self. The grotesque's forbidden, suppressed memories or urges rush headlong to the surface and are voiced or acted upon and then they withdraw again as suddenly into unapproachable depths. Revelation or confession is not attended by catharsis; the private pathos of the incident is not shown to serve a general good. By the level of expectations that Bakhtin and Rourke placed upon the mode, the grotesques of Winesburg fail to achieve any degree of redemption in culture or society. Folkloric traditions in general, according to Bakhtin, are the crucial means through which common humanity confronts the forces in nature and society whose seeming superiority induces "the fear of the immeasurable, the infinitely powerful" (*Rabelais*, 335). In Bakhtin's estimation, the grotesque proves to be inexhaustible in resources and inventiveness as it pursues an "act of becoming" that guarantees that it always "outgrows its own self" (*Rabelais*, 317). Through the sheer magnitude and multiplicity of its regenerative momentum the grotesque triumphs over "cosmic terror" (*Rabelais*, 335).

Most of Anderson's grotesques are atomized, and they are shown to abide as arrested and scarcely felt presences within the Winesburg community. Their tales often culminate in perverse, momentary expenditures of emotion and spirit that in the event prove to have no lasting, reinvigorating power for a society that has drifted far from basic, necessary human truths. By default and with repeated admissions of their aborted condition, the tales in written form nonetheless still hope to convey some of the grotesque's redemptive potential.

In the 1920s Thomas Mann, reflecting upon the conditions of culture in the new century, judged "the striking feature of modern art" to be the general rupture and fragmentation among traditional aesthetic categories with the result "that the grotesque is its most genuine style."[9] Mann makes this assessment from his position as a master of literary traditions and complex narrative structures, as a writer determined to mold together into fitting patterns the great incongruities of modern cultural forms. For Anderson, by contrast, grotesque style is an authenticating mark of social failure and of literary malfunctions in communication of experiences that are preliterate in nature.

At the time of the publication of *Winesburg, Ohio*, Anderson had an idea for a new book to be entitled "Industrial Vistas." Though he never carried through the project, Anderson conceived it in terms of the following substance and approach: "It is to be the autobiography of a man's secondary self, of the queer, unnamed fancies that float through his brain, the things that appear to have no connection with actualities. In me, and, I fancy, in most men, odd, detached fancies are born, blossom, sometimes like flowers, sometimes like evil-seeming weeds, then appear to pass. My notion is that no man knows himself or can arrive at truth concerning himself except by what seems like indirection. I have a desire to take hold of indirection as a tool and use it in an attempt to arrive at truth. . . . I hope to make an odd, insane-seeming man emerge into actuality." The book was intended to embody the "jangle and ugliness" of such origins.[10] By comparison to Thomas Mann's sense of the broad cultural reach of the grotesque, Anderson's understanding here seems private and narrowly particularized.

Anderson's first writing career, it is well to remember, was not literary at all. Starting around 1902 he took a position in the advertising business as a solicitor and copywriter, and he periodically continued in this line of work into the 1920s. In the years 1903–1904 he contributed regular, signed columns to the trade journal *Agricultural Advertising* under the banner heads "Rot and Reason" and "Business Types." In one of these pieces, Anderson cautions against the urge for novelty in advertising as a breach of the sole imperative in commerce, which is "to put money in the till": "It is this everlasting effort for the new and the strange that leads to all the freakish, absurd stuff" that appears in print.[11] Set against this message of conformity, however, in another column for *Agricultural Advertising* that same year (1903) entitled "The Lightweight" Anderson imagines the fate of a nondescript employee in a world ruled by profits.

The title introduces a contemporary parable of the grotesque that applies to the common man who takes a routine desk job in an office in the city only in time to discover himself to be weak and inadequate by the standards of business success. With such a realization he becomes one of the city's "discontented spirits." When a manager notices this condition the employee is fired and replaced by someone optimistic and energetic, as the jaded employee once was. In sympathy with the fired man, Anderson understands that such social dislocation can well cause a desperate, violent reaction: "He'll make news now if he isn't careful, for he's on a fair way to the horror column" (*Early Writings*, 26).

Distinct registers of meaning for the freakish and the extreme are apparent in the two articles. From a business standpoint, these tendencies interfere with the profit motive, while in life they express a margin of humanity that eludes the social forces of practicality and conformity. Once Anderson's artistic life as a writer began, the two registers of meaning entered into a complicated relationship that persisted for the duration of his career in large part because he never overcame an acute self-consciousness about his status as a published fiction writer. His initial aspirations for an artistic life are expressed alternately in terms of menial work in a warehouse or a field and in those of craft, vocation, and apprenticeship. From the outset there coexisted within him an idealistic yearning for humble creative honesty and a worldly desire for literary success. The model persona of the artist long remained for Anderson a forthright, unselfconscious workman engaged in nonindustrial labor or handicraft as opposed to assembly-line manufacture and the prevailing Fordism. Within this scheme of values, the production of advertising copy amounts to no more than a mechanical application of words.

Regardless of Anderson's aesthetic standard of clean, simple hand labor, on paper his own script appeared to be an indecipherable mess, as he stated on several occasions. And it was through handwritten manuscript form that Anderson first placed for publication several Winesburg stories in small literary magazines. In that period Anderson was quick to characterize his own handwriting as a "scrawl" whose effect was bound to be "atrocious" to the eye of any reader (*Letters*, 12). At the same time Anderson could conceive of the following benchmark of lucidity for his work: "I have had the notion that nothing from my pen should be published that could not be read aloud in the presence of a cornfield" (*Letters*, 21). In "An Apology for Crudity," issued in 1917 in the pages of *The Dial*, Anderson extends the dualism of coarseness and craft to include literary style. Since, by his reasoning, American culture now generally manifests itself in anonymous, mindless, and inarticulate ways, with daily life turned "as ugly as modern war," any honest and truly contemporary style needs to embody these limitations through "crude and broken forms." Under the circumstances, at both particular and integral levels there is no longer any necessity in literary structure for "subtlety of plot and phrase."[12] For Anderson the writer it is only in such conditions and through a crafted application of crudity that the underlying poetry of American life can be recovered.

Even while the promise of *Winesburg, Ohio* is through the grotesque to arrive at earlier, more original truths of humanity, truth value within the grotesque is liable to further, severe distortion through the process of writing itself, no matter how skillful, and through any subsequent mediation in print. More than a decade after publication of the book, Anderson returned to the experience of its inception as the moment of his discovery of artistic purpose. Within the full manuscript of his last autobiography, begun in 1933 and left unfinished at the time of his death in 1941, Anderson recounts the outset of writing *Winesburg* as a genesis scene and he does so in three separate places. He also confesses that by its measure he feels even more acutely at present "the shame of my many failures since that, the greatest moment of my life."[13] In a foreword drafted for the autobiography Anderson erroneously states that he had *published* three books by the time when in 1915 he wrote the first Winesburg stories. In fact, these three volumes appeared in the interim 1916 to 1918, *after* he began to write what would become *Winesburg, Ohio*. The error in memory is symptomatic of Anderson's conflicted sense of identity as a professional writer, even in a phase of widespread public recognition.

Another symptomatic lapse in memory is apparent in Anderson's repeated claim that composition of the tale "Hands" marks the inception of his Winesburg book when in fact he had drafted "The Book of the Grotesque" first. By his account Anderson completed "Hands" in one inspired, unselfconscious evening of work and it required no substantial revision: "I wrote my first authentic tale and having . . . completed it cleanly at one sitting, I jumped up and again walked but I walked now with a new gladness" (*Memoirs*, 237). As Anderson portrays them, he had spent the business hours of that day partly at the advertising company on assignments as a copywriter, partly in saloons with another ad man seeking escape from the numbing boredom of their work. He judges himself at that point in life to have been socially a go-getter who was "pretty slick" with customers and associates, while privately he led in his off-hours a largely aimless existence as a "scribbler" (*Memoirs*, 238). The breakthrough moment marks a divide between print culture in service to commercial end uses on one side and on the other creative writing in longhand as honest handiwork. The cardinal value of manual labor for Anderson extends to his lifelong preference for writing by hand rather than by machine: "I have never developed any skill on a typewriter and, besides, when I become absorbed in writing there is always a queer internal excitement that leads me to press the keys of a typewriter too vigorously. . . . And besides I like the smell of ink. I like the physical feeling of the words flowing out of a pen on the paper" (*Memoirs*, 13).

Anderson's earlier, published autobiographical volume *A Story Teller's Story* (1924) depicts the consequences for him as a fiction writer of the relative success of *Winesburg, Ohio* with critics and readers. For one thing the simplest of verbal exchanges with nonliterary acquaintances and friends, Anderson observed, became subject to the distortions of self-consciousness, on both sides. Such was the case with his grocer, who was now studied in his speech, adopting the style of "a very movie hero: . . . his tales, that had been [once] so naturally and humanly told, became grotesques of tales. . . . I remembered almost with tears in my eyes the little homely real stories he had formerly been in the habit of telling of himself."[14] "Grotesques of tales" is meant here in the sense of an impersonal, derivative contrivance, whereas a tale of the grotesque entails the disclosure of raw, authentic emotional matter through honest, directly-spoken outer forms.

The 1924 autobiography conjoins violence, human authenticity, and the grotesque in an office scene when Anderson's imagination is overpowered with thoughts of the untold story that would explain a long, vivid scar that marks the face of a company executive he has chanced to meet. During a business conference the sight of this scar leads Anderson into a reverie where he envisions an ideal community of wounded souls in which each person is completely free from practical concerns and social inhibitions and becomes a candid storyteller. As at the outset of his creative writing career, Anderson here asserts the ideal mode of storytelling to be oral, casual, immediately interpersonal, and based in powerful visual stimuli. With national attention paid to his own published fiction now in the 1920s, Anderson worries more than ever that any writing distributed in print is liable to the taints of machine-made culture. Its sound, should the writing be vocalized, may not be able to rise above the cacophony of modern society whose component noises, as he imagines at one point, include the clatter of the typewriter and the false chatter issued by the commercial press.

Over the course of extended reflections upon the professionalization of authorship, either to serve the aims of commerce through advertisements or to cater to popular reading tastes through mass-circulation magazines, Anderson willingly arrives at the conclusion that often the closest a dedicated writer comes to the ideal of storytelling is, perversely, through failure and futility. By any standards of modern industry or capital enterprise, a man's solitary dedication to prose craft must inevitably appear to be an unnatural act. A refrain scene within the 1924 autobiography is that of Anderson the writer lying in bed at night in a rooming house, holding his hands up in the moonlight in order to observe them more clearly. With confessional intensity he identifies these hands as his secret, sworn, forbidden lover. Anderson's intense self-awareness in the role of writer, with its mixture of naive wonderment and insurmountable anxieties, is quite removed from the reflexivity of a writer like Poe, who freely and gladly optimizes the possibilities offered through intricate, elaborately mediated textuality.

In summation of his creative experience over the decade since his breakthrough in 1915, Anderson is content to make a generalization that would be damning for many published authors. He considers frustration in one's artistic aspirations to be inescapable for the writer and to constitute in fact "a part of the joy of his fate." This situation does not warrant pity, for it is the writing not yet achieved that offers the greatest promise: "Before him always there is the unsolved problem, the clean white unwritten sheets. . . . There will always be the moments when he is lost in wonder before the possibilities of the materials before him" (*Story Teller*, 296). Yet, once written upon, the sheets become new testimony to the author's shortcomings: "To the writer of prose who loves his craft, there is nothing in the world so satisfying as being in the presence of great stacks of clean white sheets. The feeling is indescribably sweet and cannot be compared with any reaction to be got from sheets on which one has already scribbled. The written sheets are already covered with one's faults and oh, it is seldom indeed these sentences, scrawled across these sheets, can compare with what was intended!" (*Story Teller*, 290). In response to the predicament, the writer need only destroy the scribbled sheets until "there, lying before him, will be again the fresh white surface." In celebration of this option, Anderson delivers a good-humored public retraction: "Makers of paper, I exclude you from all the curses I have heaped upon manufacturers when I have walked in the street breathing coal dust and smoke" (*Story Teller*, 293).

Although Anderson published seven novels in his lifetime, the long narrative form ill-suited him. His fictional world is not one of sustained, unfolding events or of a longitudinal development of character. Rather, its milieu largely consists of half-formed emotions, confused thoughts, abiding compulsions, unrealized individual potential, and intense, fleeting revelations. The books of fiction where his best writing is to be found—*Winesburg, Ohio, Poor White* (1920), *The Triumph of the Egg* (1921), and *Horses and Men* (1923)—work mainly as assemblages of anomalies and exceptional cases conveyed through a focus upon incongruity, absurdity, failure. Rather than a subsidiary to narrative, description in his tales often has equal standing with story and in several instances takes priority over it.

Anderson's prose commonly uses synopsized events in order to intensify characterization and descriptive particulars as is the case with Tom King, a man much feared around Winesburg, who "always carried a wicked-looking walking stick in his hand." In introducing this character the tale explains immediately: "Once he killed a dog with the stick. The dog belonged to Win Pawsey, the shoe merchant, and stood on the sidewalk wagging its tail. Tom King killed it with one blow. He was arrested and paid a fine of ten dollars" (*Winesburg*, 99). The anecdote is not offered in the service of a backstory that would trace the development or history of the character's violence. Rather, it stands as a laconic portrait stroke in establishing his innate viciousness.

Among fellow writers as distant from one another in sensibility as William Faulkner, Henry Miller, and Ben Hecht there is consensus that both the attainments and liabilities of Anderson's prose arise from his devoted efforts at word choice. In a faint "Appreciation" of Anderson delivered in 1953, Faulkner said of his style: "His was that fumbling for exactitude, the exact word and phrase within the limited scope of vocabulary controlled and even repressed by what was in him almost a fetish of simplicity."[15] Faulkner's respect is reserved for Anderson's sheer dedication of purpose, despite the faults in its premises and outcome. Henry Miller considers the older writer's commitment to plain craft and simplicity in language to be admirable. But in total effect Anderson's prose is distinguished for Miller chiefly through its "mania for trivia."[16] In remembering Anderson from the Chicago years during the creation of the Winesburg material, Ben Hecht indicates that at the time the stories in their quest for descriptive precision struck him as "very mystic and a little illiterate" when the author read them aloud to friends, which he would do repeatedly over the months to any willing listeners.[17] Ernest Hemingway extends no professional courtesy whatsoever with *The Torrents of Spring* (1926), which thoroughly burlesques Anderson's high seriousness and prose mannerisms, especially his indecisiveness over specific means of expression. In matters of style *The Torrents of Spring* impeaches Anderson as a writer unable to construct or sustain a sensible storyline as infrastructure to his prose.

As every reader of American modernism knows, the one eminent contemporary to have extolled the artistic virtue of Anderson's style is Gertrude Stein. In Stein's thoughts on prose writing over the 1920s the values of "composition as explanation" and of "intellectual passion for exactitude in the description of inner and outer reality" held priority.[18] Her views on temporality and prose operated far outside conventional ideas of narrative progression or recession. Stein understood modern prose composition as a matter of "beginning again and again and again and again, it was a series it was a list, it was a similarity and everything different it was a distribution and an equilibration" (*Selected Writings*, 522). The resultant "continuous present" within the composition means that the act of telling, within its virtual present tense, takes precedence over the substance of what is told (*Selected Writings*, 517). It is according to these standards that Stein credits Anderson's fiction with "a genius for using a sentence to convey a direct emotion" (*Selected Writings*, 205). Perhaps as notable as the attribution of genius here is the clear suggestion that Anderson's abilities extend no further or higher than the level of the sentence.

One Anderson story that involves a host of the differentials in theme, images, and reflexivity discussed thus far is "The Man Who Became a Woman," which he wrote in the fall of 1922 and published the next year in the collection *Horses and Men*. As in Anderson's most realized fiction, these differentials constitute figure-ground relationships that prove inherently ambiguous or reversible and that in the end cannot be resolved into a final or stable gestalt. The story's speaker is an inexperienced author named Herman Dudley, and he begins with a self-effacing account of another man, named Tom Means, "who has since become a writer of some prominence."[19] That name reiterates a basic distinction between the two men: the authorial mode of Means is writing, that of Dudley is speech. Their brief friendship has had a marked influence over Herman, one achieved through a somewhat indirect process: "He had some notions about writing I've never got myself around to thinking much about but just the same maybe his talk, working in me, has led me to want to begin to write this story myself" ("The Man," 367). The story thus within its first pages aligns principal differentials of female/male (Her/man), telling/writing, and talk/print. The latter correspond to a linguistic differential: transparency of spoken words/substantiality of language in print, in black and white.

To these differentials the story quickly adds ones of boyhood/adult-hood, bachelordom/marriage, horses/men, and—most importantly in regard to the published story's reflexivity—black/white social relations. Customarily, Herman Dudley conforms to the social mandates of racial separation: "With a Negro you couldn't be close friends like you can with another white man. . . . There's been too much talk about the difference between whites and blacks and you're both shy, and anyway no use trying" ("The Man," 371). This situation prevails specifically within the domain of social discourse. But when it comes to a private realm, in this instance the story as Herman confesses it in writing, segregation is no longer an absolute and indeed a reversed situation seems likely: "Some-times, these late years, I've thought maybe Negroes would understand what I'm trying to talk about now better than any white man ever will" ("The Man," 375). As events unfolded in the past, one night while fast asleep in a hayloft Herman was mistaken for a white woman by two lustful black stable hands. Terrified but physically unharmed, Dudley escaped into the "black dark" of a moonless night outside ("The Man," 392). Recalling the pursuit now, he envisions his predicament in the fol-lowing way: "Of course, my body being white, it must have made some kind of a faint streak in the darkness as I ran, and anyway I thought they could see me and I knew I couldn't see them and that made my terror ten times worse" ("The Man," 392).

Herman's situation inverts the figure-ground of social relationships in a segregated world. And it shifts the alternate conditions visibility/invisibility understood as fundamental to a system of racial segregation by African-American cultural observers from W. E. B. Du Bois through Ralph Ellison. The isolation and fragility of Herman's white identity are exposed as they never could be in socially normative circumstances, where white is the pervasive context and standard against which all nonwhite figures are poised and determined. The story's descriptive situ-ations are literally grotesque in the sense that they configure "darkness" brought to light, though in this case darkness pertains paradoxically to the social privilege of white skin. The circumstances through which Herman's whiteness becomes newly foregrounded and self-conscious are overdetermined and become even more so when Herman stumbles into the bleached, upturned ribcage of a horse's skeletal remains. Once he finally returns from this ordeal back to the stables, the only fellow worker to try to protect Herman from social ridicule is a Negro named Burt. He specifically is the Negro Herman had found it impossible to befriend earlier because of the color line. At the story's conclusion, Herman sneaks away from the scene and ends that part of his life without offering Burt any thanks. The published story stands in some sense as compensation for Herman's sin of omission, for it intends to convey a powerful integrity to black life that otherwise largely passes unexpressed and invisible within sanctioned, print culture.

This intention is also apparent in Anderson's *Dark Laughter*, a novel published in 1925 that concerns the aspiring author Bruce Dudley who will have some success in love but absolutely none in art. His motivation toward literature is based in the familiar Anderson belief that "the beginning of education might lie in a man's relations with his own hands, what he could do with them, what he could feel with them, what message they could carry up through his fingers to his brain, about things, about steel, iron, earth, fire, and water."[20] This unprofessional writer despises the kind of feature copy done for the Sunday supplements as impotent stuff hammered out unthinkingly on a typewriter. Genuine poetry on the other hand grows from words cast like seeds by hand onto the soil. Bruce Dudley's ideal of a physical and elemental poetic is formed through his experiences of travel by riverboat on the Ohio and Mississippi rivers, where he absorbs the work chants and blues hollers of black workers on the boats and along the waterways. (*The Torrents of Spring*, which Hemingway subtitled "A Romantic Novel in Honor of the Passing of a Great Race," parodies this kind of fascination with black life.) To his mind, these workman are original "word-lovers, sound-lovers" possessed of an "unconscious love of inanimate things lost to the whites—skies, the river, a moving boat—black mysticism—never expressed except in song or in the movements of bodies."[21] It is no exaggeration to say that Anderson, devoted to subject matter he considered rudimentary and unassuming, aspired for his words when they appeared finally in print an equivalent, nonliterary "black mysticism."

"Elephantine Close-Ups"

Nathanael West

OVER THE COURSE OF 1932 Nathanael West published four "Miss Lonelyhearts" stories in *Contact,* a newly revived little magazine edited by William Carlos Williams with West as an associate editor. The opening lines to the first story printed, under the title "Miss Lonelyhearts and the Lamb" in the February 1932 issue, indicate West's awareness of the *Winesburg, Ohio* antecedent and at the same time they mark a point of departure from its example: "After a cold morning and a rainy afternoon, the evening had turned warm. Thomas Matlock, the Miss Lonelyhearts of the New York Evening Hawk (Are you in trouble? Do you need advice? Write to Miss Lonelyhearts and she will help you), decided to walk from the Hawk Building across the park to Delehanty's speakeasy."[1] In place of the Winesburg town newspaper the *Eagle,* a designation with overtones of acuity, attentiveness, and sweeping vision, West titles the city daily here the *Hawk.* In addition to its associations with a keen-eyed, soaring bird of prey, that name has obvious, disagreeable resonances with verb forms meaning to cough up and to utter harsh guttural sounds. And of course the verb *hawk* also means to vend by means of street cries, as for cheap goods and the latest or extra editions of a newspaper.

West's choice of the name "Thomas Matlock" for his central figure is obviously caricatural and emblematic in comparison to the "George Willard" of *Winesburg, Ohio.* In light of events and symbols that follow, the given name suggests the predicament of a "doubting Thomas." Within its story context, the *Mat* in Matlock signals a matte quality to the character's experiences and responses, which are by turns dull in feeling and spirit, crude, thick-witted. And the second syllable in the surname is indicative of his entrapped situation. West substantially revised the sentence in making it the lead-in to *Miss Lonelyhearts,* which was published in April 1933. Throughout the novel West has removed all overt acknowledgment of the example of *Winesburg, Ohio.* The novel's rewritten opening (now under the chapter title "Miss Lonelyhearts, Help Me, Help Me") reads: "The Miss Lonelyhearts of the New York *Post-Dispatch* (Are-you-in-trouble?—Do-you-need-advice?—Write-to-Miss Lonelyhearts-and-she-will-help-you) sat at his desk and stared at a piece of white cardboard. On it a prayer had been printed."[2] The novel gives no individualized name to its protagonist here or at any later point. In contrast to the story's opening, no wider world outside the newspaper offices is suggested at first. The advice columnist is confined within the medium of print, the letters penned by petitioners, and the prayer inscribed on cardboard.

Situated in the opening scene with less than fifteen minutes until deadline, Miss Lonelyhearts is still struggling at the typewriter to compose the lead paragraph to his advice column. He gets only as far as the unnerving promise of a "faith that burns like a clear white flame on a grim dark altar" and then abandons the effort (*Novels,* 59). Tellingly, the image reverses the conventional figure-ground relationship of type to the page, and for him as a newspaperman it in effect records his defeated attempt to effect through his column a leap of faith. Unlike Sherwood Anderson, Nathanael West does not assume in his writing that oral expression possesses greater sincerity and immediacy than the printed word. For West, speech is no less liable to deformation and inauthenticity than language in the published domain. All language in his fiction ultimately falls within the purview of the print media and mass culture. Later in the novel, Miss Lonelyhearts imagines himself to have the ability of a priest at confession to soothe suffering through a power of speech, but he quickly recognizes that he "had merely written a column for his paper" in an assumed, literary voice (*Novels,* 115). Then, in a complete reversal Miss Lonelyhearts begins to rant of "the black Christ-fruit, the love fruit," but he recognizes in his delivery the tone of a scripted "stage scream" (*Novels,* 115). Feature editor Willie Shrike converses as though he were giving dictation, no matter what the situation. The editor's wife Mary "always talked in headlines" (*Novels,* 81). In all these ways, the newspaper and sensational entertainments mark the boundaries of the characters' known world.

In the piece "Some Notes on Miss L." published in 1933, West indicates that he had in mind the prospective subtitle "A novel in the form of a comic strip" from early on as part of his working plan for the book (*Novels*, 401). Above all else, his approach was graphic in its conception of the literary text: "The chapters to be squares in which many things happen through one action. The speeches contained in the conventional balloons" (*Novels*, 401). During the college years West, according to his biographer, had a stronger interest in graphic art than in literature, and he devoted much time to pencil-and-ink drawings featuring facial caricatures, mythological creatures, and religious subjects, with an emphasis often on suffering and martyrdom.[3] Once he became a writer and an editor West maintained professional relationships with several designers and artists. For the second and third issues of *Contact* West devised the cover layout himself, using a simple but bold typeface. Literary contributors to the issues included West, William Carlos Williams, James T. Farrell, S. J. Perelman, Erskine Caldwell, Yvor Winters, and Louis Zukofsky.

Contact was published without illustrations or any typographical decorations, but in the same period West became associated with *Americana*, a New York little magazine dedicated to humor and satire whose inaugural issues were entirely pictorial. The first three numbers of 1932 featured captioned cartoons grouped under headings like "Entertainment," "Society," "Fashions," "Politics," "Harlem," "Sport," and "Science." The fourth issue (July 1932), with the cover subtitle "Indignation Number," contained a few pages of text. At about this time West developed a close friendship with the magazine's publisher, Alexander King. Under a new policy, revised to give substantial space to literary and opinion pieces, *Americana* restarted in November 1932 as a monthly; it ceased publication at the end of 1933. In all, seventeen issues of *Americana* appeared in the course of two years. Its contributors included the artists George Grosz, John Heartfield, Al Hirschfeld, Jose Clemente Orozco, John Sloan, William Steig, James Thurber, and the writers Kenneth Burke, e. e. cummings, Joseph Mitchell, and Gilbert Seldes. West published in its pages two brief segments from *The Dream Life of Balso Snell* (1931) and in the "Hollywood Number" of October 1933 "Business Deal," a story about a movie mogul outwitted by a screenwriter. Grosz contributed many graphic pieces from the outset of publication in February 1932, and he became associate editor in November of that year. With the August 1933 issue West joined Grosz as associate editor.

While West did not adhere strictly to his first intention, "Some Notes on Miss L." states that the finished novel "retained some of the comic strip technique: Each chapter instead of going forward in time, also goes backward, forward, up and down in space like a picture. Violent images are used to illustrate commonplace events" (*Novels*, 401). Spatial position and the dynamics of a *spectator's* attention across a picture plane take priority over a *reader's* impression of the passage of time. West disfavors any grand schemes of temporal or aesthetic design: "Forget the epic, the master work" (*Novels*, 401). He offers no careful psychological development or gradually disclosed motivation: "Leave slow growth to the book reviewers" (*Novels*, 401). The present-day conditions of culture mean that, for the writer, "you only have time to explode" (*Novels*, 401). Though he does not in fact use the word, West seems to have in mind here the *squib*, a term from the press and popular entertainments with which he would be familiar. From its origins in the sixteenth century the word has meant equally a common type of firecracker, derision, and a short satirical piece. In the newspaper world it also came to identify a small, often comical or offbeat item used to fill up space in a column of print.

The actions and encounters within each section of the book are treated in digest fashion through mock summary titles such as "Miss Lonelyhearts and the Fat Thumb," "Miss Lonelyhearts in the Dismal Swamp," and "Miss Lonelyhearts Pays a Visit." In the manner of spiritual allegory, the headlined sections announce the stations along a latter-day pilgrim's path, though in this case one of descent rather than of progress. While Bunyan's pilgrim Christian is mired in the Slough of Dispond for only a brief spell at the outset of his journey and then travels well beyond it, Miss Lonelyhearts inhabits such a region exclusively. It will be remembered that in *The Pilgrim's Progress* (1678, 1684) the Slough of Dispond is the first major impediment in the path of Christian's flight from the City of Destruction and in the ultimate direction of the Celestial City. The Slough is a sinkhole "whither the scum and filth that attends conviction for sin doth continually run." And the place has remained wretched for more than sixteen hundred years (that is, from the time of Christ) despite "Millions of wholesom Instructions, that have at all seasons been brought from all places of the Kings Dominions."[4]

For his part, West is specific in geography and history in the symbolic designation "the Dismal Swamp," the name of a vast territory extending from Virginia to North Carolina. In West's topography of the American scene it is a foundational place, meant to stand in contraposition to idealizations of the City on a Hill. Four times greater in size during colonial times than at present, on any physical map of the thirteen colonies the Great Dismal Swamp shows prominently and centrally. In the 1760s George Washington surveyed the Great Dismal Swamp as part of a commercial effort to drain it for agricultural use, an enterprise that was partially undertaken during the nineteenth century but never fully achieved. And as first president, Washington surveyed and selected the exact site for the nation's capital in a location that included expanses of marshland but which he deemed of great potential as a commercial center. For decades many visitors considered the locale of the new capital to be little better than a boggy wilderness.

To defend *Miss Lonelyhearts* against moralistic objections, in 1933 William Carlos Williams issued a statement entitled "Sordid? Good God!" in which he reasserts his earlier poetics of the grotesque. Williams singles out for praise the quality in West's writing of a "downward motion" accelerated by "the teeming vulgarisms of our speech."[5] For the poet, it is such momentum that makes graphic and incisive West's imaginative reach into the obscured, corrupted areas of American culture and social life. Paradoxically, these areas are often already conspicuously public, and taken for granted, in the media. Two other, recent commentators interpret West's fiction largely as a critique of mass culture. Rita Barnard views the role of consumer goods and the media in the fiction as expressions of collective desires that result from mystification and distortion. She identifies in the work a "special obsession" on the author's part over the loss in originality, authenticity, and presence caused by the consumer market and mass communications.[6] Jonathan Veitch approaches West as a social artist who carries out an avant-garde, anti-aesthetic mandate of negation in order to construct a critique of political power. Veitch also traces through the fiction West's reflexive responses to the problem of representation within a modern culture industry.[7] In a consideration of American popular theater of the time, Mark Fearnow with his study *The American Stage and the Great Depression: A Cultural History of the Grotesque* argues the general conclusion that in times of social anxiety and conflict the grotesque in popular forms is a cultural expediency that makes unresolved dualities seem tolerable.[8]

While critique and censure are surely motivations, only Williams among these commentators recognizes the vulgar energy that West's fiction releases in the course of penetrating the shallow yet mythic surfaces of the American scene. In this West is much like another great mythologist of his own times, Roland Barthes. To decode any contemporary mass-produced myth, Barthes understood, the mythologist first must be capable of participation within it. The participant-interpreter "consumes the myth according to the very ends built into its structure: the reader lives the myth as a story at once true and unreal." Since mass-mediated myth endows commonplace persons, things, and events with meanings that far exceed their actuality, the interpreter for his or her part is "condemned for some time yet always to speak *excessively*" about the reality of the situation.[9] A critique of the myths of one's society involves a dialectical negation of the forces of irreality, which is to say that in advancing toward fuller comprehension the process cannot help but subsume some elements of myth and irreality. From Barthes' perspective, this double bind is a source of writerly pleasure for the mythologist. In the case of West, at the same time that the novelist exposes the deadening grotesqueness of many myths within the culture at large, his imagination fabricates a new, spirited, patchwork grotesque from available cultural materials.

To be recognized as grotesque, features of mass culture that have become commonplace must be defamiliarized, as through the pronominal declension "Miss Lonelyhearts . . . he" that functions like a refrain in the novel. The novel's principal mode of defamiliarization is through descriptive devices that reduce appearances to tonalities of dark and light. This method fulfills a premise that the mass circulation of words and images has already abridged much of experience down into black and white. Miss Lonelyhearts occupies a room "as full of shadows as an old steel engraving" with barren walls except for an "ivory Christ" removed from its cross and renailed with large spikes directly onto one surface (*Novels,* 67). On his way to a speakeasy after a day at the newspaper office, Miss Lonelyhearts rests on a park bench and contemplates the heavens for a spiritual sign: "But the gray sky looked as if it had been rubbed with a soiled eraser. It held no angels, gleaming crosses, olive-bearing doves, wheels within wheels. Only a newspaper struggled in the air like a kite with a broken spine" (*Novels,* 64). Mundane surroundings are full of menacing configurations: "He walked into the shadow of a lamp-post that lay on the path like a spear" (*Novels,* 63). Seeking refuge in the countryside with his fiancée, Miss Lonelyhearts' gloom proves a stronger force than nature's vitality: "Although spring was well advanced, in the deep shade there was nothing but death—rotten leaves, gray and white fungi, and over everything a funereal hush" (*Novels,* 101). Even when a color value is mentioned its original vibrancy is obliterated: "new green leaves hung straight down and shone in the hot sun like an army of little metal shields" (*Novels,* 102).

The suppliant Peter Doyle, in addition to being crippled in one leg, has facial features that are completely askew. To describe this quality, the novel resorts to an unexpected analogy: "He looked like one of those composite photographs used by screen magazines in guessing contests" (*Novels,* 110). Needless to say, Doyle is in status and appearance the farthest thing from a movie star. The analogy suggests that deformity— whether actual like Doyle's or a trick effect—is received among the general public as a media construct for one's passing diversion. The only answer to the misfortunes of Doyle and others that Miss Lonelyhearts can think of anymore is a spiritual one, even as he recognizes this message to be nowadays a dead letter. Seated at his office desk he lapses into writer's block after typing the word Christ. His attention wanders to the view through his window, where "a slow spring rain was changing the dusty tar roofs below him to shiny patent leather. The water made everything slippery and he could find no support for either his eyes or his feelings" (*Novels*, 104). For him, the written word has proven to be an especially slippery slope. Situated at the bottom of the slippery slope in *The Pilgrim's Progress* is the Valley of Humiliation, the place of degrading lessons in the costs of pride. At the bottom of Miss Lonelyhearts' humiliations the spiritually forlorn newspaperman meets a senseless end.

Often a skeptic in such matters, contemporary novelist Don DeLillo in *The Body Artist* (2001) imagines a meaningful empathic consciousness through his central character's vicarious encounters with human experience rendered in newsprint. For the body artist Lauren Hartke the daily newspaper is something of a spiritual mystery in that it can provide a full, genuine measure of humanity: "there are endless identical lines of print with people living somewhere in the words and the strange contained reality of paper and ink." She is prone to the uncanny sensation that "an incident described in the paper seemed to rise out of the inky lines of print and gather her into it."[10] DeLillo's own aspirations toward readers are made clear through these intimations of consubstantiation. In *Miss Lonelyhearts,* to the contrary, the newspaper becomes an instrument of destruction. This eventuality is broached first in West's novel as a morbid joke, when Miss Lonelyhearts recommends suicide in the column in the hope that he will be fired from the job. His editor Shrike responds with the mild rebuke that such advice will reduce the paper's circulation and harm business.

At the story's climax and catastrophe Doyle arrives on the scene carrying a gun concealed inside a folded newspaper that will detonate seemingly on its own accord. In a panic Doyle seeks to escape the embrace of a wild-eyed Miss Lonelyhearts and by turning away he pulls back his hand, whereupon "the gun inside the package exploded" (*Novels*, 126). The "complicated bomb" lodged in the heart of this newspaperman since the beginning of the story has finally burst (*Novels*, 74). In "Some Notes on Violence," published in a 1932 issue of *Contact*, West's attention is directed solely toward the role of violence in *print* culture for the gratification of a mass-circulation readership: "In America violence is idiomatic. Read our newspapers. To make the front page a murderer has to use his imagination, he also has to use a particularly hideous instrument" (*Novels*, 399). And, in turn, so has the reporter who wants the event to become a lead story, through the instrument of lurid description. Given the cultural conditioning of American audiences, West observes, there is no need to make violence personally motivated in order for it to seem convincing and thus there is no responsibility to unfold a story that explains a violent act.

Indeed, in West's practices the grotesque mode is often a matter of hypertrophy in description and a corresponding atrophy of narrative. Soon after publication in *Contact* of the first Lonelyhearts story *The Criterion*, edited by T. S. Eliot at the time, printed a dismissive assessment of West's literary treatment of violence. Reviewer Hugh Sykes Davies faults the story's "attitude of impersonal observation, of scientific and photographic reproduction" but not the subject of violence per se. In Davies' opinion the story through a nearly exclusive attention to descriptive particulars leaves the content unnarrativized, which means that the reader's reaction of horror is not "anticipated and catered for in a proper way."[11] As we have seen, the novelist was fully aware already of the disparity between the axes of description and narration in his fiction. With a proposal for creative work that West submitted in 1934 to the Guggenheim Foundation, for support that he did not in the end receive, a chapter plan is provided but his synopses do not chart any plot line. Each chapter is cast instead in terms of intellectual reflection ("Ideas about conduct. The morals of sport") and exposition ("A first attempt at definitions. . . . A discussion of values"). Conscious of the structural anomaly, West concludes his proposal with the following assurance: "The ideas I have briefly described will be hidden as carefully as possible in the body of my narrative" (*Novels*, 465–66).

When in the 1950s W. H. Auden offered a generally favorable critical overview of the American writer, he prefaced his assessment with a caveat that "West is not, strictly speaking, a novelist." By this statement Auden means that in West's books the wide social world is not a significant narrative presence. That world is instead the object of a single-minded act of dissection. Auden considers it suitable to approach West only as a modern, cultural symptomatologist who specializes in the diagnosis of one disorder, namely "a disease of consciousness which renders it incapable of converting wishes into desires." This condition condemns an individual to despairing, guilty inaction, or to impulsive attempts at escape through violence.[12] For West's own part, we should add, violence and the grotesque are both presenting symptoms of society's disorders *and* the literary means through which he formulates a diagnosis.

In West's first book *The Dream Life of Balso Snell* culture is examined from the position of a recessed, darkened space, specifically from inside the mythic Trojan horse, now equipped with a functioning alimentary and excretory system. From the mock canonical premise "Art is not nature, but rather nature digested" West draws a dadaist conclusion: "Art is a sublime excrement" (*Novels*, 9). The perspective also entails a figure/ground conundrum in which the differentials of dark/light are not sufficiently distinctive. One consequence of the situation is expressed in an entry Balso Snell reads from the diary of a madman: "It is as if I were attempting to trace with the point of a pencil the shadow of the tracing pencil. I am enchanted with the shadow's shape and want very much to outline it; but the shadow is attached to the pencil and moves with it, never allowing me to trace its tempting form" (*Novels*, 16–17). *Dream Life*'s own textuality traces the most profound grotesque within its contents. West told an interviewer that he published the novel "as a protest against writing books."[13] At its grossest, such protest takes the form of a revenge fantasy. The novel imagines a devoted audience that attends the latest experimental play. While spectators dutifully watch the performance onstage, which they do not comprehend in the slightest, the denouement comes from an unexpected direction: "the ceiling of the theatre will be made to open and cover the occupants with tons of loose excrement" (*Novels*, 28).

During his odyssey through the entrails of the Trojan horse, Balso is besieged by authors eager for an audience for their amateurish, derivative work. West renders this material mainly in a graphic, descriptive way through "elephantine close-ups of various literary positions and their technical methods" (*Novels*, 398). Thus, grand storytelling traditions appear within West's small book grossly magnified beyond its confines and are left in a fragmented and scarcely recognizable state. One such instance is the Janey Davenport and Beagle Darwin episode, a modern attempt to write in the epistolary style of sentimental fiction. Literary traditions survive for West only as waste products of the consumption process, after their breakdown through the digestive acids of mass communications. The fundamental relationship of art to excrement is held to be especially true in the case of the realist movement. At the end of *The Dream Life of Balso Snell* all the literary techniques and story forms crudely rehearsed within its pages culminate, in a variation upon the theme and manner of Molly Bloom's soliloquy, with a solitary man's wet dream.

Another West piece of the early 1930s that literalizes a grotesque perspective is "The Adventurer," an unpublished story. Its narrator is one of West's underground men, a monomaniac who at the outset inhabits a world of books. He burrows among their pages every spare moment, "stuffing my eyes, ears and mouth with them" (*Novels*, 448). In the end, he designates himself merely a talker, and not a narrator, for "a story is—and then something happened and then something else happened. This was simultaneous, like a great picture" (*Novels*, 455). By this point he has become a kind of anchorite, furtively inhabiting New York's Central Park. There he has fashioned a makeshift urban grotto: "I made a nest for myself near the top of the hill . . . , a little hollow in the midst of a tangle" (*Novels*, 455). Whether in the library or in this hollow, his mental context remains "the same dark picture" (*Novels*, 455). He is unable to construct a story and he thus remains bound and static within his fixation.

West's third novel, *A Cool Million: The Dismantling of Lemuel Pitkin* (1934), brutally parodies the mythos of a common man's rise to importance. Another pilgrim figure, the ambitious yet innocent young Pitkin suffers many misfortunes along the path of the American way. The book's grotesque reflexivity stems chiefly from its exaggerations of the already exaggerated stylizations that are a staple of pulp magazines, the tabloid press, radio programs, action-suspense serials, and B movies. Its short chapters are structured like episodes to a serialized adventure tale in weekly installments. In a matter of months Pitkin runs a gauntlet of dangers derived from scenarios of white slavery, crime and imprisonment, international Communist espionage, and the Wild West. Rather than triumph over adversity, however, he falls prey to each and every danger that he encounters. With a story action reminiscent of Poe's "The Man That Was Used Up," the novel in quick order reduces Pitkin to a one-eyed, stooped, penniless, toothless wreck.

Eventually, after having further suffered a scalping and the amputation of one leg, Pitkin is persuaded to seek his fortune as the freak attraction in a tent show, which is soon incorporated into a larger traveling exhibition called the "Chamber of American Horrors, Animate and Inanimate Hideosities" (*Novels*, 226). After a stint there, he takes the part of the slapstick stooge in a vaudeville comedy routine. A feature of modern life as common as newsprint has its own part to play in the brutalization and exploitation of Lemuel Pitkin: "One of Lem's duties was to purchase newspapers and out of them fashion the clubs used to beat him. When the performance was over, he was given the papers to read. They formed his only relaxation, for his meager salary made more complicated amusements impossible" (*Novels*, 233). In the end, Pitkin's true destiny is fulfilled as a martyr to the cause of the Leather Shirts, a band of street agitators within the fascist National Revolutionary Party.

Principal targets of parody in *A Cool Million,* Jay Martin has argued, include Horatio Alger books *and* Hitler's *Mein Kampf,* which are treated as equally perverse expressions of social faith in individual success and in personal triumph over great adversity.[14] Kenneth Burke understood the grotesque to be an attitude toward history that, in the context of the 1930s, provided a means by which to account for ideological peculiarities within extremist politics, particularly those of "national absolutism" (*Attitudes,* 58). In a consideration of *Mein Kampf* upon its full translation into English in 1939, Burke weighed Hitler's objectives in fostering a Nazi collective mythos. Burke approaches Hitler's autobiography as the textbook of "Nazi magic; crude magic, but effective." In the conjunct rationalizations of Aryan racial purity and worldwide Jewish conspiracy, Nazism puts forth a deformed version of "contemporary neo-positivism's ideal of meaning, which insists upon a *material* reference," and the movement advances irrationalism under a banner of Reason.[15] Through political rhetoric and public spectacle fascist culture promotes a new primitivism.

Beyond the specific Alger and Hitler intertexts, West's diacritical imagination is drawn to confusions in the figure-ground relationship of idea to reality within American society. These can range from the absurdities of consumer life to atrocities motivated by political and racial fears. Modern America's Great Awakening, West foretells, is to come from mass politics and mob violence, not from religion per se. A decade earlier William Carlos Williams voiced a similar expectation in the poem "At the Ball Game" (1923):

> . . . in detail they, the crowd,
> are beautiful
>
> for this
> to be warned against
>
> saluted and defied—
> It is alive, venomous
> it smiles grimly
> its words cut—
>
> The flashy female with her
> mother, gets it—
>
> The Jew gets it straight—it

is deadly, terrifying—

It is the Inquisition, the
Revolution.[16]

Hollywood provides West in *The Day of the Locust* (1939) with an
opportunity to explore the American grotesque on its grandest scale and
in its gaudiest light. To make a screen epic on the Battle of Waterloo, for
instance, the National Films studio has raised a replica of Mont St. Jean
on its lot. The set, however, is built upon a substructure of mere lumber
and canvas and once filming begins it collapses under the weight of
movie extras. The impressive interiors and facades of other movie spectacles, "having first been made photographic by plaster, canvas, lath and
paint," are destined after a single use for a backlot that serves as a dump
for "a gigantic pile of sets, flats and props" (*Novels,* 326). No quarter
of Los Angeles described in the novel escapes the influence of Hollywood. To obtain distinction, a screenwriter with the personal features of
a "postal clerk" occupies a house designed as the exact reproduction of
a famous antebellum Mississippi mansion (*Novels,* 252). SunGold Market,
a grocery store, features an interior as brilliantly lighted as a production
set. Spotlights with color filters are trained on the counters and displays
to intensify the natural hues of different items: "The oranges were bathed
in red, the lemons in yellow, the fish in pale green, the steaks in rose and
the eggs in ivory" (*Novels,* 274).

The book's habits of description are in keeping with the sensibility of
its central figure Tod Hackett, an art school graduate with the aspirations
of a visionary painter but who in plain fact earns a living as a movie
costume and set designer. Through this character West displays a deep-
running anxiety, as had Sherwood Anderson before him, that hackwork
can become the grotesque professional fate of the aspiring artist. In the
novel's account of Tod's creative efforts emphasis falls upon the graphic
basis of his medium, the planar and contour forms his imagination takes,
and the techniques that he uses with light/dark tonalities to produce
histrionic contrasts in mood and theme. For the novel as a whole, the
perspective upon people and objects is presented as two-dimensional
in almost every respect. Whatever impression of depth and substance
that an appearance possesses proves to be a temporary illusion attained
through optical effects.

In actuality, for example, the old vaudevillian Harry Greener, has "very
little back or top to his head. It was almost all face, like a mask, with

deep furrows . . . plowed there by years of broad grinning and heavy frowning. Because of them, he could never express anything either subtly or exactly. They wouldn't permit degrees of feeling, only the furthest degree" (*Novels*, 311). The physical features of Earle Shoop, a bit player in Westerns, are so geometric that they could be all copied by ruler and compass. Faye Greener, Tod's lust-interest, is introduced by way of a photograph chapters before she appears in person. The photograph is a publicity still from a screen farce in which Faye had one line of speech. Two dimensions suffice for a rendering of Faye's physique ("a tall girl with wide, straight shoulders and long, swordlike legs") and the same holds true for her personality once Tod comes to know her (*Novels*, 250). Faye is devoid of emotional or erotic depth. Tod learns to recognize that her customary come-hither look "seemed to promise all sorts of undefined intimacies, yet it was really as simple and automatic as the word thanks. She used it to reward anyone for anything, no matter how unimportant" (*Novels*, 355).

West's early literary technique of "elephantine close-ups" further evolves in *The Day of the Locust*. One manifestation registers in the form of verbal gigantism, as when Homer Simpson, overwhelmed by confused feelings, releases a torrent of speech in which what sounded like "long strings were really one thick word and not a sentence. In the same way several sentences were simultaneous and not a paragraph" (*Novels*, 368). The disorder is recognizable as an "elephantine" condition in the paradigmatic functions of language and a "dwarfish" one in the syntagmatic ones.

Language also becomes disproportioned whenever Harry Greener launches into a sales spiel or a show business reminiscence. Another manifestation occurs reflexively, through the novel's own hyperdetail in description. The book's second paragraph offers an enumeration of distinctive features of the uniforms to cavalry and foot soldiers from different armies involved in the Napoleonic Wars. The description, in part, details "The dolmans of the hussars, the heavy shakos of the guards, [and] Hanoverian light horse, with their flat leather caps and flowing red plumes" (*Novels*, 241). These features are noted in passing as Tod is said to look out from an office window upon troops of extras marching off to a sound stage. Irrespective of the specificity in descriptive vocabulary, from Tod's vantage such details are visually "all jumbled together in bobbing disorder" (*Novels*, 241). The hodgepodge of residential architecture along one of the city's canyon streets is succinctly noted in a paragraph that heaps together diverse cultural terms for period, style, and region. In a later scene Faye Greener recounts her ideas for movie stories in the hope that Tod will serve her and write scripts from them. Her ideas are a stockpile of utter clichés; each predictable scene is synopsized with a well-worn phrase.

In his mind's eye, Tod views the world in the light and dark of divine judgment and retribution. It is worth remembering that the biblical plague of locusts is, before all else, a force that darkens the earth. The darkness that comes when, in the Book of Exodus, the Lord causes locusts to cover the land of Egypt is a prelude to a time of "darkness *which* may be felt" (Exodus 10:21). And the spread of locusts upon the earth in Revelation issues from the dark smoke of the bottomless pit. As for the iconography of West's own times, from the depth of the Great Depression Franklin D. Roosevelt acknowledged in his first inaugural address, delivered in March 1933, that "only a foolish optimist can deny the dark realities of the moment." The overall tone of the new president's speech, however, promises that "we are stricken by no plague of locusts" and that "our common difficulties . . . concern, thank God, only material things."[17] Some six years later, with the worst of the Depression behind for many Americans, *The Day of the Locust* nevertheless insists that society's difficulties, pity the common individual, are precisely the material promises and illusions promoted through its media culture.

Not surprisingly Homer Simpson, the novel's commonest of common humanity, has been limited in experience to a world rendered mainly in black and white. Homer's occupation for twenty years in the Midwest had been as a bookkeeper, and his horizons reached little beyond ink and ledger: "he had worked mechanically, totaling figures and making entries with the same impersonal detachment" (*Novels*, 275). Now that he has come to Southern California with not even this little to do, he feels besieged by his surroundings. The bright profusion of color in sunlight paralyzes Homer in daytime. His sole comfort is that "sleep was at the far end of it, a soft bit of shadow in the hard glare" (*Novels*, 290). Tod, as an artist, is also paralyzed. Work on his projected, visionary canvas "The Burning of Los Angeles" remains arrested at the stage of preparatory sketches of single figures or small groups and a preliminary cartoon of the massive, chaotic scene blocked out "in rough charcoal strokes" on one large canvas (*Novels*, 387). So far, the painter has been able only to imagine, through an inner eye, colors appropriate to the scene. He has not yet applied color to canvas.

One challenge Tod faces in regard to color selection is the brightly hued, pellucid tonality of American life in the public sphere, perpetuated through advertising illustrations, Hollywood screen fantasies, and sunny optimism in the rhetoric of political figures and spiritual promoters.

Looked at generally in America of the 1930s, colors that enhance the mass media are often saturated and intensely primary in value, from market displays and billboards to picture magazines and big-budget releases in Technicolor like *The Adventures of Robin Hood* (1938), which was advertised with the claim "Only the rainbow can duplicate its brilliance!" A technological irony of Technicolor, introduced by studios in 1922 and perfected in 1932, is that the process is based upon black and white film. To produce a color image, dyes are transferred to three black and white film prints separated by sensitivity to different portions of the spectrum and then the dyed prints are laminated together. In other words, color in motion picture and still photography is not in the least intrinsic to the medium, it is an artificial additive.

Occasionally the world Tod occupies is colored in an alternative manner, as with the Fauvist juxtapositions in this landscape scene: "The path was silver, grained with streaks of rose-gray, and the walls of the canyon were turquoise, mauve, chocolate and lavender. The air itself was vibrant pink" (*Novels*, 303). But Tod's aesthetic preferences are for Goya, Daumier, and "Salvator Rosa, Francesco Guardi and Monsu Desiderio, the painters of Decay and Mystery" (*Novels*, 325). Goya and Daumier, both masters of the grotesque, are of course as well known for their work in the black and white medium of prints as for their paintings. A favorite Goya etching for West was *El sueño de la razon produce monstruos* (1799; "The sleep of reason produces monsters"), a theme whose relevance to his fiction is immediately apparent (fig. 5.1). In this connection we can also think of the enthusiastic response by Baudelaire to Goya's etchings for their "modern attitude of mind [and] feeling for violent contrasts" and for the somber and cruel temper of their grotesque inventions (*Art and Artists*, 236).

In the case of paintings by Salvator Rosa (1615–1673), several of his canvases in oils are deeply shaded to a point where the color range is contracted into darks and lights. The prolific Francesco Guardi (1712–1793) is famous for his view paintings of Venice, some of which show deterioration to the city's architectural features. As for Monsu Desiderio, there were in point of fact three different artists working in Naples during the first half of the seventeenth century who were known by that name. Attributed to one painter by this name are many scenes of ruins, several of which feature the process of destruction itself in massive scale and by a full spectrum of forces—man-made, natural, mythological, and divine.[18] Tod in *The Day of the Locust*, in envisioning "The Burning of Los Angeles" as a prophecy of final destruction, sets the event at high noon on a clear day so that the conflagration is nearly outshone by the desert

Figure 5.1. Francisco de Goya, *El sueño de la razon produce monstruos*, from *Los Caprichos* (1799).

sun, with the result that the scene seems perversely celebratory. While this prophecy is blindingly bright, for the most part Tod's sensibility is preoccupied by the soul's night thoughts.

As a variant to the principle advanced by Kenneth Burke that "incongruity *without* the laughter" produces the grotesque, laughter itself in *The Day of the Locust* can operate as a cruel psychological weapon. When quarrels between Harry Greener and his daughter Faye turn bitter he resorts to stage laughter, she to crudely delivered popular song. In these situations his "masterpiece" laugh is a horrifying effect that evokes "an insane asylum or a haunted castle" (*Novels*, 284). Under other circumstances the grotesque in West's novel involves a fierce transformation in personality "from apathy to action without the usual transition" (*Novels*,

301). Such an unexpected shift into action is enough to prompt involuntary laughter among observers. With violent conduct the response among observers can be mercilessly good-humored, as among people at the movie premiere in the novel's last chapter when talk spreads of the vicious rape of a child.

The grotesque in Sherwood Anderson's fiction is often handled as an outward sign of redemptive truths concealed within the individual and as a medium through which the authentic poetry of life can be expressed. Regularly among West's characters, by contrast, there is no inner self. The superficiality of Faye, for instance, is consummate, "uncontaminated by thought" or conscience (*Novels*, 336). This condition can reveal a self possessed of brutality at heart or it can provoke others to violence, as in the cock-fighting episode. Faye's placid self-absorption provokes in Tod, who seems otherwise docile, an urge "to break its smooth surface with a blow" (*Novels*, 336). Early on, the characterization of Homer Simpson seems closest in spirit to one of Anderson's grotesques. In an incident from his past in the Midwest, Homer becomes smitten with Romola Martin, a hotel guest. Infatuated, Homer refuses to acknowledge the plain fact that she is a drunken prostitute. In their one direct encounter Homer impulsively embraces her: "His suddenness frightened her and she tried to pull away, but he held on and began awkwardly to caress her. He was completely unconscious of what he was doing. He knew only that what he felt was marvelously sweet and that he had to make the sweetness carry through to the poor, sobbing woman" (*Novels*, 271). The embrace goes no further and, as impulsively, he leaves the room, never to see her again.

In the end, West's portrayal of Homer constitutes a rebuttal of sorts to the sentimentality of the tale in *Winesburg, Ohio* of Wing Biddelbaum. Where Wing's hands are revealed to be the true organ of his genius as a teacher of the young, Homer's hands are always alien, seeming to him "like a pair of strange aquatic animals" (*Novels*, 267). Clearly evoked here are the "ragged claws" from T. S. Eliot's "The Love Song of J. Alfred Prufrock" (1915). When Homer is agitated his hands compulsively repeat the child's game "here's the church," a habit Tod finds "particularly horrible [in] its precision" (*Novels*, 359). With this characterization there is no promise of innocence redeemed and indeed in the novel's closing chapter Homer stomps to death the child actor Adore Loomis. For his part, Adore is the troubled, ill-tempered creature of a stage mother's relentless ambitions.

A unique instance when West claims authentic emotion and genuine innocence from within the grotesque arises not from reality but from total illusion. The occasion is a nightclub act by a female impersonator dressed in a tight, red silk evening gown and singing a lullaby. The prose depiction claims great credibility for the performance: "What he was doing was in no sense parody; it was too simple and too restrained. It wasn't even theatrical" (*Novels*, 342). Faye reacts to his performance as an indecent offense against motherhood and she declares a hatred for homosexuals. For its part, the novel fully honors the event: "This dark young man with his thin, hairless arms and soft, rounded shoulders, who rocked an imaginary cradle as he crooned, was really a woman" (*Novels*, 342). Circumstances here are quite different from the storyline in Anderson's "The Man Who Became a Woman," which is told by a man now married and adamantly heterosexual who for a limited period of his youth imagined himself to resemble a woman in respect to facial features and some emotions but who never voluntarily acted out such a role. What proves "awkward and obscene" in the episode from *The Day of the Locust* comes after the song, when the performer exits with a showy "imitation of a man" who has just played the role of a woman (*Novels*, 342). In concession to the paying, conventional-minded audience, he provides a drag-show curtain routine by tripping on his dress and revealing a pair of garters.

Despite the perfection of the impersonator's lullaby, the most powerful impressions of authenticity in the novel are inharmonious, often literally so. The book's very first paragraph conveys the sounds Tod hears coming from the studio grounds. The "groan of leather" combines with "the jangle of iron" and a percussive "tattoo of a thousand hooves" to make "a great din" (*Novels*, 241). These opening notes achieve prophetic fulfillment in the concluding chapter with the bedlam roar of shouts, laughter, screams, and catcalls from the premiere crowd outside Kahn's movie palace. Louder still, as the crowd turns to riot, are the piercing sirens of police cars, the wailing signal from an ambulance, and the sobs and howls of suffering from victims in the melee. At the very last Tod emits a primal cry which is born from physical pain and spiritual anguish but that takes audible form as laughter twisted into an imitation of an emergency siren. By ending with an inarticulate, confused howl, West's novel gives the lie to any confidence in spoken language, held by Sherwood Anderson for one, as the medium closest to humane, liberating truth. What a reader encounters at the conclusion to *The Day of the Locust*

Figure 5.2. George Grosz, *Maul halten und weiter dienen* (1928). Art © Estate of George Grosz/Licensed by VAGA, New York, NY.

is the comedy Baudelaire explained as absolute and grotesque, as an aggrieved outcry that rises from lost innocence and joy.

The visual artist of the contemporary scene with a sensibility close to West's in several respects is George Grosz, who during the 1920s created in his Berlin studio a number of graphics and paintings that fiercely caricatured postwar German society, from top to bottom, and that denounced the rising Nazi campaigns of militarism and social hatred. His drawing *Maul halten und weiter dienen* ("Shut your mouth and keep on serving"), published in 1928, shows a crucified Christ wearing combat boots and a gas-mask and perched on the cross in a posture that, given the circumstances, approximates a soldier's stance at attention (fig. 5.2). By the early 1930s West was familiar with this particular image as well as with Grosz's book of lithographs and watercolors *Ecce Homo* (1923), a panorama of moral decay in German life.[19]

Several images in the Grosz book had been judged to be pornographic by a German court. The "Christ with a Gas-Mask" drawing, as *Maul halten* is commonly known, was one among three images the state additionally used as grounds for the prosecution of Grosz and his publisher on charges of blasphemy. The trial, one of the most elaborate of its kind in the nation's legal history to that time, became a *cause célèbre*. Started in 1928, the court action led to an initial acquittal, but the state restarted pro-

Figure 5.3. George Grosz, *Proven Proverbs* from *Americana* (1932). Art © Estate of George Grosz/Licensed by VAGA, New York, NY.

ceedings that ended finally in 1931 with a guilty verdict against Grosz, a fine, and destruction of the original plate for the image. He later created several variations upon this theme and image. Grosz's earliest contributions to the little magazine *Americana* consisted of images drawn in Germany and for which the editor composed captions in English, at times adding an Americanized context. Grosz spent four months of 1932 in the United States, from June until October, teaching at the Art Students League in New York City. In letters he wrote of the American scene as an odd, stimulating mixture of brutality and laughter. At the end of 1932 the artist returned to Germany, but only for a few months. In January 1933, shortly before Hitler's seizure of power, Grosz left with his family permanently for the United States; in 1938 he became a naturalized American citizen.[20]

While Grosz and West can each imagine a distinctly modern martyrdom for Christ, there is a deep political grain within Grosz's social views, whereas politics are not definitive in West's work. The artist came of age personally and professionally within a progressive political culture, and he was a member of the German Communist Party for a period of years as a young man. For all the savagery in his attacks against contemporary society Grosz at times would voice also a strong note of utopian promise, though far more often in words than in pictures. In an autobiographical statement for the pages of *Americana* in 1932 he wrote: "I still believe in certain forbidden metaphysical concepts like Truth, Justice and Humanity."[21] When Grosz left the ideological and class conflicts of Germany and established himself in the United States, his work lost its urgent sense of conscience and spirited tone of resistance to established power. Of the transition Grosz later commented: "In Germany, I had poured forth venom in the form of pen-and-ink caricatures. Hate and proselytizing rancor seemed out of place here."[22] The change is evident in early graphic work Grosz prepared in contexts specific to the United States, as in several *Americana* cartoons published in 1932 and 1933 (fig. 5.3). Events in Europe later in the decade, however, would provoke a return to previous themes and attitudes.

Nathanael West, though sympathetic with many causes within the American Left, remained as skeptical of Communist promises and programs as of those issued by other ideological factions. He rarely relinquished his inclinations as a disengaged, caustic observer to serve in any common political purpose. The two principal exceptions in which West took limited part in the 1930s were the Screen Writers Guild and the anti-fascist movement based in Hollywood.[23] Even so, West explained in a letter to Malcolm Cowley that he had failed in an attempt to include any serious political material in *The Day of the Locust*: "I tried to describe a meeting of the Anti-Nazi League, but it didn't fit and I had to substitute a whorehouse and a dirty film. The terrible sincere struggle of the League came out comic when I touched it and even libelous" (*Novels*, 795). The persuasive political impact *The Grapes of Wrath* achieved immediately upon its publication in 1939 caused West to reflect on the absolute separation of art from politics in his own life: "Take the 'mother' in Steinbeck's swell novel—I want to believe in her and yet inside myself I honestly can't. When not writing a novel—say at a meeting of a committee we have out here to help the migratory worker—I do believe it and try to act on that belief. But at the typewriter by myself I can't" (*Novels*, 795).

The other two American writers most often associated with the grotesque in the 1930s are William Faulkner and Erskine Caldwell. Faulkner adopts the mode masterfully for the dramatic arc of an epic, burlesque funeral journey in *As I Lay Dying* (1930) and for plot incidents in it like the early augury of events to follow when the boy Vardaman bores holes in his mother's coffin and mutilates her face in the process. The book unfolds mainly, however, as an exploration into the varieties of human consciousness of mortality through its multiplicity of interior monologues, from family members, neighbors, spectators, and the deceased herself. The novel's attitude toward the story material, in the end, is not in essence grotesque, nor is that of *Sanctuary* (1931), even for all its sensational, macabre incongruities in situation and characterization. In reaction to Caldwell's commitment to a grotesque vision Faulkner confided in a letter he wrote in December 1932, after receiving a copy of *God's Little Acre* (1933) in galleys from Caldwell's editor at Viking Press: "I read it with a good deal of interest, but I still think the guy is pulling [Viking editor] George Oppenheimer's leg."[24] Many years later Faulkner, in the preliminary draft of his acceptance speech for the 1949 Nobel Prize in Literature, named Caldwell, Hemingway, and himself as "all of us children of Sherwood Anderson."[25] The assertion was not retained in the final text of his speech, nor did Faulkner ever claim any definitive literary kinship with an American tradition of the grotesque. In truth, Anderson's sensibility and style had been the object of an early parody by Faulkner, in the foreword he contributed to the collection of sketches by William Spratling *Sherwood Anderson and Other Famous Creoles* (1926).

Stories by Erskine Caldwell appeared in the pages of *Contact*. Upon a request from West, and for the purpose of a brief statement to be cited on the dust jacket to *Miss Lonelyhearts*, Caldwell said in praise of West's book: "I can easily imagine that the bulk of its audience will applaud it for being a clever and amusing novel, and I believe it will have a large audience; but to me it is a tragic story."[26] This last remark, which I think misjudges the novel's tone and final effect, is indicative of the strain of high earnestness in Caldwell's literary persona, which is quite at odds with the popular response to his work. His book *Tobacco Road* (1932) and the immense commercial success of its stage production on Broadway, which opened in late 1933 and which would run continuously until May 1941, established for the public mind a grotesque vision of the American South that interbreeds lurid sex, crude dialect humor, and social documentation on rural idiocy.

Adaptation of the book for the stage was handled by writer Jack Kirk-land with the approval of Caldwell. In publicity and interviews the novelist praised the play as an effective dramatization of his book and he insisted that the production—beyond its sensational, humorous, and crowd-pleasing elements—presented a serious, documentary portrait of America's Southern poor. The drama scholar Mark Fearnow, on the other hand, attributes the box-office success of the stage production of *Tobacco Road* to a cultural process of overcoming social fears through mockery.[27]

In an assessment of Caldwell's popularity during the 1930s, Ken-neth Burke is of the opinion that his work consistently performs "an astounding trick of oversimplification" by placing characters possessed of "the scant, crude tropisms of an insect" into complex social situations. Burke estimates that Caldwell's underlying intentions are "to blaspheme and profane for our enjoyment" and that consequently his characters can never amount to more than "subnormal mannikins." Burke places the fiction of Caldwell within the lowest, crudest ranks of comedy, and he considers it thus incapable of achieving the incisive critique of one's own time possible through the grotesque.[28] Burke additionally remarks upon a quality of "balked religiosity" within the fiction, and in this one respect we can place Caldwell meaningfully in the company of Nathanael West and Flannery O'Connor.

All God's Grotesques

Flannery O'Connor

IN MANY STATEMENTS on the craft of fiction Flannery O'Connor made explicit the place of the grotesque in her imagination and its role in her writing. For O'Connor, as a Catholic author living within a largely irreligious culture, exaggerated and overdetermined methods seemed necessary in order to convey matters of faith: "You have to make your vision apparent by shock—to the hard of hearing you shout, and for the almost-blind you draw large and startling figures" (*Mystery*, 34). In turn, the dominance of the secular and the material in modern life has meant the distortion, often to a point of exclusion, of genuine spiritual considerations. To her mind, advertising agencies answer most conscious needs in American society since "everybody wants the good things of life, like supermarkets and cellophane."[1] As to media culture O'Connor, in observing the new public frenzy over Elvis Presley, anticipated that her challenge was to find subject matter and perspectives that are not superficially grotesque. O'Connor was aware that she shared such jaundiced reactions to popular culture with Nathanael West but, finding Miss Lonelyhearts to be "a sentimental Christ figure, which is a contradiction in terms," she felt no meaningful connection to the earlier writer.[2] Mindful of a humorous tradition of the grotesque, of the kind Constance Rourke delineated, O'Connor traces the modern grotesque to intractable "prophetic vision" instead: "In nineteenth-century American writing, there was a good deal of grotesque literature which came from the frontier and was supposed to be funny; but our present grotesque characters, comic though they may be, are at least not primarily so. They seem to carry an invisible burden; their fanaticism is a reproach, not merely an eccentricity" (*Mystery*, 44).

If in one sense the social grotesque is embodied in the mindless, material norms of everyday experience, the grotesque O'Connor creates in fiction is a homeopathic countermeasure designed to re-embody the mystery of spiritual life. Where religious faith itself is concerned, the general public is impaired by great blind spots. Given this situation, the literary grotesque becomes necessary in order to disclose intrinsic truths that would otherwise remain unnoticed: "It is the extreme situation that best reveals what we are essentially" (*Mystery,* 113). The writer centered in Christian concerns resorts to the grotesque as a means to rejoin the material and the spiritual, which for most contemporaries are separated by great distances: "He's looking for one image that will connect or combine or embody two points; one is a point in the concrete, and the other is a point not visible to the naked eye, but believed in by him firmly, just as real to him, really, as the one that everybody sees" (*Mystery,* 42). A unifying grotesque mode is achieved through what O'Connor terms prophetic vision, which is a matter of "seeing near things with their extensions of meaning and thus of seeing far things close up" (*Mystery,* 44). She offers a more theological explication of the term in a letter from 1959: "According to St. Thomas, prophetic vision is not a matter of seeing clearly, but of seeing what is distant, hidden. The Church's vision is a prophetic vision; it is always widening the view. The ordinary person does not have prophetic vision but he can accept it on faith. St. Thomas also says that prophetic vision is a quality of the imagination, that it does not have anything to do with the moral life of the prophet. It is the imaginative vision itself that endorses the morality."[3] This capacity makes her unlikely prophet figures the sole "realist of distances" in the stories, irrespective of how out of touch with reality these figures may seem (*Mystery,* 44). These prophets' discrepant perspectives are the source of many profane and violent effects in her fiction.

For O'Connor the Christian presupposition of fallen humanity is not a cause for sentiment or even for compassion but rather it is a call for the close scrutiny of our necessarily mortal status. In her hierarchy of values, moral judgment is always superior to intellectual discriminations and emotional reactions. Prophetic focus directs attention toward the "fierce and instructive" mystery of life on earth as the phase of human existence that is "Christ-haunted" (*Mystery,* 44–45). With an ingenious eye and ear for mundane detail her fictions present many tokens of the concrete and the here and now in the process of conveying a more essential immateriality and spiritual displacement. O'Connor assessed her own imagination to be other-directed in a religious sense, well outside positivist purviews like behaviorism and toward instead the unknowns of faith. In a letter written in 1955, she comments sardonically that college had prepared her to be "the stinkingest logical positivist you ever saw" and she offers thanks to Providence: "The only thing that kept me from being a social-scientist was the grace of God and the fact that I couldn't remember the stuff but a few days after reading it" (*Letters*, 97–98). Having renounced the seeming certainties offered by various schools of determinist thought, which she deems to be a kind of creature comfort for contemporary humanity, O'Connor is drawn instead toward the disruptive uncertainty of eternal matters.

From the outset of her writing life O'Connor felt no affinity with litera-ture of earnest social conscience, as with portrayals of the American South by Erskine Caldwell and James Agee in the 1930s and 1940s. Included in the story collection O'Connor submitted for her Master of Fine Arts in 1947 is "The Crop," a burlesque on the writing craze for poor, rural Southern subject matter. Unpublished in O'Connor's lifetime, "The Crop" served in her apprenticeship as a symbolic renunciation of genre fiction and social commitment. The story's own aspiring writer, Miss Willerton, is always on the lookout for a topical and marketable subject: "Social problem. Social problem. Hmmm. Sharecroppers! . . . 'I can always capitalize,' she mut-tered, 'on the hookworm'" (*Works*, 733–34). The characters and plot that Miss Willerton ineptly contrives center around a dirt-poor tenant farmer named Lot Motun. "The Crop" gives O'Connor an occasion for shorthand satire on *Tobacco Road* and its whole genre and she takes as a given their ineptitude in plotting, characterization, dialogue, and prose style.

O'Connor associates her own writing generally with the American literary tradition of romance rather than with realism or naturalism. She aligns it with the fiction of Nathaniel Hawthorne and Henry James on the basis of a shared predisposition to render "dark and divisive" forces at work within a pragmatic and optimistic American scene (*Mystery*, 46). In her judgment realism and naturalism, even at their most powerful, are limited to ephemeral perceptions, while a specifically Christian romance can convey a firm potential for the action of divine grace. In matters of lit-erary technique, O'Connor acknowledges Joseph Conrad as the strongest influence and states that she aspires to Conrad's famous purpose toward the reader "before all, to make you *see*" (quoted in *Mystery*, 80).

Comments O'Connor made about her youth identify two early literary sources for her sense of the grotesque. In a letter of 1955 the author recalls that the only reading of quality she did in childhood was about Greek and Roman myth in a juvenile encyclopedia, and that the rest was "Slop with a capital S" (*Letters*, 98). Surely one appeal classical mythology held for her is its repertory of metamorphoses and the unpredictable ways of divine power toward humanity. The next memorable literary encounter for O'Connor was fiction by Edgar Allan Poe. Gathered in a collection labeled "Humorous Tales," it was favorite reading "before the age of reason" in her development and it started a fascination with Poe that lasted for years. Intrigued by their "walled-in monsters" and other oddities, she recognized that these tales were "anything but funny" (*Works*, 911).

In the same 1955 letter she recalls three stories in particular from this time, and notably they are not among the best known by Poe nor are they tales of terror in any essential way. Rather, they revolve around distortions and transformations in visual perspective that in the end thoroughly, and thankfully, reconstitute the meaning of appearances in the storyteller's world. She remembers the three by plot situation rather than by specific title and their plots merit some consideration here. One ("The Spectacles") involves a mistaken identity and the romantic deception that entangles a young man too vain to wear glasses in public. In the end he manages nonetheless to marry well. Another ("The Man That Was Used Up"), which I mentioned in connection with West, reveals that a formidable public figure, a man of great outward physical and social endowments with a reputation as a fierce Indian-killer, is in truth a nondescript weakling once all his artificial devices (including false teeth, a wig, and two wooden limbs) are removed. The third ("The System of Doctor Tarr and Professor Fether") follows a visitor into a mental institution where he observes increasingly odd behaviors among the director and his staff. He struggles to explain these as normal human eccentricities only at last to discover that lunatics have taken over the asylum, and with this discovery he gains his freedom. These are tales of elucidation rather than of gothic horror. While there is some passing anxiety, each protagonist at the end welcomes with grateful wonderment the conversion of confused appearances into a clear picture of the underlying truth.

To a defining degree, O'Connor's practices of the grotesque in fiction are graphic in nature and they proceed from a descriptive level of expression.[4] Her interests in drawing and caricature became evident early, and she contributed cartoons to high school publications and then regularly to campus publications when she attended Georgia State College for Women in Milledgeville. The undergraduate cartoons often include a stylized self-portrait of O'Connor as an outsider and gadfly reacting against the narrow uniformity of college life. While studying in the graduate writers' program at the University of Iowa she did some course work in advanced drawing and political caricature.[5] In her early twenties O'Connor made efforts to place her cartoons commercially, including submissions to *The New Yorker*, but these proved unsuccessful and she concluded that her abilities in the medium would develop no further. Of her experience in creating line figures, O'Connor has written: "I enjoyed that greatly, there is something immediate about it, it either is successful or it isn't, there are never any doubts, such as you feel over a piece of fiction, that you can't see all at once" (*Works*, 1112). Later in life she recommended to apprentice writers the practice of drawing as a means of developing their powers of observation and description.

To regard the world solely on a basis of obvious appearances, however, is to see only "in the fashion of a camera," whereas in her fictional world Christian "beliefs will be the light by which you see" (*Mystery*, 181, 91). In the late 1950s O'Connor read Erich Auerbach's important study on the representation of reality in Western literature, *Mimesis*, and she was especially struck by connections between its ideas on figural interpretation of the Bible and her own beliefs ingrained through Catholic liturgy. Auerbach traces the evolution in meaning of *figura*. The term evolves from original denotations of outward appearance and plastic form into, during the Roman period of Cicero, a primary idea about rhetorical form. The concept of *figura* was adapted in early Christianity "to show that the persons and events of the Old Testament were prefigurations of the New Testament and its history of salvation." In such cases of figural prophecy "the figure had just as much historical reality as what it prophesied."[6] Thus, the dynamic of prophetic realism shadows forth Christ as a carnal and historical truth, but one attendant consequence is "antagonism between sensory appearance and meaning" (*Mimesis* 49). For O'Connor outsized deformation and profound misapprehension are the collateral effects of just such a process.

Within a figural context of meaning, Auerbach elaborates, "the horizontal, that is the temporal and casual, connection of occurrences is dissolved; the here and now is no longer a mere link in an earthly chain of events, it is simultaneously something which has always been, and which will be fulfilled in the future; and strictly, in the eyes of God, it is something eternal" (*Mimesis*, 74). Thereby the figural is "an intrinsically irrational interpretation" (*Mimesis*, 75). Which is to say, it cannot be rationalized through positivist explanation or a narrative logic. By standards of the two axes of language that Roman Jakobson has presented, the figural is aligned with the paradigmatic and the synchronic (the domain to which description belongs) as opposed to the syntagmatic and the diachronic (the domain of narration). In terms of O'Connor's storylines, her strange prophet and pilgrim figures in the end do not arrive at a spiritual state unprecedented or unforeseen, rather they finally answer and return to promptings of the spirit eternal to humankind and personally suppressed or denied for a time.

Though clear, total delineation is not the final effect O'Connor sought through fiction, description serves her as the means to sustain a literal, apprehensible level in an ultimately mystical, anagogical structure of meaning that "has to do with the Divine life and our participation in it" (*Mystery*, 111). In elaborating this idea, she turns to a mundane act of graphic representation: "A good story is literal in the same sense that a child's drawing is literal. When a child draws, he doesn't intend to distort but to set down exactly what he sees, and as his gaze is direct, he sees the lines that create motion" (*Mystery*, 113). O'Connor's fiction cannot be said to be limited by its nature to description, as is often true in the cases of Anderson and West. Her work is oriented toward matters of eschatology, and it thus entails a figuration of the potential for transformation. On this matter O'Connor has reflected: "The hardest thing for the writer to indicate is the presence of the anagogical which to my mind is the only thing that can cause the personality to change. . . . We are not our own light" (*Letters*, 503).

Because human existence is inseparable from mortality in O'Connor's judgment, it is as well inescapably marked by deformity and moral failings. Only the dead, once saved, are whole. In life, the secular world establishes pliable standards of evil with which most people become dispassionately familiar. Her fiction often aims to defy such complacency: "I have found that violence is strangely capable of returning my characters to reality and preparing them to accept their moment of grace" (*Mystery*, 112). It is with the axioms of evil and violence and the absolutes of joy and innocence, whose intersection can produce the grotesque, that O'Connor unexpectedly shares views with Baudelaire. As explained by Baudelaire, grotesque laughter "is satanic; it is therefore profoundly human. . . . It is at one and the same time a sign of infinite greatness and of infinite wretchedness, infinite wretchedness in relation to the absolute being, of whom man has an inkling, infinite greatness in relation to the beasts" (*Art and Artists*, 148). O'Connor describes one aspect of such a spiritual legacy in this manner: "Good is another matter. Few have stared at that long enough to accept the fact that its face too is grotesque, that in us the good is something under construction" (*Mystery*, 226).

During her life O'Connor maintained an interest in graphic art and she especially admired prints by Daumier, over which she once exclaimed:

"They kill me—but it isn't the form, the motion or anything, just the expressions on their faces" (*Letters*, 494). Here one recalls Baudelaire's appreciative reaction to the "trivial and terrible" power of the appearances Daumier depicted. For her part, O'Connor finds that where "the almost imperceptible intrusions of grace [and] the nature of the violences which precede and follow them" are concerned the French poet understood one cogent truth: "The devil's greatest wile, Baudelaire has said, is to convince us that he does not exist" (*Mystery*, 112). In the face of this situation, her fiction has developed an eye for the sinister and for humanity's deformed spiritual condition. O'Connor has said that "to disconnect faith from vision is to do violence to the whole personality," a consequence for many characters that is explored in excruciating detail (*Mystery*, 181).

And like Baudelaire, O'Connor's sense of comedy is absolute rather than significative. On the subject of "the Comic and the Terrible, which two things may be opposite sides of the same coin," she wrote to a close literary friend: "In my own experience, everything funny I have written is more terrible because it is funny, or only funny because it is terrible, or only terrible because it is funny" (*Letters*, 105). This attitude does not allow for tragicomedy because O'Connor does not accept a tragic vision: "Naw, I don't think life is a tragedy. Tragedy is something that can be explained by the professors. Life is the will of God and this cannot be defined by the professors; for which all thanksgiving. . . . Altogether it is better to pray than to grieve; and it is greater to be joyful than to grieve. But it takes more grace to be joyful than any but the greatest have" (*Works*, 928–29). Her ideas on the matter are remarkably similar to Baudelaire's concept of grotesque laughter. The elements of prayer and grace are for O'Connor, however, first principles.

Over the years O'Connor did oil painting and in 1953 she finished a freely representative self-portrait, accompanied by a pheasant cock, that she far preferred over any photograph taken of her. With friends and literary people she elaborated a humorous yet half-serious phobia over the camera. Of one photo portrait she said that it "looked as if I had just bitten my grandmother and that this was one of my few pleasures" (*Letters*, 31). She had a particular dislike for the author's picture on the dust jacket to her first novel, *Wise Blood*, published in 1952, which she thought made her look "like a refugee from deep thought" (*Letters*, 33). She became no more accustomed to such publicity over time. A decade later she protested that a magazine photograph portrayed her as "one of the Okies with the burden of world peace on my shoulders" (*Letters*, 525). Writer Katherine Anne Porter thought that none of Flannery O'Connor's physical appeal and personal charm was captured in photographs of her: "I am always astonished at Flannery's pictures which show nothing of her grace. . . . She had a fine, clear, rosy skin and beautiful eyes. I could wish I had some record of her as she appeared to me" (*Letters*, xi). Two pronouncements O'Connor made in the 1960s sum up a lifelong opinion on the subject: "I think it would be great if the camera had not been invented" and "Photographers are the lowest breed of men" (*Letters*, 401, 534).

In some respects, however, O'Connor offered the public an image made in a vein of American backwoods grotesque, as with the childhood anecdote she often retold about a prized chicken that could walk backwards and that drew reporters' attention far and wide, including a motion picture news crew from the Pathé company. Since then, she told an interviewer on the occasion of the publication of *Wise Blood*, "my life has been an anti-climax" (*Conversations*, 4). At a conference on fiction held at Vanderbilt University in 1959 she appeared before faculty and students in the company of Robert Penn Warren. While Warren's statements were discursive and broadly allusive, hers were limited and tersely pointed. Warren allowed himself academic notions of "the muse," "feeling envisaged and pre-felt," and "a dramatic need of fiction, a need of pace" (*Conversations*, 21, 23). Wanting not to "intellectualize it too much," O'Connor avoided speaking at any length and for some remarks she assumed a down-home idiom. To a question on plot construction, for example, she explained "I just kind of feel it out like a hound-dog. I follow the scent" (*Conversations*, 20, 19).

Though O'Connor cultivated the grotesque both as a serious means to understand her fiction and as part of a self-styled public image, once her writing entered the common sphere it became subject to forms of simplification and exaggeration well beyond her intended purposes. The response to *Wise Blood* included letters that struck her as "from people I might have created myself." Among them was "a message from two theological students at Alexandria who said . . . that I was their pin-up girl—the grimmest distinction to date" (*Letters*, 82). Her second novel, *The Violent Bear It Away* (1960), was reviewed in *Time* magazine as the story of "God-Intoxicated Hillbillies." The unsigned piece treats the book as an "ironic jape" and portrays its author as a "retiring, bookish spinster who dabbles in the variants of sin and salvation like some self-tutored backwoods theologian."[7]

Intrinsic to *Wise Blood* are tropes of dark/light that figure the inevitably grotesque reckoning of flesh with the spiritual. From the outset Hazel Motes, the book's inverse pilgrim and evangelist, seeks utter blackness.

Traveling overnight in a Pullman berth he draws the curtains tightly together: "He wanted it all dark, he didn't want it diluted" (*Works*, 9). This compulsion is explained as an outward sign of "a deep black wordless conviction in him . . . to avoid Jesus" (*Works*, 11). By the end of the novel, as the leader and only parishioner of the "Church without Christ," he professes one doctrine: "it was not right to believe anything you couldn't see" (*Works*, 116). This conviction brings a desired blankness: "His face seemed to reflect the entire distance . . . that extended from his eyes to the blank gray sky that went on, depth after depth, into space" (*Works*, 118). But even blankness proves insufficient for his mission. O'Connor, who considered Motes "such an admirable nihilist," has after all drawn his name from Christ's parable (Luke 6: 39–42) of the blind leading the blind (*Letters*, 70). In a final perverse testament to his beliefs, Motes blinds himself, yet the act oddly endows his face with "the look of seeing something" (*Works*, 120). The ultimate scene offers a contorted version of Christ's healing of the man born blind and the teaching "I am the light of the world" (John 9:5). Through death the face of Motes gains composure and an unearthly "point of light" can now be seen at the depths of his eye sockets (*Works*, 131). In an author's note for the second edition of *Wise Blood* O'Connor terms Hazel Motes "a Christian *malgré lui*" and explains his "belief in Christ" as hereditary. With an antic retort to Darwinian explanations, the novelist compares this belief to a "ragged figure who moves from tree to tree in the back of his mind" (*Works*, 1265 n.1).

Often in O'Connor's fiction the visible world is filtered through the perspective of a character's untested confidence, easygoing adages, or mundane self-interest. Seen as such, the world is cast in simplified, black and white terms, unilluminated by eternal truths of the spirit. For their part, eternal truths can appear suddenly in splendid, vivid hues. The farm owner Mrs. Cope of "A Circle in the Fire" (1955), for example, is land proud, and she regards her property with "black eyes that seemed to be enlarging all the time behind her glasses" (*Works*, 232). Her pastures are bordered by a "fortress line of trees" but she lives in holy fear of a fire danger to these woods (*Works*, 247). When in the end the woods are set ablaze by a group of vagrant boys the story's narrator likens the spectacle to the biblical scene of prophets "dancing in the fiery furnace, in the circle the angel had cleared for them" (*Works*, 251). To a fatalist like Asbury in "The Enduring Chill" (1958) there is a monochrome tonality to the world, but against this stands juxtaposed a secret craving for signs of a promised "majestic transformation": "The sky was a chill gray and a startling white-gold sun, like some strange potentate from the east, was rising beyond the black woods" (*Works*, 547).

The hired help Mrs. Shortley of "The Displaced Person" (1955) falls into an anxious reverie, cast fully in black and white, when she fears losing her position to a Polish refugee family. Her reverie starts with a battle of words and ends with movie news images of the death camps. Mrs. Shortley began "to see the Polish words and the English words coming at each other, stalking forward, not sentences, just words. . . . She saw them all piled up in a room, all the dead dirty words, theirs and hers too, piled up like the naked bodies in the newsreel. God save me! she cried silently, from the stinking power of Satan!" (*Works*, 300). She has amplified her peevish worries into a personal apocalypse. At the same time the old priest, a visitor oblivious to the worldly concerns of the farm's various occupants, marvels at the peacock on the place. Its tail, "full of fierce planets with eyes that were each ringed in green and set against a sun that was gold in one second's light and salmon-colored in the next," might be taken for "a map of the universe" (*Works*, 290–91). With an eye toward Apocalypse, the priest utters joyfully at the splendor of this sight: "'Christ will come like that!'" (*Works*, 317).

A pathway toward spiritual awareness is often traced in O'Connor's stories by means of colorless, contrasted lights and darks. In "The Life You Save May Be Your Own" (1955) the drifter Mr. Shiftlet utters the startling claim that he is possessed of "a moral intelligence" at a point when his devious schemes are already well underway. As Mr. Shiftlet makes this perversely apt declaration "his face pierced out of the darkness into a shaft of doorlight and he stared . . . as if he were astonished himself at this impossible truth" (*Works*, 176). In O'Connor's rendering, such intelligence is usually more wicked than righteous in its conscious purposes. At the moment when this confidence man outwits the old country-woman O'Connor provides this depiction: "in the darkness, Mr. Shiftlet's smile stretched like a weary snake waking up by a fire" (*Works*, 179). For O'Connor there is unimpeachable authority for rendering evil as a sign that stands along the direction toward good: "In the gospels it was the devils who first recognized Christ and the evangelists didn't censor this information" (*Letters*, 517). On other occasions O'Connor explained this circumstance through the exemplum, devised by St. Cyril of Jerusalem, of the dragon by the roadside. Good in the instance of "The Life You Save May Be Your Own" is glimpsed in the form of the deaf and mute Lucynell, portrayed at the outset in terms of her "long pink-gold hair and eyes as blue as a peacock's neck" (*Works*, 173). An innocent virgin still at nearly thirty years of age, she is already among the saved and by story's end she is recognized as "an angel of Gawd" (*Works*, 181).

"Greenleaf" (1956) reverses the relationship of figure (color, grace) to ground (light and dark, utter worldliness) in the stories considered thus far. Against a backdrop of insistent, often vivid colors, spiritual mystery in "Greenleaf" transpires in forms of black and white. Its establishing descriptions extend from the "even piercing blue" of the sky in spring to the name Greenleaf itself, which belongs to a tenant family whose matriarch has small eyes "the color of two field peas" (*Works*, 506, 520). Mrs. May, the proud owner of the acreage on which the Greenleafs work, judges the family to be the worst of white trash, especially the wife and particularly on account of that woman's fervent practice of prayer healing, always accompanied by cries of "Jesus!" Mrs. May finds this last habit particularly objectionable: "She thought the word, Jesus, should be kept inside the church building like other words inside the bedroom" (*Works*, 506). Yet, the true nemesis to Mrs. May, and the agent of spirituality in the story, is a dark, rogue bull who has invaded her garden. The animal is first glimpsed in moonlight, while at intervals night "clouds crossing the moon blackened him" (*Works*, 501). The next night Mrs. May watches the invader angrily "until the iron shadow moved away in the darkness" (*Works*, 519). Their final confrontation takes place in an open pasture under a bright sun that bathes the scene in "white light" (*Works*, 522). All coloration vanishes from the story at this point. When she sights the bull approaching Mrs. May remains stock-still "not in fright, but in a freezing unbelief" and the "violent black streak" gores her (*Works*, 523). The fatal encounter opens "a dark wound in a world that was nothing but sky—and she had the look of a person whose sight has been suddenly restored but who finds the light unbearable" (*Works*, 523).

Sometimes human vanity in O'Connor's fiction assumes the form of intellectual superiority, as with Joy-Hulga of "Good Country People" (1955) who takes cardinal pride in her academic training in existentialism: "I don't have illusions. I'm one of those people who see *through* to nothing" (*Works*, 280). Joy's confidence in the complete transparency of the world to her mind is undone by the traveling Bible salesman bearing a large black sample case that seems to have a momentum of its own: "It was rather as if the suitcase had moved first, jerking him after it" (*Works*, 269). Her experience of revealed truth begins when the salesman meets with Joy in private and opens the suitcase to show its contents: one actual Bible and a fake one hollowed out to make room for a whiskey flask, a pornographic deck of cards, and a pack of condoms. The revelation comes as a shock to Joy mainly because she had believed in earnest that he was just a naive Christian boy. At least the salesman has the integrity to be a genuine atheist. Upon departure, he announces triumphantly "you ain't so smart. I been believing in nothing ever since I was born!"

(*Works*, 283). The vision of the nonbeliever, which enables him or her to see through to nothing, is unobstructed by light/dark differentials and figure-ground meanings such as grace/evil or eternity/mortality. At the same time, this nonbeliever does spread the word of God through his Bible sales.

For all the contrastive and contrarian formulations in her fiction, O'Connor's sense of reality is unrelated to dualism. She considers ancient Manicheanism to have a detrimental counterpart in contemporary thought through the categorical separation of spirit from matter. Also Manichean, in her opinion, is the materialist premise that evil is essentially a social problem answerable through enlightened public policies. For her, the central spiritual mystery of life is instead "that all creation is good and that evil is the wrong use of good and that without Grace we use it wrong most of the time" (*Letters*, 144). Since worthwhile fiction to O'Connor is an "incarnational art," she considers it impossible to write about matters of the spirit, good or evil, without the mediation of the flesh and dull reality (*Mystery*, 68). The tropes of dark and light prominent in her work are in no sense Manichean.[8] Rather, they can function as figure-ground gestalts useful in rendering evil and in evoking intimations of the divine.

In O'Connor's assessment, the presence of spiritual concerns is experienced by readers "when the writer puts us in the middle of some human action and shows it as it is illuminated and outlined by mystery" (*Conversations*, 17). Such a presence can "cast strange shadows, very fierce shadows" in the story (*Conversations*, 72). The light/dark differentials and their correlations to either spirituality or godless materiality are treated here as variable rather than absolute. On another occasion, she recast these formulations: "The writer who emphasizes spiritual values is very likely to take the darkest view. . . . The sharper the light of faith, the more glaring are apt to be the distortions the writer sees" (*Mystery*, 26n). The fictional world rendered through such tonal contrasts has strong affinities "for the perverse and for the unacceptable" (*Mystery*, 33).

With elaborate play upon differences in visual perspective and upon the differential bright/dark, the late story "The Lame Shall Enter First" (1962) examines matters of good and evil, of faith and denial. In a letter years earlier O'Connor had irreverently conjectured that the phrase, which refers to the miracle of the lame man healed at the gate of the temple in Acts 3, may well be true "because the lame will be able to knock everybody else aside with their crutches" (*Letters*, 117). Though dedicated to the betterment of young people, the widowed father Sheppard proves altogether ill-equipped to guide his ten-year-old son Norton let alone the juvenile delinquent Rufus Johnson, a fourteen-year-old afflicted with a club foot who is sheltered in the household for a time. A complete set of the encyclopedia holds pride of place in Sheppard's sizable library, but no Bible is to be found in the home. When Rufus brings a copy of scripture and reads together with Norton from it, Sheppard condemns the Bible: "'It's for cowards, people who are afraid to stand on their own feet and figure things out for themselves'" (*Works*, 627). Since Sheppard dismisses religious belief the only assurances he can offer Norton, who remains grief-stricken over the loss of his mother, is that there is neither a hell nor a heaven and that after death nonexistence awaits. Sheppard is a nearly tireless do-gooder, conceited in his pragmatism and humanitarianism. He draws inspiration from science, technology, and social reform, and he has brought into the home a microscope and a telescope for the education of the boys. But his own vision is blind to the plain sight of evil in the person of Rufus.

After all, during their first encounter when Sheppard visited the reformatory one Saturday as a volunteer counselor, Rufus declared that he was under the power of Satan. As he said so there was a "a black sheen" to Rufus's eyes and an expression on his face "set with pride" plain as can be (*Works*, 600). Nonetheless, Sheppard holds to a ready-made explanation that the boy's misdeeds are a form of compensation for the psychological damage he suffers over his club foot. The unfolding irony of "The Lame Shall Enter First" lies in Sheppard's failure to grasp the obvious truth established for the reader in the story's visual depictions and comparisons, which in places evoke terrible beasts from Revelation. Rufus's "monstrous" foot is encased in "a heavy black battered shoe," its leather split open to show "the end of an empty sock [that] protruded like a grey tongue from a severed head" (*Works*, 599–600). The would-be benefactor Sheppard is blinded by his inability to believe in evil, while the devil in Rufus is "clear-eyed" (*Works*, 632). None of his Enlightenment principles have enabled Sheppard to detect the resemblance of Rufus to a "black figure on the threshold of some dark apocalypse" (*Works*, 628).

O'Connor's second novel, *The Violent Bear It Away*, contests the very terms through which its characters perceive and interpret the world. At their core, one set of terms approaches life as a question of eternal existence, another treats it as simply a matter of individual self-determination. The outcome is decided in the fate of the fourteen-year-old Tarwater, who is ensnared in a struggle of wills between his great-uncle Mason Tarwater, a countryman in his eighties when he dies, and his uncle Rayber, a teacher who lives in the city. The great-uncle is a religious fanatic guided by the conviction that he is an agent of the Lord chosen to awaken the world to the coming Judgment. He once believed that his calling was to take the message to the city and proclaim "from the midst of his fury that the world would see the sun burst in blood and fire" (*Works*, 332). Failing this apocalypse, the old man took the infant boy from his uncle's care in the city and out to the backwoods in order to prepare him for the life of a prophet. The fundamental legacy which he intends to impart to the boy is the "rage of vision" by means of which the righteous make their way through a wicked world (*Works*, 332). For much of his young life the boy has rebelled against inheriting this burden of spirituality.

While the Raybers are equally the boy's direct relations, through the course of the story he bears the family name Tarwater exclusively. This name, through its evocative juxtaposition of an impenetrable blackness and translucence, marks a mystical possibility in the midst of a largely nonbelieving world. And the Tarwaters, great-uncle and nephew, are tar babies of sorts in that they have become a mystery and a fixation for Rayber. The Tarwaters draw the schoolteacher, despite his best efforts to normalize and rationalize everything, into questions of the spirit unanswerable by his secular standards. The prophecies spoken by the old man and that reverberate in young Tarwater's imagination are infused with the searing intensity of sun, blood, and fire. Nonbelief, on the other hand, is colorless. It strives to prevail through conventionalities that schematize the world into black-and-white terms that seem to hold primacy and finality. Here, as in many O'Connor stories, the rationales of nonbelief rely on modern psychology, the social sciences, pragmatism, and a utilitarian concept of benevolence.

The city uncle Rayber is a man of facts and rational explanations determined to ward off any promptings from the spirit by dint of what amounts to a rigid ascetic denial that includes the discipline of not looking at any mystery in the world too long or too deeply. For vision Rayber is dependent upon heavy, black-rimmed spectacles. Their rims and lenses, not his eyes themselves, are what characterize his face. These eyeglasses are a sign of the narrow instrumentality of his view of the world: "Every living thing that passed through [Rayber's] eyes into his head was turned by his brain into a book or a paper or a chart" (*Works*, 341). Rayber confronts the Tarwaters as a challenge to his own enlightened atheism and exults "'I can read you like a book!'" (*Works*, 438). When old Tarwater discovers that he has become the subject of a case study that Rayber published in a professional journal he decries the betrayal of being "laid out in parts and numbers," of transformation entirely into information (*Works*, 341). The teacher's home, though sparsely furnished, seems to overflow with an accumulation of printed matter of all kinds. To the old man and to young Tarwater it is an appalling place of "dead words" (*Works*, 341). Once the old man reads the case study in print he senses himself captive in a "mysterious prison" that traps the spirit, as the whale trapped Jonah, the lion den Daniel (*Works*, 342).

The novel entails an intricate, uneasy conjunction of visual-verbal properties. Young Tarwater's fate hinges in effect on choices between competing claims over sight and the word. The word, like the world, once put into print and scanned for mundane purposes yields an impaired, dispirited meaning. While print is the medium upon which an irreligious world relies, speech is a faculty of greater truth in *The Violent Bear It Away*. The Word and its infinite expanse belong primarily to the voice rather than the page and they promise human transcendence. To convey the note of prophecy within the old man, the novel explains that "his voice would run away from him as if it were the freest part of his free self and were straining ahead of his heavy body to be off" (*Works*, 342). By general rule, the world's words operate as positivist tools designed to compress human possibility down into black-and-white truisms. But for eventualities of the spirit inflamed and visionary speech is required. By the end young Tarwater possesses the rage of vision that foresees final destruction *and* salvation: "His scorched eyes no longer looked hollow or as if they were meant only to guide him forward. They looked as if, touched with a coal like the lips of the prophet, they would never be used for ordinary sights again" (*Works*, 473). The allusion is to the biblical prophet Isaiah, who is purged of sin in just such a manner and then is instructed to spread the warning "Hear ye indeed, but understand not; and see ye indeed, but perceive not" (Isaiah 6:9). O'Connor's image incorporates speech into sight.

In addition to the eyeglasses for sight, Rayber is dependent upon a bulky mechanical aid for his hearing. It became necessary after Rayber was wounded on the ear by a shotgun blast fired by old Tarwater to thwart Rayber's efforts to return the boy to the city. With the old man's death years later young Tarwater returns to the city on his own, drawn, despite his conscious efforts, by the great-uncle's obsession with the matter of baptizing Rayber's retarded boy Bishop. At night from a distance the city is noticed by the young man through its garish but shallow light, too cold and "too far away to ignite anything" (*Works*, 347). By day, the city is a place of "dried light," its appearances are pale and tin-colored or gray in tone (*Works*, 349).

Yet, spiritual intensity can be experienced within the city, most powerfully inside a storefront Pentecostal tabernacle where a crippled girl preaches. In following young Tarwater one night Rayber comes upon the tabernacle. Despite his intention to dismiss the scene and move on, Rayber remains listening by the window, transfixed by the child preacher as she elaborates the evening's text ("The Word of God is a burning Word to burn you clean!") in high, clear tones (*Works*, 414). While the episode offers the reader some details of what Rayber sees, it is conveyed mainly through the girl's sermon, which is punctuated by the refrain "'Listen you people . . . Listen world'" (*Works*, 412, 414). After listening to most of her message Rayber reasserts his reason and switches off the hearing aid to protect himself, an action that consigns the Word to oblivion and brings "silent dark relief" (*Works*, 415).

By the end of *The Violent Bear It Away* young Tarwater has perversely baptized the boy Bishop in the process of drowning him. To answer for the negative logic of the world in her fiction O'Connor declared: "If you live today you breathe in nihilism. In or out of the Church, it's the gas you breathe" (*Letters*, 97). In explanation of the prevalence of violence in her fiction over any benevolent spiritual promise she said that "the times do seem a bit apocalyptic for anything so sane" as "Christian humanism" (*Letters*, 360). *Caritas* is not essential in her understanding of Christianity, though she acknowledged its place as a Catholic duty: "I share [a] lack of love for the race of man, but then this is only a sentiment and a sentiment falls before a command" (*Letters*, 335). On matters of Christian fellowship O'Connor indulged in much frank humor, reflecting for instance that there is a "great natural grace is finding the good in people. It's a real gift. I never been bothered with it myself" (*Letters*, 587). In defense of her literary sensibilities, she responded to criticism "about the vacuum my writing seems to create as to (I suppose) a love of people" thusly: "Fiction writing is not an exercise in charity, except of course as one is expected to give the devil his due—something I have at least been scrupulous about" (*Letters*, 103).

When praising her work, novelist John Hawkes placed O'Connor in the select company of Nathanael West for "their employment of the devil's voice as a vehicle" to advance a "reductive or diabolical value judgment" of the world they inherited.[9] Though an admirer of Hawkes's fiction, O'Connor vigorously refused any such characterization of her own work. In making a defense she cites Thomas Mann's understanding of the grotesque in contradistinction to the merely perverse, in which the secular sensibility can find gratification.[10] Instead the grotesque is an alternative, necessary perspective in a time when dominant values stunt and deform the spiritual capacity of human life. Innocents too are to be counted among creation's grotesques.

In 1960 O'Connor received a request from the Sisters with Our Lady of Perpetual Help Free Cancer Home in Atlanta to write an account of the life of a cancer casualty who died at age twelve after spending nine years at the Home. Notwithstanding tributes by the Sisters to the girl's courage and joyous spirit and their claims for her saintliness, O'Connor responded chiefly to the fact of her physical suffering: "What interests me in it is simply the mystery, the agony that is given in strange ways to children" (*Letters* 394). A tumor on one side of her face had caused the loss of an eye and disfigurement to many features. In her introduction to the published *A Memoir of Mary Ann* (1961) O'Connor does not hesitate to focus on her deformity: "The defect on Mary Ann's cheek . . . was plainly grotesque. She belonged to fact and not to fancy" (*Mystery*, 216). And the facts of her appearance and fatal condition confirm for O'Connor an active belief that goodness, like evil, can be manifest in malformed, unfinished states.

On the matter of one's personal response to such affliction, O'Connor finds modern, ordinary pity to be a wholly inadequate substitute for an orthodox religious response: "If other ages felt less, they saw more, even though they saw with the blind, prophetical, unsentimental eye of acceptance, which is to say, of faith" (*Mystery*, 227). Even in the face of the hereditary, debilitating disease lupus erythematosus that caused her father's death at age forty-five, and that would cause her own at thirty-nine, O'Connor questioned the motives of any purely emotional reaction to suffering: "I think it is impossible to live and not to grieve but I am always suspicious of my own grief lest it be self-pity in sheeps [*sic*] clothing. And the worst thing is to grieve for the wrong reason, for the wrong loss" (*Works*, 928). For O'Connor genuine compassion is a profound and "forbidding" response with potentially grotesque consequences that puts us "in travail with" the immediate world "in its subjection to vanity" and that forces upon us both "a recognition of sin [and] a suffering-with" (*Mystery*, 165–66).

Having declared a "lack of love" for humanity in general, O'Connor's sympathies were rarely stirred by issues of race relations or civil rights, and in some respects she remained an unreconstructed white Southerner. Too devout to be an out-and-out misanthrope, O'Connor nonetheless defended her right to create in fiction "colored idiots" to go along with the many white ones (*Letters*, 547). Critical assessment of O'Connor's views on race ranges widely. To one side Ralph C. Wood concludes that in her stories "the way to real fellowship" between blacks and whites is achieved through "their common imprisonment in the bonds of sin and mortality."[11] Robert Coles finds that O'Connor "has no interest in sparing blacks the burdens (but to her theological mind, the dignity) that go with being a sinful human being."[12] While noting stereotypes in early stories, novelist Alice Walker asserts that the *"essential* O'Connor is not about race at all, which is why it is so refreshing, coming, as it does, out of such a *racial* culture."[13] On the other hand, Frederick Crews finds in her life and work "complacency about social injustice" and "twisted feelings about segregation."[14]

On the subject of segregation, privately in the 1950s O'Connor made a frank admission: "I observe the traditions of the society I feed on—it's only fair" (*Letters*, 329). In the fiction she freely used racial stereotypes of blacks in characterizing the thoughts and perceptions of white characters. An atypical vision of racial equality comes in the 1958 story "The Enduring Chill" at the point where Asbury imagines "moments of communion when the difference between black and white is absorbed into nothing," but the passage serves only to portray Asbury's narrow vindictiveness toward his mother, with her sense of white superiority, and as another indication of his own nihilism (*Works*, 558).

O'Connor's fiction has its share of caricatures of shuffling, malingering, or grinning blacks, as with the hired dairymen Randall and Morgan of "The Enduring Chill." On several private occasions she deployed racial stereotypes as a basis for satiric provocations, as in letters to her friend Maryat Lee, a longtime advocate of civil rights born in Kentucky. It should be acknowledged that under O'Connor's caustic scrutiny no person, group, or organization was exempt from her sharp commentary, not even Catholicism or its clergy. She held the Church responsible, for example, for the accumulation in prose of a "large body of pious trash," at the top of which she placed Cardinal Francis Spellman's 1951 bestseller *The Foundling* (*Mystery*, 180). For all that, there is a significant difference between prejudicial opinions and informed, specific assessments. In truth, racial tolerance was a matter of minor concern through much of her life, while the social facts of an American racial grotesque and the segregated South often served the purposes of metaphor for her fiction through which to render matters of spiritual mystery.

When asked which was her favorite story O'Connor often named "The Artificial Nigger," which was first published in *Kenyon Review* in 1955. Upon accepting the story the journal's editor John Crowe Ransom urged that she change the title in order to avoid offending some readers or stirring racial tensions, but O'Connor steadfastly refused to make any such modification. On the semantics of this term William Styron has observed that "'nigger' remains our most powerful secular blasphemy."[15] Yet O'Connor seemed to sense no complication in putting the word in the mouths of Southern whites who become recipients of divine grace. In explanation of the origin of her story's title, O'Connor indicated that she had first heard the term a few years earlier, in reference to the distinctive decorative feature of a home located in the white section of town.

As in many O'Connor stories of spiritual mystery, depictions in "The Artificial Nigger" of both outward appearances and characters' states of being are conducted largely through an iconography of darks and lights. In this story such depictions are often strictly maintained in intense tones of black and white to illustrate proverbial insights that pride leads to destruction and a haughty spirit to a fall. They also bring to light the mystery of divine mercy. The story's two proud white individualists, one a man of sixty the other a boy of ten, are evenly matched. In his own estimation, Mr. Head is a wise man who has been "awakened by a blast of God's light," while his grandson Nelson appears to Mr. Head in the opening scene to amount to no more than "a dark spot" obscured "underneath the shadow of the window" (*Works*, 210). When they venture into town and become lost in the Negro section, "black eyes in black faces were watching them from every direction" (*Works*, 221). There, in the presence of a large black woman, Nelson experiences an intimation of humility and mortality that makes him feel as though he were "reeling down through a pitchblack tunnel" (*Works*, 223). Later Mr. Head and Nelson become lost in an elegant white suburb where "the big white houses were like partially submerged icebergs in the distance" (*Works*, 228). Mr. Head's mortification occurs in this locale and it is marked with his desperate outburst "'Oh Gawd I'm lost! O hep me Gawd I'm lost!'" (*Works*, 228).

After they are given proper directions by a white stranger, the pair encounters the plaster figure of a Negro about Nelson's size and perched precariously atop a low brick wall. Crafted originally as a mirthful "darky" in the minstrel tradition, the figure's decayed condition has left it with "a wild look of misery" (*Works*, 229). The two stand rapt before the artificial Negro, "as if they were faced with some great mystery, some monument to another's victory that brought them together in their common defeat" (*Works*, 230). In context, "another's victory" has little to do with white supremacy or racial oppression and everything to do with the grace of "an action of mercy" upon Mr. Head and Nelson (*Works*, 230). Mercy is invoked here, as throughout O'Connor's writings, in the root Church sense of divine love in its response to misery.

Newly united in humility, grandfather and grandson return home to the country. Arriving at nighttime, their familiar surroundings have been cleansed by a moon "restored to its full splendor" that irradiates the scene in "shades of silver" and "a fresh black light" and that makes all the more prominent "gigantic white clouds illuminated like lanterns" in the sky (*Works*, 230). In commenting upon the story's iconography, O'Connor wrote to a literary friend: "What I had in mind to suggest with the artificial nigger was the redemptive quality of the Negro's suffering for us all. You may be right that Nelson's reaction to the colored woman is too pronounced, but I meant for her in an almost physical way to suggest the mystery of existence for him. . . . I felt that such a black mountain of maternity would give him the required shock to start those black forms moving up from his unconscious" (*Letters*, 78). While this is the closest to a social context that O'Connor ever gives for the image, even here the artificial Negro is not expressive of a cause for public concern or political redress, rather it and the story's other black figures are immutable symbols of mortification and of the soul's dark mysteries.

Asked in 1960 why black characters are not given active roles in her stories, O'Connor explained unapologetically: "I don't understand them the way I do white people. I don't feel capable of entering the mind of a Negro. In my stories they're seen from the outside. The Negro in the South is quite isolated; he has to exist by himself. In the South segregation is segregation" (*Conversations*, 59). This is not to say, however, that blacks cannot be agents, knowingly or not, in the spiritual process that some white characters undergo, as is the case with the maternal figure in "The Artificial Nigger." The Negro named Buford Munson in *The Violent Bear It Away* is a more active, conscious agent even though he only appears briefly in two scenes. He gives a half day of hard, unpaid work to bury old Tarwater's body "in a decent and Christian way, with the sign of its Saviour at the head of the grave" (*Works*, 331). Buford has done so in defiance of young Tarwater's contemptuous declaration "'I don't want no nigger-mourning'" (*Works*, 357). At the end, Buford is witness to the transformation within young Tarwater ("he sensed it as a burning in the atmosphere") that sends forth a new prophet with a rage of vision.

In a 1963 interview O'Connor defended blacks against a stereotype that on occasion appeared in her own fiction: "The uneducated Southern Negro is not the clown he's made out to be. He's a man of very elaborate manners and great formality which he uses superbly for his own protection and to insure his own privacy" (*Conversations*, 103). At the same time O'Connor exempted herself from any responsibility for taking a political stand: "The fiction writer is interested in individuals, not races; he knows that good and evil are not apportioned along racial lines" (*Conversations*, 109). Somewhat belatedly, O'Connor now applied spiritual values in her thinking on the matter: "It requires considerable grace for two races to live together, particularly when the population is divided about fifty-fifty between them and when they have our particular history. It can't be done without a code of manners based on mutual charity." Ever skeptical of humanity, O'Connor immediately modified her statement: "When the charity fails—as it is going to do constantly—you've got those manners there to preserve each race" (*Conversations*, 103).

As far as O'Connor was concerned, then, for resolution to the problem the nation would have to rely upon Southern traditions of social manners between the races rather than upon religion, rights legislation, or equal protection under the judiciary. In views expressed privately in 1963, O'Connor thought that public debate on behalf of Negro rights never failed to "romanticize" the issue. Exasperated at one time over the national attention directed on the South, she erupted: "I say a plague on everybody's house as far as the race business goes" (*Letters*, 537). With the news of riots in the ghettos of Northern cities in the summer of 1964, O'Connor expressed some satisfaction that racial unrest was not limited to her region. Writing close friends that same year, she conveyed her lack of sympathy with the public pleadings of James Baldwin for racial reconciliation and her agreement with the separatist views of Cassius Clay, who had newly adopted his Black Muslim name Muhammad Ali.

In O'Connor's late story "Judgment Day" (1964) the difference between faith and unbelief is represented to be as categorical as separation of the races within a segregated society. This difference is rendered through a heated and ultimately physical conflict between T. C. Tanner, an old white man from the rural South, and a sophisticated black Northerner who is an actor by profession. The two have recently become neighbors in the New York City apartment building where Tanner now lives with his married daughter and her husband. To Tanner's patronizing but not intentionally derogatory greeting "'Good evening, Preacher'" the black man reacts with vehemence: "'I'm not a Christian. I don't believe in that crap. There ain't no Jesus and there ain't no God.'" Tanner responds instinctively to this heresy: "'And you ain't black . . . and I ain't white!'" (*Works*, 690). The storyline confirms Tanner's retort as a creditable defense of Christian faith. Their dispute culminates with brutalities committed by the black actor that contribute to Tanner's death. The story's closing imagery suggests that Tanner dies a martyr, leaving this world as a man prepared spiritually for judgment.

For a writer concerned with spiritual mystery O'Connor might strike readers as inordinately engaged by physical appearances and fleshly matters. It is this seeming contradiction that in her imagination points precisely to the core of Christian mystery: "For my part I think that when I know what the laws of the flesh and the physical really are, then I will know what God is. We know them as we see them, not as God sees them. For me it is the virgin birth, the Incarnation, the resurrection which are the true laws of the flesh and the physical. Death, decay, destruction are the suspension of these laws. I am always astonished at the emphasis the Church puts on the body. It is not the soul she says that will rise but the body, glorified" (*Letters*, 100). In formal literary respects O'Connor's fiction, through its practices of grotesque figural realism, is as involved as Poe's work with the possibilities for linkage among verbal and visual categories. Through its attention to prophetic word and vision O'Connor's fiction shares with Anderson's an ear and eye for distinct registers of meaning in spoken language as compared to written modes. In terms of the axis of description in their prose, O'Connor, Poe, Anderson, and West share a reflexive alertness to matters of figure-ground and black/white configurations in rendering scene, character, and the story's own textuality.

New York Sights
Weegee

IN AMERICAN PHOTOGRAPHY the first genuine adherent to a grotesque attitude was the New York freelance press photographer Arthur Fellig, known from about 1938 by the professional name Weegee. Born Usher Fellig in 1899 in Austria, he was given the Americanized first name Arthur by immigration authorities when his mother and the Fellig children arrived in 1910. His adolescence was shaped by the experiences of a large, poor Jewish family living in the tenement districts of New York's Lower East Side. Among a succession of after-school jobs, Arthur worked as a newsboy around his neighborhood, but the pursuit lasted no more than a week since so few people in the area could read English. Arthur's father, whose ambitions to become a rabbi would be realized later in life, scraped up meager earnings as a pushcart vendor and, along with his wife, worked as a janitor in exchange for rent on the family's tenement rooms. To help support the family Arthur quit school at age fourteen, and his professional life can be said to have started at that point. With a modest set of equipment, Arthur went into street trade as a tintype portraitist. Since its origin in the 1850s, the tintype remained in wide use well into the next century because of its inexpensive and relatively simple processing, which produced a unique image. The tintype is in fact a negative that appears to be a positive print when viewed against the dark background that has been lacquered or enameled onto a thin sheet of iron. (Thus *tintype* is something of a misnomer. The image is more properly termed a ferrotype, as it is commonly known in Great Britain.)

When sold, the tintype was typically placed in a simple folded card or window mat, and in this form it served immigrant and working-class customers as a durable portrait.

For slightly better pay and an opportunity to learn more of the craft, Fellig became an assistant in a commercial studio that specialized in photographing large manufactured goods. Though much of the work proved menial, at the studio he did gain basics in lighting and darkroom technique. One of the firm's regular commissions on location involved the documentation of factory fires for the purpose of insurance settlements. On these assignments Fellig was given the task, as he phrased it decades later in his autobiography, "to blow the flash powder": "I would put a tube into my mouth and blow the flash powder onto a rag soaked in alcohol, which would ignite the powder. It would go off like a bomb and illuminate the scene."[1] At about age seventeen Fellig bought a second-hand 5 × 7 inch view camera. With a hired pony brought to the streets in the Lower East Side on weekends, he attracted children for a short ride and a portrait. Once he had made proofs from the glass plate negatives, Fellig would return to the neighborhood and take orders from parents. Negative-positive processing afforded far greater control over the final image than with tintypes, and Fellig made tonal retouching a major selling point: "I would finish the photographs on the contrastiest [sic] paper I could get in order to give the kids nice white, chalky faces. My customers, who were Italian, Polish or Jewish, like their pictures dead-white" (Weegee, 18). In the end, however, what income he could make did not cover expenses for the pony, and he quit the trade. Through these early working experiences with the tintype process and its dependence upon a dark ground for the image's legibility, with explosive illumination through flash powder, and with the varying effects of photographic contrast Fellig began to shape a sensibility in the black and white medium that formed the basis for the trademark urban style of Weegee.

Arthur Fellig left home at age eighteen and for a period of months he led a transient existence in Lower Manhattan's districts, taking what temporary employment he could find and sleeping in charity missions and parks when he could not afford lodging. Eventually he was hired at a passport studio near the Custom House downtown. His duties included sales and camera operation and he continued in this position for nearly three years. In time, tiring of the routine and predictability of such minor studio work, Fellig joined the darkroom staff on a major photo syndicate. There he found a vocation in the medium: "Here was the kind of photography that I had been looking for; no more still lifes at the commercial studio, no more retouching wrinkles . . . from the portraits of girls, no passport photos" (*Weegee,* 26). The autobiography, which is noticeably casual in handling such details, dates the new employment 1923 and identifies a position at Acme Newspictures.[2]

Fellig remained with Acme Newspictures for nearly the next ten years, principally as a darkroom technician and photo printer. The syndicate, which was later acquired by United Press International Photos, supplied pictures for three papers in New York City and for several hundred newspapers nationwide. Fellig's daily involvement with the preparation and marketing of photograph images for the popular press intensely influenced his eye for subject matter and his visual rationale. Three decades later in the overheated prose of his autobiography, the prose style itself a sure sign of the lasting effects of this influence, the photographer recalls: "Over the developing trays in the dark room at Acme, history passed through my hands. Fires, explosions, railroad wrecks, ship collisions, prohibition gang wars, murders, kings, presidents, everybody famous and everything exciting" (*Weegee,* 28). Patently, his attitude toward history is stopped down to the day's most startling events and is focused on disaster and notoriety. On occasion in the dead of night when no staff photographer was available, an editor at Acme would send off Fellig with a camera to cover the scene of an emergency or calamity, typically a fire. According to statements made later in interviews and in the autobiography, from this early point on there persisted in the photographer no less of a craving for sensation than in the daily audience for the photo press.

Another vivid glimpse into the world of New York tabloid newspapers of the period, one that confirms Weegee's characterization of it, is provided in the memoirs of the Hollywood film director Sam Fuller. While still in public school during the late 1920s Fuller began work as a copyboy for the *New York Journal,* and he quickly learned that "what really sold newspapers was violence, sex, and scandal." He adds a wry qualification: "There were exceptions. Big trials, labor strife, filibusters, sunken treasure, daring exploits, and political upheaval might make front-page news."[3] At age sixteen Fuller joined the staff of the *New York Evening Graphic* and, after a brief trial period, he worked there as a crime reporter until he left for the West Coast in 1931. Earlier in his career the *Graphic*'s editor-in-chief had harbored a murderer so as to take down his confession and be the first to publish it. (The incident later provided a plotline for the hit play and movie *The Front Page.*) Among New York dailies the *Evening Graphic* became known for its "composographs," photograph composites that superimposed the heads of people in the news onto the bodies of models posed in staged situations. The counterfeit was offered as a photographic record of the spectacular incident described in the accompanying story. Soon after he was hired, Fuller stood in as a body double for a composograph that portrayed a pilot desperately trying to control his airplane moments before it crashed. This kind of illustration of the event, which included a clear portrait of the pilot's face, of course in actuality was not possible with the photojournalist's camera alone.

Fellig left Acme Newspictures in 1935 to begin freelance work as a press photographer, and around 1938 he established his identity in the news business as Weegee. The spelling and pronunciation is his self-fashioned version of the trademarked parlor novelty, the Ouija or "talking board." Introduced commercially in 1890, the Ouija device claimed psychic abilities to send and receive messages from the spirit world. While a few practitioners still take such claims seriously, in most homes during its greatest popularity the Ouija was regarded simply as an amusing pastime. Weegee adopted the name with a purpose akin to a sideshow spiel, loud in its promises of uncommon sights and experiences. The name advertised his claim of having a sixth sense for news of calamities that enabled him to arrive on the scene before police or fire crews and to file his photographs first with the news agencies. In truth, Weegee spent much time at Manhattan Police Headquarters where he could monitor emergency calls and dispatches. When Weegee rented a room one block away, he had it specially wired to receive such signals. By the end of the 1930s the photographer was extended official permission for the installation of a police radio in his automobile.

Once he went freelance in 1935 Weegee produced his signature photography of crime, accidents, and disaster over the next ten years, and it received wide circulation in New York's city press and national distribution through picture syndicates. Also on occasion *Life* magazine featured Weegee's work. He was hired as a regular contributor to the New York evening paper *PM Daily* when it started publication in 1940. A quality newspaper of liberal views, *PM Daily* was headed by a former chief editor in the Time-Life organization. Given substantial latitude in his assignments, Weegee maintained a nonexclusive contract with the paper for five years. The photographer expanded his range of subject matter to include benign human interest stories such as Coney Island crowds in summer, the opening of the opera season, the circus, and the Macy's parade on Thanksgiving. In this period Weegee photographs were exhibited in New York galleries and museums, first in the one-man show *Murder is My Business* at the Photo League in 1941 and subsequently in two group shows at the Museum of Modern Art, *Action Photography* in 1943 and *Art in Progress* in 1944. Weegee's book *Naked City*, in which his untutored version of hardboiled prose accompanies his pictures of New

York, was published in June 1945, and it went through six printings by the end of the year.[4]

In comparison to Weegee's "naked city" perspective the prose and the photographs within the Federal Writers' Project *Panorama* (1938) and *Guide* (1939) publications on New York contain nothing to suggest a grotesque attitude toward the city. For all of its attention to particulars of cultural history, demographics, ethnicity, and social geography, the *Panorama* volume celebrates its subject as the contemporary cosmopolis nonpareil, "not only the symbol of America but the daemonic symbol of the modern, . . . the world city whose past weighed least heavily upon its future." Along the way, the volume acknowledges some inequities of the recent past and the present, such as slum tenement districts and riots in Harlem. But the character of the city's future is to be determined by an ongoing process that directs "the terrific flume of her energy into the orderly dynamos of social realization." In deploying another trope, the *Panorama* imagines that the great diversity and incongruities within the city's populace are coordinated into the instruments and voicings of a "New World Symphony."[5] Not one image among the book's one hundred photograph illustrations offers a contradiction to this tone of promise.

Published one year later, the *Guide*, its text divided into sections by localities within the city's five boroughs, is more receptive to disparities in circumstances and experience. The description of the Times Square district, for instance, ruminates: "Here midnight streets are more brilliant than noon. . . . Here, too, in a permanent moralizing tableau, appear the extremes of success and failure characteristic of Broadway's spectacular professions: gangsters and racketeers, panhandlers and derelicts, youthful stage stars and aging burlesque comedians, world heavyweight champions and once-acclaimed beggars." Urban colorism in this scene obviously follows the example of Damon Runyon's fiction. Although a "midway side" to Times Square and the "freak shows" at Coney Island are mentioned, the guide avoids depiction of the exact nature of such attractions. The guide locates the city's lowest depths in Harlem and the Bowery, but it does not etch the trivial, terrible, lived details such conditions entail. The section on the Bowery, for example, limits its social commentary to the rather generic language contained in two sentences: "Here flophouses offer a bug-infested bed in an unventilated pigeonhole for twenty-five cents a night, restaurants serve ham and eggs for ten cents, and students in barber 'colleges' cut hair for fifteen cents. Thousands of the nation's unemployed drift to this section and may be seen sleeping in all-night restaurants, in doorways, and on loading platforms, furtively begging, or waiting with hopeless faces for some bread line or free lodging house to open."[6]

Only two photographs in the *New York City Guide* relate to issues of human degradation; one presents a back alley view of a tenement on the Lower East Side, the other abandoned buildings in a Harlem slum. The emphasis in them falls upon environment, not upon people. The human costs of poverty and dereliction are expressed to a degree in illustrations by graphic artists Mabel Dwight and Eli Jacobi styled in a mannered proletarian realism. While the prose entry on Times Square offers morality tale exempla of the city's incongruities, the guide's photograph of the famous intersection ignores the passing scene of life at street level. The picture's vantage upon Times Square is from an elevated panoramic nighttime view that directs attention mainly upon towering, illuminated business and advertising signs. The scene contains no suggestion of social contrasts; it comes no closer to life on the street than the expansive, bright theater and hotel marquees above the sidewalks.

The attention of Weegee's camera roamed from Bowery drunks to socialites at the Met, from three-alarm blazes to vice arrests and murder scenes. Many familiar Weegee photographs provide nighttime glimpses of crime, accident, and fire victims. These kinds of events warranted the kind of momentary attention and descriptive rendering characteristic of his visual style. Such news events, and such images as Weegee made of them, held little claim to narrative depth or lasting historical significance. The quotidian sensationalism in many of these photographs surely exemplifies features of mass culture that Walter Benjamin associates with the new sensorium of urban experience and a modern temporality first expressed fully by Baudelaire. While nothing could be farther from Weegee's intentions or probably even his comprehension, when in the course of the 1930s Benjamin contemplated the medium of photography such features defined a new register of experience and time fundamental to a materialist understanding of history. The consumer of modern media culture—particularly in cases of the illustrated press and motion pictures—is subject to reflex processes that Benjamin characterizes as "perception in the form of shocks" and "reception in a state of distraction."[7]

In *Naked City* Weegee features under the heading "Psychic Photography" a pedestrian accident and a street explosion, each event "photographed before and after it happened."[8] Given camera technology in the 1930s, it was rare to record photographically a purely accidental event over its duration. The fact that such a record was made in 1937 of the airship *Hindenberg* disaster is a part of the historic nature of the event. Really what Weegee and news photographers like him offered the daily press were documented instances of the *aftermath* to catastrophe. Where Benjamin generalizes on the medium of photography and its intrinsic temporality, "the camera gave the moment a posthumous shock, as it were," a quality of the posthumous is literally contained within many crime and accident photographs.[9] With the denouement to such an event having run its violent course, Weegee arrives soon after to conduct through the camera a visual postmortem to the episode. A murder victim is documented dead on the spot where he has fallen. Casualties in an auto wreck are shown pitched askew within a vehicle or on the pavement. The deceased from a fire are registered as shrouded figures laid out at the scene.

The equipment with which Weegee covered local New York stories, many in the night hours, was the Speed Graphic camera with a high-intensity flash attachment. In production since 1912, with many technical improvements the Speed Graphic became by the 1930s a standard portable camera for professional photographers, including journalists, and remained so well into the 1950s. By the time Weegee turned freelance the disposable flash bulb had replaced powder for illumination and synchronization between flash and shutter was a regular camera feature.[10] Weegee often relied on a common professional camera practice with the Speed Graphic in the event of a sudden photo opportunity. With focus preset at ten feet, exposure time at 1/200th second, and lens aperture at f16, at the scene the photojournalist need only position his camera some ten feet from the principal subject. The small aperture guaranteed an adequate depth of field in focus for the area of flash illumination. Fall-off in light intensity from the flash could leave the background and edges of the scene vague and unfocused. Weegee worked in the conventional press format of the 4 × 5 inch picture negative, which is relatively large for a camera with such mobility. This negative size also provided the photographer ample latitude in the darkroom for cropping the image, editing its content, and manipulating densities of black and white. Key to Weegee's camera and darkroom methods was his purpose in making photographs for mass reproduction and distribution. Knowing their end use, Weegee made photographs designed to withstand the diminishing effects on clarity and contrast that were a result of cheap printing processes used by tabloid newspapers. The more expensive hot ink process used by *PM Daily* was an exception, and it provided magazine print quality for Weegee's photographs.

Weegee's New York is most often evoked as a city of night. In a typical Weegee image of urban misfortune a stark, brief radiance from the photographer's flash attachment has penetrated the city's impersonal darkness to yield a perspective on human fate. With such a flashlit image the scene's background and edges might remain pitched in night. For some

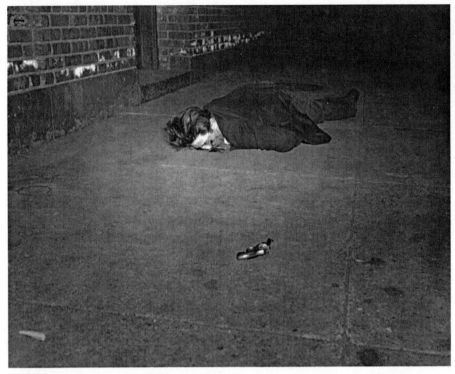

Figure 7.1. Weegee, *Gunman Killed by Off Duty Cop at 344 Broome St.*, February 3, 1942. International Center of Photography/Getty Images.

photographs Weegee would contribute further to this effect in the dark-room while printing his negatives by burning in areas of the composi-tion to produce deep, flat, funereal blacks. Within Weegee's iconography, flash illumination is as sudden and brief as it is brilliant and disturbing, preserving for clear view what belongs originally to darkness. In this as much as in subject matter his iconography shares qualities inherent to the grotesque, a mode that in its original sense involves the adumbration of some incongruous, unsettling sight.

One effect of Weegee's use of a powerful flash and fast shutter speed for a nighttime image is to compress the picture composition within a plane of visual interest defined by limited light. The resultant contrasts in tone between lights and darks can be abrupt, without much intermediary gradation in gray. These attributes are exemplified in his photograph *Gunman Killed by Off Duty Cop at 344 Broome St.*, which appeared in the February 3, 1942 issue of *PM Daily* (fig. 7.1). This sidewalk spectacle of violent death is shot with light. Unmistakably, the camera has been aimed and the flash discharged in the direction pointed by the pistol barrel. This trajectory aligns the picture and viewers with an act of homicide, irrespective of the fact that the pistol on the pavement may well belong to the victim and not the cop who shot him. In this alignment and as was customary, Weegee adopted a perspective that accentuates crude designs caused by sudden death and left for ironic notice among the living. Another such note is registered with the victim's slim cigar, still poised between his lips. These effects differ somewhat from the "trivial and terrible" details Baudelaire noted in the death scene imagined by Daumier. The Weegee photograph displays death trivialized by cheap ironies readymade within the public sphere, present within everyday scenes of violence and suffering themselves. Almost as terrible as the event itself is the trivialization.

Often the ironies and the trivialization attached to individual disaster are overstated in Weegee photographs. An obvious instance is *Joy of Living,* published in *PM Daily* on April 17, 1942 to report on a traffic accident that caused one fatality (fig. 7.2). Most prominently, the moviehouse marquee provides a deadpan commentary on the incident. But no less a part of the photograph's grotesque reflexivity is the bystander at the left border of the frame. Through cropping, the image easily could have eliminated the figure without sacrificing any other important element in the composition such as the text on the marquee, but Weegee chose to retain him. With the two police officers and other bystanders attentive to the fatal truth of the moment, this figure alone breaks the self-contained, intimate drama of the sight. Consisting only of a face and hat, the rest of him matted from view by the picture border, the figure is present as a synecdoche for a greater mass of spectators, those who look upon the event in the form of a press photograph, as we do now.

The presence of a photographer is for him for the moment of greater interest than the lifeless human being. The movie title and this figure break the security and immunity that would otherwise be available through a voyeuristic "fourth wall" effect in the photograph and that would allow one to consume a spectacle of death entirely without self-consciousness. The curious look of this curiosity seeker betokens a small component within the everyday diversions and satisfactions of the living, no matter how grim their source.

Grotesquely reflexive as well are the layers of newspaper used to cover the corpse. They have been used in this way presumably "out of respect" for the dead until a more proper cover is provided, as the police appear

Figure 7.2. Weegee, *Joy of Living*, April 17, 1942. International Center of Photography/Getty Images.

to be doing at this point. Many pages are heavily illustrated with press photographs and picture advertisements. The pile of newsprint eliminates from the scene the victim as a human figure. The only remaining vestige of his humanity is a pair of shoes, splayed apart in a posture of rest. Several such Weegee street photographs register the debris left in the wake of everyday living, and the newspaper figures as the most familiar and readily disposable of such items. Over this fact Weegee displays none of the furor of a Jeremiah as Nathanael West does in *The Day of the Locust,* which says of the onlookers gathered for a premiere outside a movie palace: "Their boredom becomes more and more terrible. They realize that they've been tricked and burn with resentment. Every day of their lives they read the newspapers and went to the movies. Both fed them on lynchings, murder, sex crimes, explosions, wrecks, love nests, fires, miracles, revolutions, wars. This daily diet made sophisticates of them. . . . Nothing can ever be violent enough to make taut their slack minds and bodies. They have been cheated and betrayed" (*Novels,* 381). While the novel's invoice of tabloid sensationalism is remarkably similar to the ones provided by Weegee and Sam Fuller, these two men accepted the situation as a plain inescapable fact of a media culture—one ripe with thematic and stylistic opportunities for the knowing participant, as they were. Of course Nathanael West was also a knowing participant during much of the 1930s with professional contracts with movie studios despite the deep misgivings expressed in private, in his novels, and in a public talk "Makers of Mass Neuroses," delivered November 1936 to a writers congress and focused on the power of Hollywood to corrupt the minds of its audience.

Weegee crafted a sensationalist yet detached style that has retained much currency in the tabloid, fashion, and art worlds. Asymmetries in composition and lighting and disproportions among a scene's elements are prominent in his camera and darkroom style. There results in some Weegee photographs a visual effect of disequilibrium that can border on vertigo. Some art critics consider his photography to belong to a stylistic trend of "American abstract sensationalism."[11] The designation, however, overstates a claim of abstraction for his news scene photographs, which remain resolutely representational. His rendering of violence or calamity often entails contradiction in the emotional mood of the aftermath to an event, but that moment is delineated as an actuality. The outlook on human mayhem generally offered by Weegee is bemused and impassive. That outlook suggests an uncynical stoicism, one endowed with a ready sense of the absurd.

Within Weegee's photography the eventful and the accidental pertain not only to subject matter. In his images the injured, the deceased, or a wreckage can be cast by events into a position remarkable in its awkwardness or absurdity that, beyond its factuality, takes graphic dominance within the photographic frame. Given the contingencies of such scenes, Weegee often could not reliably predict or control where shadows and reflections would fall once the flash was discharged. Admirers of his work like Colin Westerbeck and photographer Joel Meyerowitz value this unforeseen quality. In their estimation, Weegee frequently "shot in the dark, seldom being able to predict what, if anything, he would get. This reliance on blind chance to get some of his most effective pictures is obvious."[12] Bruce Downes, the editor of an amateur photography handbook, prizes the sheer, shock brilliance from the flash in Weegee photographs: "This is a world seen through the camera's artificial eye, which alone is capable of recording what happens when some 15 to 60 thousand lumen-seconds of light are concentrated into a split-second interval. This amounts to an explosion in which Weegee literally blasts the faces of his subjects with an intense spray of photons" (*Weegee*, 3–4). The camera practices of Weegee were so rooted in the use of flash illumination that the photographer often continued to employ flash for daylight images. Diane Arbus would later elaborate this technique to powerfully grotesque effect in her photography.

With some Weegee photographs the flash seems to have illuminated a curiosity as much for the benefit of spectators as for the camera shot. Some bystanders are animated by the uncommon sight, others remain expressionless in the face of it, a few on the fringes have not as yet focused their attention. For its part, the camera's attention can tend toward spectators within the spectacle more than toward the street incident in its own right. With their attention to the public, Weegee's crime scene photographs differ greatly from the conventions of pictures taken by the police as forensic documents. In his book *Evidence* Luc Sante has reproduced and annotated fifty-five pictures taken by New York City police photographers, most of them to document homicides, in the years 1914–1918.[13] For most of the photographs the police have kept pedestrians and spectators well away from the corpse and the immediate area of the crime scene. In Weegee's coverage of such events, the police seem to allow both his camera and onlookers fairly close proximity.

The body of an automobile accident victim in one 1938 Weegee photograph seems to be irrelevant for the moment to the crowd gathered, which seems uniform in their interest in the camera, probably in response to the photographer's request to look in its direction (fig. 7.3). In a 1940

Figure 7.3. Weegee, *Auto Accident Victim*, 1938. International Center of Photography/Getty Images.

photograph of the life-saving attempt made over a swimmer at Coney Island rescuers concentrate fully on the victim while a young woman in bathing suit among them has looked up and a smile has come automatically to her face for the camera. Her smile is among the disarming, unaccountable reactions of people caught by Weegee's camera on the scene of disaster. The young woman has instinctively posed, but in more candid glimpses analogous effects are evident, as with the 1939 photograph *Murder at the Feast of San Gennaro*, where a uniformed officer's amused expression is directed toward a poker-faced detective as both men stand over a corpse.

Naked City devotes its second chapter to "The Curious Ones" who congregate at such street incidents and a later chapter to "The Escapists," who consist of circus and show audiences, dancers on the ballroom floor, and tenement kids delighted with an open fire hydrant. From Weegee's perspective these people do not belong to a caste of the cheated and betrayed, as Nathanael West would have it.[14] At its outset *The Day of the Locust* identifies the city's bystanders as a menacing presence: "When their stare was returned, their eyes filled with hatred" (*Novels,* 242). There persists on their faces "an expression of vicious acrid boredom that trembled on the edge of violence" (*Novels,* 320–21). For Weegee, to the contrary, chance spectators are his desired audience, his paying customers. A later chapter in *Naked City* celebrates the spectrum of emotions displayed by a young female spectator over a performance by Frank Sinatra on stage at the Paramount Theater. The blasts of light from Weegee's flash and the instantaneous effect of his shutter in these candid portraits are consonant with the transports of a starstruck fan.

The first chapter to *Naked City,* "Sunday Morning in Manhattan," shows inhabitants of the city asleep, many in public spaces like stoops, park benches, fire escapes, parked automobiles, sidewalks. Within two chapters this motif is transfigured into portrayals of the big sleep, "Murder" and "Sudden Death," captured by the camera in similar locales. Such linkages have led critics like Ellen Handy to approach the book as a "collective portrait of the city [that] marks it as a place of infinite stories" and to esteem Weegee as an "urban storyteller *par excellence.*"[15] Beyond a few such structural parallels, however, the representational axis of the book's prose and pictures remains far more descriptive and depictive than narrative. A characteristic sample from its text, with its original elliptical mannerisms intact, demonstrates this assertion: "The men, women and children who commit murders always fascinate me . . . I always ask them why they killed . . . the men claim self defense, the women seem to be in a daze . . . but as a rule frustrated love and jealousy are the cause . . . the kids are worried for fear the picture might not make the papers" (*Naked City,* 160). The casual, blanket generalizations and a temporality in the continuous present keep the prose far removed from narrative functions. Alain Bergala reaches a similar finding when he observes of the book's properties in pictures and words of "narrative disconnection" that "the very significant general atmosphere matters more than the story."[16]

The historical survey *Photography 1839–1937* organized by Beaumont Newhall for the Museum of Modern Art in 1937 included news photographs as a distinct category within the medium. But the exhibition, the catalogue, and the Newhall book *Photography: A Short Critical History* (1938) contained only a few press images. At that point it was still too early in Weegee's career for his work to be included. When Newhall prepared *The History of Photography from 1839 to the Present Day* for publication in 1949 Weegee's work is acknowledged for a quality of "social caricature" that results from "unreal lighting of the flash from the camera." By the book's aesthetic standards of "naturalistic" composition, however, this quality is of limited value since in flash photography "the results were, for the most part, grotesque, because the harsh front light flattened out faces, cast unpleasant shadows, and fell so abruptly that backgrounds were unrelieved black."[17] Obviously, in Newhall's evaluation *grotesque* is strictly a pejorative, employed without a sense of its history or traditions within the graphic arts.

Talk of art in connection with Weegee's photography began in the early 1940s, prompted in part by its exhibition at the Photo League and the Museum of Modern Art and promoted energetically by Weegee himself and by admirers in the press world. William McCleery, an editor at *PM Daily*, was one of the first to sloganeer for consideration of his photographs as art, and a demanding art at that: "Of course Weegee, being an Artist, has his own conception of what constitutes beauty, and in some cases it is hard for us to share his conception" (*Naked City*, 6). With the development of a profitable market in photography in more recent decades, this kind of art talk has intensified. Louis Stettner, an American photographer who worked for many years in Europe and a friend of Weegee, acknowledges that a problem is presented by the man's seeming lack of aesthetic judgment: "In the course of his career he produced more than five thousand photographs and never discarded any! The classic Weegees are mixed in with many minor photographs and those taken for purely bread-and-butter commercial reasons."[18] Weegee's posture of rogue expertise in the news business did little to alter this impression: "I kept no files. I put my extra prints and negatives into a barrel. If anybody wanted a fire or a murder shot, my two daily specials, I'd tell him to come down and search for them. Or, better still, he could wait and, within twenty-four hours, I'd have new ones for him" (*Weegee*, 65). Stettner attempts to overcome the difficulty, though his rhetoric and logic quickly prove inadequate to the task: "Weegee's best works are, in essence, news photographs whose profundity and significance have lifted them up into the realm of art. True, they have come in by the back door. So what? When they were first made, he was called an artist and his photographs were deemed creative and interesting."[19]

Weegee once remarked to celebrity columnist Earl Wilson, in a line likely to have been well rehearsed: "You are amazed and mystified by the fabulous Weegee. . . . You're surprised by my oddacity."[20] To reporters in more professional contexts, Weegee was given to art comparisons, though they could prove wildly unpredictable in their relevance. With one interviewer he made this claim of sophistication in the composition of his photographs: "I use the camera like a painter uses a brush; I am the Renoir of the lens." The same article contains a contrary, but no less art historical self-assessment: "I'm very primitive; in fact, I'm the Grandma Moses of Photography." As readily, Weegee would acknowledge that all art talk was part of "*my* vaudeville act."[21] In a suggestive comparison with the early work of Andy Warhol, David Hopkins takes as exemplary a precedent set by "the way in which [Weegee] had crossed over, seemingly effortlessly, from the sphere of popular journalism to 'high' art." Within the museum world Weegee had been "elevated from the status of commercially driven opportunist to someone deemed to possess a superior personal vision."[22] In about 1959 Warhol cultivated a similar transformation by placing the kinds of work he did as a commercial graphic designer into fine arts contexts.

Extravagant aesthetic praise for Weegee has come from French commentators. The canonizing Collection Photo Poche series arranged by the Centre Nationale de la Photographie in Paris assesses Weegee's stature in these terms, authored by André Laude: "He was an authentic, a great, a genius of a photographer. He transcended the daily spectacle of horror, of ugliness and of violence. . . . Weegee's art—because it is art—resides in that grasping of the truth, captured in the immediate reality and glimpsed in the most dramatic fashion." To counter any cheapening associations with lowbrow mass appeal and sensational diversions, this commentary insists that "Weegee's anti-intellectualism is a sort of travesty of his true, profound art."[23] In the catalogue to a touring exhibition of Weegee photographs held in private hands, the praise could readily double as promotional copy intended for the collector of photography as art. This 1999 exhibition acclaims Weegee as a humanist and social documentarian in the tradition of American Depression-era photography: "He turns an eye full of melancholy and nostalgia upon the lonely, the abandoned, the wistful and despairing. Weegee the philanthropist, makes the image of mankind the centre of his research, and focuses on the transience of happiness and pride, on the instability of social standing and material security." For more contemporary tastes, the catalogue adopts an altogether separate tack in proposing that Weegee "might be regarded as an early or premature conceptual artist who counters with a commentary the image of his age."[24]

Several American art critics, however, have expressed deep reservations over the tabloid purposes of Weegee's photographs, ambiguities in their affective tenor, and questions of privacy in the cases of the sufferers depicted. For Colin L. Westerbeck their treatment of violent subject matter is problematic: "His pictures turn catastrophe to comedy too easily. . . . Weegee found it laughable." The critic acknowledges an immediacy of visual impact in this photography but imputes to the photographer "cruelty" in his motives and practices.[25] To be sure, Weegee would wisecrack in print about street murders among criminals as a "slum clearance project" (caption in *Weegee*, between 64–65). The photographs of such events might register mockery, but as just one among a range of reactions plain on the faces of onlookers and emergency personnel. *Their First Murder* (1941), with its mixed crowd of adults and children, vast variations in the direction of the individuals' attention, and disparate states of awareness over what has happened, is an emotional hodgepodge (fig. 7.4). In the tumult of the moment what might appear to be a grin may well have been in fact a grimace, indifference in fact involvement. Much the same is true in the mob scene at the conclusion to *The Day of the Locust*. Both are cases of incongruity and irony without the laughter.

Weegee images with the greatest immediacy, Westerbeck charges, are the same ones "where the greatest antipathy appears to have existed. The very qualities that are the most distressing in his work—his aggressiveness and disregard for the feeling of his subjects—are also his most durable qualities."[26] John Coplans has reached largely the same conclusion: "There is a demonic edge to Weegee's quirky endeavor that bears discussion. Many of his photographs are morally dubious, not just because of their evident prurience, or his antisocial attitudes or even his outrageous hucksterism—it's that he sold for money images that exposed and exploited the involuntary, naked emotions of people he photographed without their permission, often by deliberately spying. One does sense animus in Weegee."[27] As for intrusiveness, the kind of street coverage Weegee filed was well within the professional standards of American journalism of the time, though admittedly some would question the integrity of such standards. Weegee followed an established guideline: on "accident or rescue stories and where the pictures include policemen and firemen . . . neither permissions nor releases are needed except when photographs are used to advertise commercial products" (*Naked City,*

Figure 7.4. Weegee, *Their First Murder*, October 9, 1941. International Center of Photography/Getty Images.

242–43). The obvious presence of a camera the size of a Speed Graphic and the relatively proximate distance it requires belie charges of spying in regard to his street photography. Awareness and acceptance of the camera among onlookers is quite apparent in many images. And many of the events recorded took place after all in social spaces where the individual's behavior and appearance are directly on view to a public. The same holds true for semi-public spaces such as the movie theater, the opera house, and the beach at nighttime, where Weegee's method was in fact partly secretive, through the use of infrared photography.

The harshest critique of Weegee's sensibility has come from Max Kozloff, who detects in it an underlying "allegiance to slapstick and Keystone" that causes "his freelance crime scenes often [to] look comedic when they're supposed to be forensic." To scenes of actual violence and suffering the photographs bring, in Kozloff's judgment, a "flip and inconsequent tone" that is distracting and impertinent.[28] On the occasion of the major exhibition *New York: Capital of Photography,* which opened at the Jewish Museum in New York City in 2002, Kozloff as co-curator was obviously obliged to include Weegee images. The critic's essay for the exhibition catalog continues in the previous vein, labeling the photographer "a gymnast of disparagement, almost asking you not to take him seriously." In the aggregate, the essay alleges, his photographs "comprise a portfolio of indiscretions that could only have been motivated by the needs of a voyeur."[29] A major rationale for the exhibition is that the New York City depicted in American photography over the twentieth century is largely a product of Jewish consciousness and that the imagery reflects social and aesthetic approaches related to Jewish tradition. In this context as well Weegee, though obviously Jewish, is treated by the critic as something of a pariah. Kozloff charges that by 1940 Weegee had betrayed the traditions of social photography: "Private moments of the neglected and aggrieved ceased to be object lessons in political morality, and became fair game on the daily, human round."[30] The assault on privacy is certainly one aspect of Weegee's work, where it can be recognized as part of his photographic practices *and* as subject matter, as a prominent behavior in modern urban culture.

The varied dynamics of spectatorship recorded within so many of Weegee's photographs document, for one thing, that voyeurism in public places is widely stimulated by mass culture and that it is in truth a social rather than a private practice. The comparison to Andy Warhol's early work, specifically in this instance to the *Disaster* silkscreen series of 1962–63, lead David Hopkins to conclude that Weegee's habitual inclusion of spectators exemplifies "the historical instantiation of a vacant or neutralized subjectivity." Even where Weegee's spectators display obvious affect in their responses, his argument continues, "subjectivity reasserts itself precisely in the neutralized mode described by Warhol."[31] But Weegee's camera vision and the looks in the eyes of his spectators are too demonstrably sentient to be generalized in such a way. To be sure, the deadpan is one among a full repertory of responses, but in addition to being psychologically neutral the deadpan can be an assumed, calculated stance. Complicating matters, it is manifest in some Weegee pictures that emotions of the moment are uncertain or they misapprehend the enormity of the event. A grotesque attitude toward the scene is reflected in the indeterminacy among the spectators who have gathered, attracted variously by the scene or by the crowd itself, by a presence of the police or firemen, by the sight of Weegee's camera.

The life of black Americans in New York City receives some consideration in Weegee's work of the 1930s and 1940s, but the photographer's sense of race relations is not inflected by an attitude of the grotesque. As a matter of fact, his images of African Americans are ingenuously respectful toward their suffering, their joys, their formal public occasions, and their entertainments. All these aspects of experience are represented within the Harlem chapter to *Naked City*. In a sequence of three photographs the daytime scene of shrouded victims who had been trampled to death at a social event contains no contingent elements (such as a public sign) or variations in emotional tone that would contradict the temper of disbelief and anguish. Among the police and survivors no untoward expressions or gestures appear.

Two other photographs depict the celebratory occasion of Easter Sunday. Leaving services, black church members dressed in finery appear as a congenial, dignified group that welcomes a photograph portrait. These two images stand in diametric opposition to the book's earlier portrayal of society patrons at the opera in their opulence and with their air of condescension. A well-spirited sense of humor, shared by photographer and subject, is conveyed in a photograph of a young African American man contained in the "Fires" section. Descending an escape ladder while clad only in a trench coat and hat, the man is fully aware of the comedy of the sight he makes and he has paused to greet the camera with a broad smile.

The chapter's attitude toward public disorder and crime in Harlem is by turns lenient or lightly comedic. Either way, its attitude is devoid of parodic and grotesque elements. In a large nighttime crowd scene, reported in a caption as "the actual birth of a riot in Harlem," the atten-

Figure 7.5. Weegee, "Here is the actual birth of a riot in Harlem," in *Naked City* (1945). International Center of Photography/Getty Images.

tion of all but two or three individuals is directed elsewhere than the camera and overall the crowd appears watchful and restrained (*Naked City*, 192) (fig. 7.5). The object of their interest is off-frame and to the side, and this arrangement deflects any tension that would arise if the crowd were positioned frontally, with the viewer of the photograph in the path of its intent focus. The caption reads as a gross overstatement since nothing in the image indicates that these people are about to break into destructive action. In portraying subsequent events, the chapter descends into the kind of inept and tasteless jokes to which Weegee was often prone. The picture of a jumble of female mannequins in a broken shop front is accompanied by the tag line "America's pure white womanhood is saved from a fate worse than . . . Death" (*Naked City*, 194). And the pictures indulge in a cartoonish visual pun when the photograph of a black man under arrest is paired with one on the facing page of a smiling black man in prison stripes at a costume party. None of these pictures or words demonstrate a mature engagement with the racial grotesque.

Weegee prefaces the Harlem chapter with brief comments on discrimination ("that's the one ugly word for it") and on the causes of race riots (*Naked City*, 190). His remarks, however, disregard entirely New York City's history of race politics, activism, and riots, and they misunderstand the meaning of recent events. Though contemporary Harlem is the stated context, the chapter explains riots in terms of "poorly paid white people" who react to social change "by throwing rocks into the windows of the colored occupants" who have recently moved into white, working class districts (*Naked City*, 190). The explanation is irrelevant to this context, obviously, and it ignores completely the roots of the serious civil disorder in Harlem that occurred in March 1935 and again in August 1943. Both events had been a prominent subject of news stories and official inquiries in the period when Weegee worked for the daily press. Of the 1935 riot the Federal Writers' Project *Panorama* volume on New York City reports that the mayor's investigating committee determined that "the outbreak had its fundamental causes in the terrible economic and social conditions prevailing in Harlem" (*Panorama*, 142). The riot photographs in *Naked City* depict the 1943 event, but this fact is apparent only through internal evidence and a reader's prior knowledge since the captions and commentary provide no reportorial context.

Over the same period portrait photographer James Van Der Zee continued to concentrate on the "talented tenth" of Harlem society as he had done through the 1920s. Aaron Siskind of the Photo League attended to many other elements within Harlem's population. In 1936 Siskind organized a Feature Group for the League, and his first undertaking was a comprehensive record of domestic and commercial life in the area, which he had been photographing since 1932. Though some images were exhibited and published over the years, Siskind's *Harlem Document* was issued in book form only much later, in 1981.[32] His work exemplifies a social documentary style and purpose where Weegee's images on the same subject clearly do not. Siskind's interests encompass a full expanse of locales, from litter-strewn air shafts, abandoned buildings, rooming houses, and cramped kitchenette apartments to storefront churches, local shops, restaurants, the Apollo Theater, and the Savoy Ballroom. The activities and social roles depicted also reflect great diversity. These include daily routines within tenement flats, kids at play in the street, sidewalk vendors, followers of Father Divine, an orderly protest at the relief office, a meeting of the Brotherhood of Sleeping Car Porters, nameless entertainers, common laborers, and churchgoers. Siskind's composition in regard to scale and the frame typically makes the immediate surroundings as important to the picture as its human subjects. While Weegee often sought a quality of candor and the momentary in his portrayal of individuals, Siskind seems to have informally arranged a good number of his portrait subjects into typifying postures or gestures.

With the publication of *Naked City* in 1945 Weegee went on a national promotional tour. The book received laudatory reviews in weekly news and culture magazines like *Newsweek,* the *Saturday Review,* and *Time,* which acclaimed the photographer as a "poet with a camera."[33] Even the *New York Times* included some reluctant words of praise in a negative review. *Vogue* was now interested in his services and Weegee redirected his energies toward fashion and society photography. With rights to the title *Naked City* sold to a studio producer for a feature film, in 1947 Weegee left for Hollywood. For a period of five years there Weegee worked as a production consultant and a bit movie player, and he made experimental short films. By the time of his return to New York in 1952 Weegee had begun to use distortion lenses and other mechanical devices to manipulate photographs. His contorted, caricatural portraits of celebrities and politicians began to appear in major magazines. From this time until his death in 1968 Weegee contracted to photograph advertising campaigns, official functions, and public figures but no longer crime or disaster. He also lectured widely, traveled in Europe on assignment, and wrote an autobiography remarkable mainly for its braggadocio.

In 1946 the photographer published *Weegee's People,* an anodyne compilation of recent images. The book presents New York as a city without danger or wrenching dereliction. Photographs of the homeless sleeping in doorways are fully illuminated, out to the margins of the frame. The darkness of night does not intrude upon the scene; there is no incipient blackness to disturb this local color sight. The book's only coverage of a fire, in two photographs, is presented with the reassurance "Everyone was saved."[34] Most of its pictures contain no spectators within the frame. Its street views are typically on the order of the familiar and harmless (lovers on park bench) or the comfortably humorous (the floating, over-sized hand of an inflated clown in the Macy Thanksgiving Day parade). City streets at night are depicted without a hint of disaster or terror. In fact, nighttime is portrayed as essentially joyous through indoor photographs of clubs, cabarets, dance halls, rent parties, jam sessions, and masquerades.

The 1953 book *Naked Hollywood,* prepared in collaboration with Mel Harris, presents Weegee's responses to the American dream factory and mass culture.[35] Its purview, however, does not take in the dark and grotesque side to this segment of society that for Nathanael West was its most prominent feature. *Naked Hollywood,* it must be said, adopts a tritely humorous approach to its subject, with a heavy dependence upon distortion photographs. It exhibits an adolescent mentality in portraits that focus exclusively on the backs of heads or on female cleavage and in corny joke images of fans, animal actors, and movie people, in one case matching a backstage glimpse of the Academy Awards with one backstage in a burlesque house. The book's material is all offered palatably, tongue in cheek.

As crime and disaster had been Weegee's professional specialties over the previous period, from the late 1940s into the 1960s distortions and trick shots became his trademark, which he promoted with carnival show enthusiasm. He boasted of having invented a new Weegeescope lens for the camera and he devised a "fun and art" marketing strategy in answer to the era's "fun and profit" advertising campaigns: "I've managed to turn . . . dull pictures into hilarious caricatures and artistic studies."[36] His 1959 "how-to" book, *Weegee's Creative Camera,* promises to reveal to the public for the first time the compositional innovations and "extraordinarily successful" techniques over which he has held a "kind of monopoly [that] succeeded in giving me a fine income."[37] Supporters like Louis Stettner remained loyal to such self-acclaim: "In spite of his commercial lust, Weegee was too much of an artist not to be genuinely interested in the creative possibilities of manipulation." The principal effect of caricature, however, arises in the rhetoric used to legitimize the Weegee contrivances, not in the images themselves. Stettner explicates the photographer's newfound creativity thusly: "He evolved his own symbolic sexography, satirically creating overflowing cornucopias of sensuality—three, five, nine breasts; buttocks and legs galore."[38]

Weegee, it can be said, conducted the second act of his professional life largely as a self-promotion campaign. Weegee's autobiography, published in 1961, does not possess the grotesque attitude manifest in many photographs of the 1930s and 1940s. The book presents no darker aspects to his personality meant to be illuminated in the course of the life story. Instead, its prose cracks wise in the clipped bravado of a street tough designed along the lines of a Damon Runyon type. The description of the precinct headquarters on East Fifty-first Street, for example, explains: "For a guy to be booked there, he had to make an advance reservation and bring two letters of reference from the wardens of Alcatraz and Sing Sing. There the detectives looked like capitalists and read the *Wall Street Journal*" (*Weegee*, 60). Elsewhere, in pretending insider knowledge of mob activities, Weegee praises its members' sense of professionalism: "Each murder was a masterpiece . . . perfect . . . each displayed the unmistakable stamp of the Old Masters" (*Weegee*, 73; ellipses original to the text).

The autobiography likens the freelance press photographer to an urban knight errant and private eye. In this character role Weegee makes a quest through the city equipped with an automobile, photographic gear, cigars, snacks, and fresh underclothes. Such a self-portrait is, at best, amusing low comedy. In his own final estimation, properly cast for the occasion in the third person, "Weegee is the last of the giants of photography's roisterous adolescence" (*Weegee*, 159). Like the rhetoric of his autobiography, Weegee's camera caricatures and distortions are all immature artifice, ungrounded in a mature imagination's more obscure reaches of shared experience or perspectives. The palpable qualities of the grotesque in his early press work, on the other hand, arise from an image's found connections and extemporaneous perspectives on the terrible and the trivial.

IN THE 1940S AND 1950S several photographers pursued an interest in New York by night, and the most significant among them are Louis Faurer, Ted Croner, and William Klein. While Weegee relied upon a sudden punctuation with light by means of flash, these three photographers tended toward nightscapes defined by city lights in locations like Times Square, Broadway, and 42nd Street. In such locales at night a myriad of lights emanates from marquees and billboards, storefronts, streetlamps, automobile headlights, and the reflections from wet pavement, display glass, and the polished surfaces of buildings and cars. For the purposes of the photographer, however, the problems of available light for the image persist in such circumstances. Faurer, Croner, and

Klein commonly had to push film speeds and developing processes to their limits. And their photographs often bear the consequences in losses to focus, perspective, contrast, and proportionality. These consequences fully separate their work from traditions of straight or objective photography. The results can entail distortion, but usually as a collateral, subordinate dimension to the photograph rather than its sole purpose, as in Weegee's manipulations.

Louis Faurer began to work in New York in 1946, at first commuting from Philadelphia, and midtown Manhattan quickly became a favored subject. For night scenes on the streets and in public buildings, Faurer used the small format Leica camera without flash illumination, experimenting with prolonged shutter times. Through this means Faurer produced a number of photographs that are suggestively intricate in their play of half-light and muted reflections and in their echoes of profiles and indefinite forms. Ted Croner came to New York in 1945 and started a fashion studio business. For personal photography Croner also gravitated toward midtown at night, the luminosity of which he explored through techniques of multiple exposure and camera movements, made with the shutter held open to create novel streaking and blur effects. He was drawn to places like cafeterias and the circus with their unique and sometimes expressionistic lighting arrangements. By comparison to Weegee's early work, photographs by Faurer and Croner possess an uneventful quality, even in the case of Croner's circus performance images. The contrasts of light and night remain dense and extensive in their photographs in order to convey abstract patterns and graceful stylizations, not grotesque revelations taken from everyday city life.

Raised in New York City, William Klein remained in Paris after army service during World War II to study painting, which he did briefly under the guidance of Fernand Léger. Klein developed a geometric abstract style that he explored further through photography, initially by putting his paintings in motion and recording the effects with a camera. Hired to photograph for *Vogue,* Klein returned to New York in 1954, after an absence of six years. Once back, he recalled decades later, he embarked on a personal project to wield the camera "with a vengeance" and with "a peculiar double vision half native, half foreigner" and take "hundreds of photos a day looting the streets." Having in mind a future book of his own design, Klein knowingly produced some of the "least publishable pictures of the day" even while he played upon "the clichés of the era's fashion photography."[39] For these purposes he adopted a mindset of sensationalism: "I saw the book I wanted to do as a tabloid gone berserk, gross, grainy, over-inked, with a brutal layout, bull-horn headlines.

This is what New York deserved and would get. The thing I took as my inspiration was all over the place, three million a day, blowing in the gutter, overflowing ashcans. . . . I was never after news, of course, just the dumbest, most ordinary stuff. But I liked, as further distancing, the garish urgency of their front-page scoops. So I would try to photograph schlock non-events."[40]

Klein named his book *Life is Good and Good for You in New York: Trance Witness Revels*. The subtitle is a calculated spoonerism that plays upon the tabloid-style headline phrase "chance witness reveals." After New York publishers refused the book, it was released in 1956 in Europe.[41] On the streets Klein had worked with a Leica mounted with a wide-angle lens as the standard equipment for his project: "I had no philosophy about it. When I looked in the viewfinder and realized I could see all the contradictions and confusion that was there with the wide-angle—*that* was what was great."[42] On location day and night without flash, Klein was willing to photograph at extreme close range, often in situations where contrast and focus were not greatly under his control. After his experiences in studio art and the fashion world, Klein sought through this photography to escape conventions of the hard edge and careful design. And indeed heavy grain, blurring, ungainly contrasts, gritty textures, accidental effects, and cockeyed compositions proliferate in *Life is Good*. Several images are remarkable for oversaturated black tones that do not shadow or obscure some important feature but rather constitute a presence of darkness in its own right.

In several images it is apparent that Klein has pressed point-blank with his camera into crowds on street corners or at public pastimes, an action paralleled in the book's pictures of children at play with guns. The parallel is a reflexive acknowledgment on the photographer's part of his playful *and* aggressive activity in shooting images of the city. Klein's close shots are not parodic and "elephantine" in the spirit of Nathanael West's stylistic giganticism. Closeups in *Life is Good* often bring a sight uncomfortably near, as when a child thrusts out with a toy revolver aimed directly toward the camera and thus perpetually toward viewers of the photograph. In these respects, more than in specifics of subject matter, Klein exhibits an intense, engaged interest that bluffs violence. Weegee's interests are typically directed toward matters of fact and found ironies left in the wake of violence. Both Weegee and Klein are engaged in a modernist project of doing violence to traditions and accepted norms of representation.

Creatural Realism

Diane Arbus

BY 1959, **WHEN DIANE ARBUS** took a portfolio of personal work to the art director at *Esquire* magazine, the photographer had been exploring New York City on her own through a camera for years. She had stopped regular professional assignments in fashion and advertising in 1956. That year, searching the possibilities of photographic vision, Arbus sought out Lisette Model and began to study with her.[1] After emigrating from Paris to New York in 1938 with her husband, Model had made a strong first impression on American audiences with the photographs published in a January 1941 issue of *PM Weekly* as the cover story "Why France Fell."[2] The story's seven photographs—taken by Model in Paris and Nice during the mid-1930s—were presented by editor Ralph Steiner with picture titles like "Greed," "Self-Satisfaction," "Weariness," and "Cynicism" to betoken the deadly political sins of Europe. Through the 1940s and 1950s Model's photographs were exhibited at places like the Museum of Modern Art and the Photo League, and they were published in *Look, U. S. Camera,* and frequently in *Harper's Bazaar.* In this period the editors at *Harper's Bazaar* offered subjects outside women's style in order to distinguish their magazine from other fashion publications. With the encouragement of art director Alexey Brodovitch, Model's assignments for *Harper's Bazaar* included Coney Island, jazz musicians, vaudeville performers, the Bowery bar Sammy's (also a favorite subject for Weegee), the blind, settlement houses, and the circus. Brodovitch valued one quality in Model's work above all else: "Her particular genius was in photographing the bizarre quality of human beings and finding beauty in the grotesque."[3] In making this statement Brodovitch has construed the grotesque narrowly as ugliness and abnormality in simple opposition to beauty and visual appeal. Faced with the editorial uses to which her published magazine work was often put, Model rejected such simplified notions of her style and subject matter.

What began in the late 1950s as a tutorial relationship between Model and Arbus developed into a mentorship and became a close personal and professional bond until Arbus's death in July 1971 by suicide. With Model's early support Arbus began to create the body of work by which she is widely known today. Asked in an interview about the value of that work, Model has said: "Most people look away when they see this subject matter, whereas Diane did not look away, and that takes courage and independence. And I think it is the first time, as far as I know, in the history of photography that somebody would photograph this kind of people who are discriminated. And we're afraid to look at them because deep down in ourselves we feel that we are still crippled somewhere, even if it isn't outside. And she photographed them humanly, seriously, and functioning in their lives. And that was an extraordinary kind of achievement."[4]

In doing so Arbus's work exemplifies the attitude of "objective seriousness" achieved in nineteenth-century literary realism and derived, ultimately, from the "creatural realism" of the closing Middle Ages, cultural features whose evolution Erich Auerbach affiliates with the grotesque. By Auerbach's account, *creatural* realism emerges as a definable style among both visual and literary arts in the 1300s and, in distinction from the *figurative*, it emphasizes the transitory and problematic aspects of human existence. It is "realism of a coarser grain" in which "the grotesque and farcical element became increasingly current" as did a gruesome vividness in the depiction of physical suffering (*Mimesis*, 159). Within late medieval prose and poetry creatural realism functions largely as a descriptive mode and it "does not shun but actually savors crass effects" through which "everything is calculated to bring out in visual clarity" human vulnerability (*Mimesis*, 247). For Auerbach the larger cultural determinant underlying creatural realism is the period's "Christian anthropology." Irrespective of all distinctions based on social rank, from such a perspective "there is nothing but the flesh, which age and illness will ravage until death and putrefaction destroy it. It is, if you like, a radical theory of the equality of all men, not in an active and political sense but as a direct devaluation of life which affects every man individually" (*Mimesis*, 249–50).

As a stylistic innovation, creatural realism marks a breakthrough that aligns art closely with observable experience: "Average everyday life, with its sensual pleasures, its sorrows, its decline with age and illness, its end, has seldom been so impressively represented as during this epoch" (*Mimesis*, 250). And it set the course of cultural developments that lead to the achievement of "objective seriousness" in the literary realism of Gustave Flaubert, which "seeks to penetrate to the depths of the passions and entanglements of a human life, but without itself becoming moved, or at least without betraying that it is moved" (*Mimesis,* 490). The modern realism inaugurated by Flaubert more broadly entails "the serious treatment of everyday reality, the rise of more extensive and socially inferior human groups to the position of subject matter for problematic-existential representation . . . [and] the embedding of random persons and events in the general course of contemporary history" (*Mimesis,* 491). The contemporary to perceive fully the creatural aspects of such realism in Flaubert's fiction was Baudelaire. The poet celebrated the technique of representation in *Madame Bovary* for its greatly exaggerated disproportions in circumstances and expression, disproportions that "imprison the warmest, the most burning feelings within the most trivial adventure" and that make "the most solemn, the most fateful words . . . fall from the lips of the most vacuous" characters (*Selected Writings*, 249).

Arbus's own development of a creatural style in her personal photography began early on, and it is evident in her first published article "The Vertical Journey," which appeared in the July 1960 issue of *Esquire.* This pictorial essay consists of six portrait images accompanied by brief informational captions edited from material written by Arbus. Subtitled "Six Movements of a Moment within the Heart of the City," the article makes leaps across the class divides of the New York City social landscape without any intermediate stops. By category, there are three images of "the other half," four if we count the unidentified corpse in the city morgue at Bellevue Hospital, and two of the upper crust. The lower stratum is presented in the persons of Hezekiah Trambles, a black sideshow performer who appears as "The Jungle Creep"; Andrew Ratoucheff, the midget actor known for his nightclub imitations of Marilyn Monroe and Maurice Chevalier; and the Bowery inhabitant Walter L. Gregory, called by locals "The Mad Man from Massachusetts." Respectability is represented by Mrs. Dagmar Patino at a charity ball and Flora Knapp Dickinson, a regent with the Daughters of the American Revolution.[5] Comparatively speaking, the first social group receives more attentive and respectful camera treatment as portrait subjects than do high-society people, who are rendered in much the same grainy, diffuse, and somewhat blurred manner as in the concluding image of the corpse. To be sure, Flora Knapp Dickinson stands much larger in scale in her portrait than Andrew Ratoucheff does in his, and her full person is given in an unobstructed view while he is shown standing behind the corner of a bed. Where the features of her face are somewhat dispersed in the strong daylight admitted through a window, however, his face is more strongly modeled by the medium's control over lights and darks. In fact, all three portraits from the city's substratum are distinctive in texture for their more intense gradients of black and white, which produce a more defined image and a greater sense of the person's visual presence.

The corpse photograph that closes "The Vertical Journey" is organized around one prominent feature in center foreground, the body's splayed bare feet. The dead individual's one potentially identifying detail is the morgue toe tag, the blank side of which faces the viewer. The identification tag would likely be unreadable anyway given the distance and dim light of the composition. And in the end the matter seems irrelevant since the picture caption already designates a "Person Unknown." The photograph stands mutely as a memento mori, devoid of the consolations of any philosophy and without even the alternative of deadpan humor. Matter-of-factly the image indicates that if human existence is to be considered a journey, for all individuals it invariably reaches the same destination. Such a conclusion is consistent with the kind of creatural anthropology Auerbach describes, but in this case obviously without any of the redemptive promises of religion. The attitude toward death here is also distinct from Roland Barthes' sense of the *punctum* within a photograph as a solicitation for mourning. For Barthes, mourning is a process conducted at a private and even narcissistic remove from fellow humanity. In the work of Arbus, the poignancy of a photograph is instead the result of a sense of humane, nearly intimate recognition among the persons, and the camera, involved.

In writing to editors Robert Benson and Harold Hayes at *Esquire* in late 1960, soon after her first publication in the magazine, Arbus explained her idea for a new picture story, on eccentrics: "Edith Sitwell says in what is the prettiest definition: ANY DUMB BUT PREGNANT COMMENT ON LIFE, ANY CRITICISM OF THE WORLD'S ARRANGEMENT, IF EXPRESSED BY ONLY ONE GESTURE, AND THAT OF SUFFICIENT CONTORTION, BECOMES ECCENTRICITY. Or, if that word has too double an edge, we could use some others: the anomalies, the quixotic, the dedicated, who believe in the impossible, who make their mark on themselves" (*Magazine Work*, 156). The quotation capitalized by Arbus is exact and it is taken from Sitwell's *English Eccentrics,* essays on the subject first published as a book in 1933 and reissued in 1957 in an American edition with newly appended material.

With the precedent set by Robert Burton's writings in mind, Sitwell offers examples of human eccentricity as "medicines . . . advised for Melancholy, in the Anatomy of this disease." The mental stage setting for Sitwell's reflections on the subject is Old London's vast waste ground located in the Battlebridge district, a humble source of "little hopeful articulations rising from the dust" of society: "We may seek in our dust-heap for some rigid, and even splendid, attitude of Death, some exaggeration of the attitudes common to Life. This attitude, rigidity, protest, or explanation, has been called eccentricity."[6] *English Eccentrics* takes much greater interest in individuals who endure in history through legend and anecdote recorded over time in print—conjurors, unusual medical cases, hermits, and alchemists—than to intellectuals like Thomas Carlyle and Margaret Fuller, whose writings and personalities are also profiled. Sitwell's energies are encyclopedic in her search through all manner of books, official records, and ephemera in search of redemptive idiosyncrasies.

Sitwell departs significantly from the Victorian tradition of rationalist accommodation for eccentrics as a natural aristocracy. John Stuart Mill legitimized their social value in *On Liberty* (1859) through the following logic: "Precisely because the tyranny of opinion is such as to make eccentricity a reproach, it is desirable, in order to break through that tyranny, that people should be eccentric. Eccentricity has always abounded when and where strength of character has abounded; and the amount of eccentricity in a society has generally been proportional to the amount of genius, mental vigor, and moral courage it contained."[7] In truth, Mill has in mind only a few exceptional individuals of conspicuous social worth. By contrast Sitwell, like Sir Thomas Browne and Richard Burton before her, sifts through the margins of book culture to retrieve a great number of oddities in human experience.

Arbus goes further by seeking out *in person* society's nonessential human beings, its outcasts, its insulted and injured, those whose worth and power are measured in existential terms, not in civic ones. For Arbus their importance derives primarily from self-made qualities, as indicated by the terms she connects with eccentricity: "the anomalies, the quixotic, the dedicated, who believe in the impossible, who make their mark on themselves." But Arbus does not attribute to such people any corrective or therapeutic powers for the ultimate benefit of society. And, to return for a moment to a previous discussion, where in Flannery O'Connor's world of belief the powers of mystery and the grotesque ultimately bespeak a divine presence, in the work of Arbus the grotesque remains a surface sign, an aspect of our creatural being and a token of the shared human lot.

Interests in eccentricity within American culture have long tended toward the outright grotesque. The immediate predecessors to Arbus on such subjects in the context of New York City are Weegee, Lisette Model, and the writer Joseph Mitchell. In later years, before displaying any of her own work in public talks or her classes Arbus would sometimes show pictures by Weegee first, with no commentary other than a long pause and an exclamation of her admiration.[8] Arbus and Weegee share the inclinations of Jacob Riis and Lewis Hine toward subject matter of the underclass, the infirm, the impaired and outcast. But Arbus and Weegee photograph without any of the intentions of social reform apparent in the work of the two earlier men.

Later in her career Arbus was hired by the Photography Department at the Museum of Modern Art to research old photograph files at the New York *Daily News* and other sources for material to be included in the Museum exhibition *From the Picture Press,* which eventually opened in 1973.[9] In October 1970 she reviewed Weegee's entire picture file, amounting to some 8000 prints, and wrote in a letter with exhilaration over the uniqueness of his best work in comparison to the standards of press photography: "Such wild dynamics make everybody look like an academician. People pushing, shoving, screaming, bits of extraneous events thrust into the main one" (*Revelations,* 212). Arbus remained interested in the tabloids exactly for their appeal to sensation in the course of everyday life. In this Arbus departed from Pop Art and its cool, indiscriminate register of appearances transmitted through the mass media, which could include anything from cleanser products to human disasters.

With support from *Esquire* Arbus in the closing months of 1959 started to take many vertical journeys up and down the social strata of New York City. Her curiosity over the lower social reaches led Arbus to make the professional acquaintance of Joseph Mitchell, whom she first contacted in 1960. Mitchell's career as a journalist in New York City had begun in 1929, and for a few years he worked on the metropolitan desks of newspapers like the *Herald Tribune* and the *World-Telegram.* Mitchell was thus exposed to many of the same formative influences as were Weegee and Sam Fuller at about the same period. The young Mitchell possessed no abiding interest in straight press reporting. Instead, he developed a talent for writing stories on people existing along the fringes of city life, such as cheesecake models, Greenwich Village types, and urban gypsies. In 1938 Mitchell joined the staff of *The New Yorker,* which gave him great latitude in matters of subject, space in print, and deadline. Over the time of his active career with the magazine, which lasted until 1964, Mitchell perfected a literary approach to reportage. In his profiles of otherwise obscure inhabitants of the city Mitchell knits together an intricate skein of facts, background, and quotations. Entailing immersion in minute particulars and an ear attuned to peculiarities in speech, Mitchell's process is truly one of thick description rather than narration. Through a primarily denotative, cumulative style his prose achieves evocative metaphoric effect while seeming to leave the work of connotation largely up to the reader's imagination. In many respects Mitchell's reportorial manner is the direct forerunner of what came to be known as New Journalism in the 1960s.

In attitude, Mitchell's profiles indicate that the marginal and the non-descript, seen from a perspective within their world and heard fully, disclose extraordinary expanses within individual existence no matter how ostracized or socially inconsequential the person may be outwardly. Arbus first contacted Mitchell out of an interest in photographing people he had written of. Among them was "Lady Olga," the subject of a *New Yorker* article reprinted in Mitchell's collection *McSorley's Wonderful Saloon* (1943).[10] Jane Barnell, a bearded attraction, first performed in carnivals at age four, and she became known over her career as Princess Olga, Madame Olga, and Lady Olga. Though she had appeared in the Tod Browning feature *Freaks* (1932), Lady Olga considered the movie to be an insult to her profession. For six seasons she traveled with the Ringling circus in their sideshow "The Congress of Strange People," which until the 1930s had been known as "The Congress of Freaks." While other sideshow attractions prefer to be called artistes or performers, Mitchell explains, Lady Olga has adopted a hardboiled attitude and she does not refuse the term *freak.* Indeed, she defiantly accepts the designation as long as it applies equally to all show people, no matter how celebrated. Mitchell reports that for her "a freak is just as good as any actor, from the Barrymores on down. 'If the truth was known, we're all freaks together,' she says" (*Saloon,* 103). Nearly seventy years old at the time of Mitchell's interview, she currently worked in the sideshow presented in the basement of Hubert's Museum on West Forty-second Street, a place that Lisette Model and Arbus would visit and photograph.[11] By Mitchell's account, Lady Olga at present looks "like an Old Testament prophet;" on the exhibition platform she discourages familiarity or pity, and "like most freaks she has cultivated a blank, unseeing stare" (*Saloon,* 92, 93). In fact, where the performers are concerned, according to Mitchell: "utter apathy . . . is the occupational disease of freaks" (*Saloon,* 94).

The one matter about which Lady Olga remains animated is that of social status *within* the sideshow world. Its natural aristocrats are *born freaks*, an estate comprised of persons with congenital abnormalities and deformities, such as Siamese twins, pinheads, dwarfs, midgets, giants, and bearded ladies. Next in order are *made freaks*, to which tattooed people, sword swallowers, snake charmers, glass eaters, and the like belong. Lastly are *two-timers*, those former athletes, criminals, and minor celebrities who put themselves on display. Where John Stuart Mill's sense of the value in eccentricity relies on its acquired or "made" qualities, the value system here prizes innate or "born" conditions. For his own part, Joseph Mitchell explains a long-held interest in eccentric and grotesque personalities this way: "I wanted not the unusual but the usual in the unusual. Or the extraordinary in the ordinary. . . . The accepted is one thing and the freak is another. The freak living in the ordinary human being is what we're after."[12] Mitchell seeks, as does Arbus after him, a normative and reversible attitude of the grotesque. That is to say, within the world of a freak, incongruity itself establishes norms and a sense of the ordinary. From such perspective the incongruities of the commonplace are more easily detectable. This perspective exemplifies the creatural realism at the heart of the modern grotesque.

Arbus's second published article, "The Full Circle," with photographs and a lengthy text written by her, appeared in the November 1961 issue of *Harper's Bazaar*, and it was reprinted with new material in February 1962 in *Infinity*, the official journal of the American Society of Magazine Photographers. Her article takes as its subject "people who appear like metaphors somewhere further out than we do, beckoned, not driven, invented by belief, author and hero of a real dream by which our own courage and cunning are tested and tried; so that we may wonder all over again what is veritable and inevitable and possible and what it is to become whoever we may be" (*Magazine Work*, 14). Among the five people it profiles, with a sixth for its republication, are Max Maxwell Landar, an eighty-year-old "Uncle Sam" who has fully cultivated the appearance of this American icon, and Polly Bushong, a well-bred woman who appears at social functions in the costume of the clumsy, uneducated Miss Cora Pratt for the purpose of causing a disruptive scene. Beyond the comical stand more dedicated and mysterious examples, such as that of William Mack, "known as The Sage of the Wilderness, The (Abominable) Snowman, Santa Claus, El Dorado, Rasputin, Daniel Boone, Garibaldi," an ex-seaman who daily makes a ritual circuit through Lower Manhattan; and Prince Robert de Rohan Courtenay, "His Serene Highness, surnamed

The Magnificent, the rightful Hereditary claimant to the Throne of the Byzantine Eastern Roman Empire," who has decorated every inch of his tiny room in a midtown boarding hotel in faux regal style (*Magazine Work*, 16–17). As these quotations make evident, it is impossible to tell where the prolific self-fashioning by these eccentrics ends and where an overlay of fabulist inventions by Arbus starts.

The fifth author of his own metaphor for life is Jack Dracula, or The Marked Man, the proud bearer of over 300 tattoos who "can outstare any stranger and causes a sensation on the subway, looking large, proud, aloof, predominantly bluegreen, like a privileged exile" (*Magazine Work*, 16). The Arbus portrait photograph presents an individual self-composed in demeanor. His *visage*, in the original senses of the "sight" of him and the viewer's perception of him, entails a look of prepossession, on the part of both parties.

A sixth self-authored individual, in a section refused by editors at *Harper's Bazaar* but added for the *Infinity* article, is Miss Stormé de Larverie, the one real woman to appear in the drag revue "25 Men and a Girl," but in the person of a man. Forty years old and married but now separated from her husband, Stormé dresses daily as a male and she "has conscientiously experimented to perfect the cut, fit, shape and style of her appearance as a man, without ever tampering with her nature as a woman, or trying to be what she is not."[13] In this instance persuasive imposture (as distinct from complete transformation) is the genuine truth about an individual, a privileged situation reached in Nathanael West's *The Day of the Locust* in the scene when a young man is "really a woman" as he performs a lullaby. For Arbus and West alike, even when imposture breaks down and proves in the end to be fraudulent there is always human significance in a person's attempts to impersonate the identity she or he most deeply desires.

Within its intentionally limited social purview, Arbus's choice of milieu is schematic ("The Vertical Journey") or concentrated ("The Full Circle"). For the lower and eccentric segments Arbus accepts the situation and outlook by which individuals gauge their world. Her photographs and prose take at face value some of the ironies inherent to the life circumstances of an eccentric, and they are receptive to the ordinariness of the grotesque. More often than not, Arbus adopts a visually underdetermined approach in comparison to the graphic overdetermination a viewer encounters in the grotesques of Goya, Daumier, Grosz, and Weegee. In the Jack Dracula photograph the body markings make the same contrast on his flesh as his person does in relation to the background in the portrait as a whole. The later *Tattooed man at a carnival, Md. 1970* allows the man's physique, self-assured posture, and forthright facial expression to dominate the portrait to the point that the markings to his chest, arms, and face seem secondary.

Over the course of the 1960s Diane Arbus was certainly mindful of political issues like race relations, civil rights, and domestic conflict over the Vietnam War, but the issues never amounted to a matter of social conscience in her photography. The nature and extent of her political awareness is made evident in letters and some unpublished material. Her article on nudist camps, a project that received initial support from *Esquire* but not the magazine's acceptance for publication, assumes for a while the blithe spirit of campers: "It is a good life. You turn one color all over in the sun and the water feels fine. Everyone leaves their cares behind. It's a little like heaven. . . . There is always the possibility that negroes will try to get in, but for the most part they seem satisfied with their own nudist camps, and, as some joker is sure to point out, 'How can they get a tan, anyway?'" Further recognition of humanity's lapsed condition comes: "Sometimes you begin to wonder. There is an empty pop bottle or rusty bobby pin underfoot, the lake bottom oozes mud in a particularly nasty way, the negroes are not there, most people don't look so good, . . . the outhouse smells, the woods look mangy" (*Magazine Work*, 69). Segregation is treated here as just one among many of life's disparities.

In 1962 Arbus changed her regular equipment from the 35 mm Nikon to the twin-lens Rolleiflex, a reflex camera that produces the significantly larger 2¼-inch-square negative, which has a much greater capacity for fine detail and clarity throughout the picture space. Once she had made the transition Arbus began to look upon her earlier work in 35 mm in these terms: "You were dealing mostly in dark and light, not so much in flesh and blood" (*Arbus*, 9). The distinction often also holds true for photographs Arbus did *within* each camera format. Subjects that possess little inherent creatural significance for her are rendered in diffuse, porous contrasts, like the society people in "The Vertical Journey," and the circus and "The Couple" assignments for *Harper's Bazaar*. The "flesh and blood" portraits often display a degree of animal self-containment on the individual's part as with, to take just two examples, Jack Dracula and the post-operative transsexual now fully a middle-class matron in appearance whom Arbus photographed for *Esquire* in 1967 (see *Magazine Work*, 89). The second photograph demonstrates that Arbus's sense of fleshly reality is not dependent upon an exposure of the body. The subject may be buttoned-up and guarded, as is Norman Mailer in his three-piece suit for a portrait commissioned for the review of his book *The Presidential Papers* (1963) in *The New York Times* (see *Magazine Work*, 31). Mailer's posture in a high-backed chair—body splayed sideways and one leg draped over an arm rest, captured by the camera in a moderately down-angled composition—immediately organizes attention to two fixed zones, the face and the crotch. Though Mailer has obviously cooperated in assuming such a physical disposition, he would later say of Arbus: "Giving a camera to Diane is like putting a live grenade in the hands of a child."[14]

When in 1969 Walker Evans praised the photography of Diane Arbus, he did so in varied terms. To begin with, Evans makes an obvious analogy on the basis of her first name: "This artist is daring, extremely gifted, and a born huntress." Evans next offers a more challenging comparison: "There may be something naïve about her work if there is anything naïve about the devil." Finally and on a significantly different note Evans characterizes her camera vision as "an eye cultivated just for this—to show you fear in a handful of dust."[15] It is in this context of common, unheroic mortality, in the direct paraphrase by Evans of a line from "The Burial of the Dead" section to T. S. Eliot's *The Waste Land* (1922), that the creatural dimension to her work is recognized.

Arbus's practices as a portraitist are often called manipulative, predatory, and destructive—both in wary appreciation, as by Mailer and Evans, and in full animadversion, as by Susan Sontag (whose critique will be engaged later in this chapter). To be sure, these qualities came to be associated with a camera style prominent after the death of Arbus, a style that often is presumed to be a result of the influence of her photography but that in truth derives much more from William Klein and Richard Avedon. Avedon's work, for example, is championed by Adam Gopnick as an "imposing collection of uglifying images" that manages to turn each camera subject into another "member of a disturbed family of the spirit."[16] Indeed, Avedon portraits can be a merciless exposé of how people appear in the flesh, particularly public figures once their cachet has worn thin. Avedon explains the psychological dynamics of his work as an exchange that "involves manipulations, submissions. Assumptions are reached and acted upon that could seldom be made with impunity in ordinary life." And he elaborates: "A portrait photographer depends upon another person to complete his picture. The subject imagined, which in a sense is me, must be discovered in someone else willing to take part in a fiction he cannot possible know about. My concerns are not his. We have separate ambitions for the image. His need to plead his case probably goes as deep as my need to plead mine, but the control is with me."[17]

In the 1960s Avedon admired Arbus for moving unstaged portraiture "away from the sneaks, the grabbers" in professional photography, whose candid comic shots of humanity would appear in the back pages of *Life* and

Look magazines.[18] It is an opinion shared by Joel Meyerowitz, a street photographer of significance who also knew Arbus personally in those years. Having himself experienced all the difficulties of working in informal circumstances, Meyerowitz prizes the quality of reciprocal interest manifest in the Arbus portraits: "If you look at her pictures, the one thing you don't see is resistance. You don't see people chin up, toughing it out. . . . People are giving themselves over to her. When you look at those pictures, their subjects are just flowing out toward her."[19] While the viewer may well also find reserve or a degree of wariness among Arbus's portrait subjects, Meyerowitz makes this tribute as a fellow professional often left with images that record mainly, and merely, visible resistance to the camera.

To convey the attribute of individuals functioning in their lives no matter how marginal their social station, Arbus conducted the portrait sessions in locales where those lives familiarly take place or where those individuals may be familiarly found. Settings typical of her work are the living room, the ball room, dressing rooms, the bedroom whether it be in a mansion or a boarding hotel, show grounds, the sidewalk, and the city park. The specifics of a given locale may not be finally central to the portrait image itself but the choice of such locales has involved a degree of mutual agreement over an appropriate balance of the public and the private. This practice is quite different from Avedon's signature habit from the 1950s through the 1990s of using an all-purpose, neutral backdrop, whether in the studio or on location, whether indoors or outside. The consistent use of this device to contextualize the portrait individual within the photographer's style is forthrightly expressive of the control Avedon claims as his artistic right.

No matter how incongruous or awry an appearance may be at first glance, Arbus's portrait treatment often conveys the integrity and self-possession of an individual. In this her work differs from the carnivalesque and utopian sense of the grotesque that Mikhail Bakhtin advances. By Bakhtin's account the medieval tradition of the grotesque "ignores the closed, smooth, and impenetrable surface of the body and retains only its excrescences (sprouts, buds) and orifices, only that which leads beyond the body's limited space" (*Rabelais,* 317–18). In the medieval conception no body is an island, living flesh intermingles to create a "bodily cosmos, ever-growing and self-renewing" and mortality is always conquered through forms of "pregnant death" (*Rabelais,* 340, 352). Utopian in vision, the carnivalesque grotesque is far from the earthbound, mortifying attitudes of creatural realism.

To Bakhtin, of all human features the eyes are the least susceptible to a grotesque rendering: "The eyes have no part in these comic images; they express an individual, so to speak, self-sufficient human life, which is not essential to the grotesque" (*Rabelais*, 316). And it is in this principal regard that Arbus's work functions independently of carnivalesque traditions. Speaking of photography as an act of attention, Arbus has said: "I think when you look anything squarely in the eye it is different from how you thought it was."[20] In many Arbus portraits the eyes are captured in strong frontal compositions. With seated subjects the composition is positioned at the camera's virtual eye-level, with standing ones the camera view is directed slightly up toward the face and eyes. From these two vantages the eyes forcefully delineate the individual as in, to take only four memorable instances, *Puerto Rican woman with a beauty mark, N.Y.C. 1965*, *A young man in curlers at home on West 20th Street, N.Y.C. 1966*, *Identical twins, Roselle, N.J. 1967*, and *Tattooed man*.

In these cases, "the beholder's share" may be said to extend from the portrait subject herself or himself to the viewer. It will be remembered that Gombrich bases this concept on a hypothesis of the viewer's behavioral responsiveness, even where static media like painting and photography are concerned: "We interpret and code the perception of our fellow creatures not so much in visual but in muscular terms."[21] With many of Arbus's photographs, to invert this formulation, evidence of visual attention on the part of the portrait subject directed toward the photographer establishes an impression of the phenomenal presence of the on-camera human being. And an impression of reciprocity that extended from the portrait subject to Arbus in the first place now extends to each viewer in her stead. In this respect Arbus's portrait work is aligned with a tradition to which Lewis Hine, August Sander, and Walker Evans belong, even while her style of treatment is often less formal. Damning critics of Arbus judge her work to be invasive, confrontational, and finally unethical. While often it can be clearly seen that Weegee, William Klein, and Garry Winogrand have thrust the camera lens into a public scene to single out an individual or two, in Arbus portraits most often it is apparent that an interpersonal encounter has begun for a significant, even if relatively brief, duration before the photograph is taken.

Within Arbus's portrait work there is a recurrent interest in squarely frontal composition. For several images already cited the encounter has been literally frontal in geometric and optical terms in the physical disposition of the camera operator directly and proximally face-to-face with another person. With 2¼-inch format equipment, the viewing glass is held at chest or waist level and the photographer is free to face the subject unobstructed in the course of a session. Frontal composition does not become exclusive or definitive in her photography, but it reflects the broad interest of Arbus in the social appearances constructed or maintained through facial appearance, clothing, make-up, masks, costumes, identifying marks, personal touches, and the like. Interviewed in 1969, Arbus spoke of her childhood and adolescence in terms of the family's pretensions to greater wealth and privilege than her father could actually afford: "It was a front. My father was a frontal person. A front had to be maintained."[22] Her photographic attitude toward such matters accords in some telling respects with ideas developed in *The Presentation of Self in Everyday Life* (1959) by the social psychologist Erving Goffman. Arbus had in her library two later Goffman books, *Asylums* (1961) and *Stigma* (1963), subjects of obviously great interest to her.[23] In the earliest book, Goffman maintains that in normative interactions an individual's identity depends upon a personal "front" and the use of "expressive equipment" involving setting, appearance, and manner. His principal research interest lies in "the dramaturgic elements of the human situation" and their consistency across boundaries of public and private spheres, work and domestic life.[24] Arbus and Goffman alike accept as inevitable the artifices and social fronts involved in human interactions, and in communicating this situation neither the photographer nor the sociologist intends an exposé.

In a psychological sense Arbus's portrait work results from a mutually frontal encounter, she with a camera and her show of interest, the portrait subject with his or her self-fashioned traits and a degree of acceptance of the photographer's presence. Of her own demeanor in relation to subject matter for the camera Arbus has remarked "I don't like to arrange things. If I stand in front of something, instead of arranging it, I arrange myself" (*Arbus*, 12). On the part of portrait subjects the presentation of self can vary from the assertively ornamented Jack Dracula to the unassuming *Man at a parade on Fifth Avenue, N.Y.C. 1969* with his hat placed over heart in a modest show of respect. The photographer has spoken of her awareness of the contrivances on her part in interpersonal relations during a portrait session:

Actually they [portrait subjects] tend to like me. I'm extremely likable with them. I think I'm kind of two-faced. I'm very ingratiating. It really kind of annoys me. I'm just sort of a little too nice. Everything is Oooo. I hear myself saying "How terrific," and there's this woman making a face. I really *mean* it's terrific. I don't mean I wish I looked like that. I don't mean I wished my children looked like that. I don't mean in my private life I want to kiss you. But I mean that's amazingly, undeniably something. There are always two things that happen. One is recognition

and the other is that it's totally peculiar. But there's some sense in which
I always identify with them. (*Arbus*, 1)

Heard as an example of speech behavior these remarks, edited from her
words either in a class or an interview, remind one of the ongoing efforts
at balance among experience, thought, and language that occupied Sherwood Anderson's attention. On the part of the photographer, the experience of recognition is attended with awareness of the peculiarities of the
situation and of the personalities involved. Just underneath the habit
in Arbus's conversation to use *terrific* as an intensifier meant to convey
approval there is also evident the word's original senses of something
frightful and awesome.

Most critics are blind to the creatural dimensions in Arbus's work,
preoccupied as they are with other issues. Shelley Rice is concerned to
separate the work of Arbus from that of Model. While, Rice contends,
Model created "universalized renditions of human types that embody the
'heroism' of modern life," Arbus produced "obsessively one-dimensional"
portraits that communicate only "an assertion of power over her sitters."[25]
Given her own professional experience from an earlier decade, however,
Model particularly valued Arbus's ability to make photographs independent of the ready-made ideological and caste perspectives dominant in
mainstream media. Another critical approach interprets Arbus's mature
photography as a deconstruction of her earlier professional experience in
the fashion and advertising world.[26] While aspects of cultural critique and
a reaction against high fashion can be attributed to her work, the power
of the photography through which Arbus helped define the sensibility
of 1960s America functions well beyond such considerations. In subject
matter and visual style Arbus shaped an inclusive yet still incisive sense
of the grotesque to gain perspective on the individual's social existence
in our time.

Key concepts I apply here toward an understanding and appreciation
of Arbus's photography as a mode of creatural realism—the grotesque,
flaw, freak, the uncanny—have been used consistently by art reviewers
and academic critics since the 1970s to denigrate her work. Fifteen months
after the photographer's death the posthumous retrospective *Diane Arbus*
opened at the Museum of Modern Art in New York, on November 7, 1972.
From New York City the exhibition traveled for a period of seven years
through the United States and abroad. *Diane Arbus* became a landmark
in the art museum exhibition of photography. During her lifetime, on the
other hand, Diane Arbus remained reluctant and ambivalent about the
presentation of her work as art.

The general tenor in both the daily press and art journals of the reception for the *Diane Arbus* exhibition and catalog is made obvious by a brief sample of title phrases from published articles: "Charade of Losers," "Photography's Greatest Primitive," "Flaw Show," "Visions of a Crazy World," "Politics of Despair," "The Hostile Camera."[27] Ian Jeffrey in the review "Diane Arbus and the American Grotesque" accepts the work only as a symptom of "the new decadence, of a violent subculture of stylish derelicts, . . . of that perverse underworld which obsessed writers during the 1960s" like William Burroughs.[28] To value Arbus as an artist of the extreme one has to discount the phenomenal evidence that very often the subjects of her portraits are people that she first encountered, and many times later photographed, in open public life. Admittedly, for someone working primarily in New York City the expanse of public life is broad indeed.

Heather McPherson approves of Arbus's "human comedy" of grotesques, but she narrowly reduces their humanity down to a matter of "marginals" immobilized by the camera "like wild animals hypnotized by the unexpected glare of headlights."[29] Significantly on this point Diana Hulick, a scholar given wide access to the Arbus archive, has examined closely the contact sheets that contain images Arbus selected for enlargement and printing. Hulick finds that the photographer passed over images in particular sessions where the appearance of the grotesque was most overt.[30] Gauged by the exhibition catalog to *Human Concern/Personal Torment: The Grotesque in American Art* at the Whitney Museum in 1969 Arbus's contributions were among the least exaggerated in subject matter and visual style of the many paintings, drawings, photographs, installations, and sculptures on display.[31] For Arbus the grotesque is more a matter of variability within human experience and appearances than one of extremes.

The influential photography critic Max Kozloff applies a concept of the uncanny in his assessment of Arbus, but its presence in her work amounts to no more than "cruel over-determinisms" and "an ongoing betrayal."[32] In a general critique of camera portraiture as antithetical to the narrative potentials of photography, Kozloff considers the pose to be a *"corrupted* form of momentum" that falsely promises the viewer "all that is needed to know to form a judgment about a human moment."[33] As for Arbus portraits, Kozloff judges the photographer to have made false promises to her subjects: "in order to get her kind of distressing pictures she breaks their trust, the trust they had in her."[34] For photographer Lou Stettner, an active member of the Photo League in the 1940s, the Arbus work promotes a logic that "only freaks were normal" and it confuses "despair, melancholy and nausea with profundity."[35]

The new, more extensive retrospective *Diane Arbus: Revelations* opened in October 2003 at the San Francisco Museum of Modern Art. Some of the same rhetoric of condemnation from three decades earlier persists in the review by Jed Perl: "Arbus is one of those devious bohemians who celebrate other people's eccentricities and are all the while aggrandizing their own narcissistically pessimistic view of the world." His bill of particulars charges further that Arbus is "intent on telling us how awful everything is [while she remains] a master of the highfalutin creep-out" and that her work "uses the fixity of the image to deny people their freedom—and in so doing she also denies them their self-esteem."[36]

Susan Sontag's critique of Arbus appeared under the title "Freak Show" when originally published in 1973. But before turning to this, the most articulate and consequential of damning commentaries, the freak as a cultural icon in the 1960s and since should be considered. When Arbus read *Stigma: Notes on the Management of Spoiled Identity* by Erving Goffman, she made a personal list of categories of people stigmatized within mainstream society. In his book Goffman examines the stigmatized individual by stipulating first that stigma is more a situational category than an inherent one: "By definition, of course, we believe the person with a stigma is not quite human. . . . We construct a stigma-theory, an ideology to explain his inferiority and account for the danger he represents, sometimes rationalizing an animosity." The book's focus falls upon the psychological situation of individuals disqualified in this way from full social acceptance. Through a generalization extrapolated from social phenomena attached to the racial grotesque, Goffman stresses his claim that in many social interactions a process of *minstrelization* takes effect, whereby "the stigmatized person ingratiatingly acts out before normals the full dance of bad qualities imputed to his kind, thereby consolidating a life situation into a clownish role."[37] Minstrelization is conveyed by Nathanael West in *The Day of the Locust* at the moment when the female impersonator caters to his heterosexual audience with the stage bit of tripping in his evening gown.

In the portrait work of Diane Arbus there is no certain dividing line nor any convenient polarity between the incongruous and the everyday. While the titles to photographs may well name particular stigmas, the persons portrayed do not oblige audience expectations of a minstrelization. *Russian midget friends in a living room on 100th Street, N.Y.C. 1963* is in its pictorial contents so predominantly mundane (the housedresses and aprons worn by the women, the personal effects such as snapshot mementos and house plants) that its extraordinary elements (the midgets, the reduced scale of the armchair prominent in the foreground) almost seem secondary. Society's stigma upon the individual is not privileged in the portrait. In remarks expressive of her own values Arbus once spoke of her admiration for one particular amateur photograph: "A whore I once knew showed me a photo album of Instamatic color pictures she'd taken of guys she'd picked up. I don't mean kissing ones. Just guys sitting on beds in motel rooms. I remember one of a man in a bra. He was just a man, the most ordinary, milktoast sort of man, and he had just tried on a bra. Like anybody would try on a bra, like anybody would try on what the other person had that he didn't have" (*Arbus*, 6).

In Arbus portraits of confirmed cross-dressers, such as *Seated man in a bra and stockings, N.Y.C. 1967*, often the ambience is prosaic and the moment of the photograph suggests nothing spectacular, nothing in the obvious incongruity that goes beyond shared principles of the everyday presentation of a self. Even when there is pronounced theatricality, as in *A naked man being a woman, N.Y.C. 1968* the scene is far removed from the show places where such incongruities are minstrelized. In this instance, drapes to the alcove in an ordinary room may serve to suggest a parted stage curtain but a hot plate and a beer can remain prosaically in view at his feet. With genitals tucked out of view, the man's pose is a variation on the "Birth of Venus" motif, yet it is presented without comic discrepancy or fey imitation. The *Revelations* exhibition catalog has enlarged a sequence of images of the same portrait subject, first fully dressed as a woman seated on a park bench, secondly in the room in stockings and undergarments, then nude, and lastly in male attire seated on a park bench. Arbus has labeled the contact sheets "Catherine Bruce and Bruce Catherine" (*Revelations*, 194). None of the individual images, nor the sequence as a whole, entail the sensationalism that mass culture of the time required for such subject matter, as in the B-movie on cross-dressing directed by Edward Wood, *Glen or Glenda?* (1953).

My responses to Arbus portraits obviously absorb the expanded cultural compass of what now falls familiarly within the visible for Americans, an expansion to which Arbus's work doubtlessly contributed. Many critics object to her attitude of inclusion as offhand and devoid of social conscience. In this regard Arbus has a place in what Gertrude Stein identified as modernity's "history of the refused in the arts and literature." For Stein the key to cultural sensibility and its changes over time is that "each generation has something different at which they are all looking." But the full assertion of such difference is undertaken first by only a few in each generation: "No one is ahead of his time, it is only that the particular variety of creating his time is the one [attribute] that his contemporaries who also are creating their own time refuse to accept" until a point when "almost without a pause almost everybody accepts" the changed attitude.[38] Undeniably, Arbus contributed significantly in the cultural process of establishing a matter-of-fact place for "freaks" within the visual mainstream.

As few need be told, in the course of the 1960s the semantics of *freak* was extended from a stigmatizing pejorative to comprehend an honorific title. It became a designation for heroic marginality or nonconformity much as *eccentric* had for Edith Sitwell in an earlier decade. In the 1970s Leslie Fiedler published an elaborate defense of the freak as a counterculture hero and as a manifestation of respectable society's secret self. His book proposes that the freak is a still-powerful remnant of the ancient mythic union monster/human and that in contemporary life it remains "capable of providing the thrill our forebears felt in the presence of an equivocal and sacred unity we have since learned to secularize and divide." For Fiedler a categorical exception must be made for grotesques, however, since they are merely "vestiges of medieval superstition which their authors only played at believing, like children scaring themselves to allay boredom."[39] Where Fiedler privileges freaks as mythic and sacred, Arbus associates them in her commentary with familiar vernacular modes like dream, legend, and fairy tale.

The recent study *Sideshow U.S.A.*, by Rachel Adams, reserves meaning for *freak* as a "performative category" rather than as an indicator of cultural or natural absolutes. In going beyond Robert Bogdan's earlier *Freak Show* to construct a social theory of the exhibition dynamic, *Sideshow U.S.A.* attributes to the event a normative cultural function in the reinforcement of onlookers' sense of centrality within society and in the confinement of freaks to a sphere of absolute difference. The sideshow trades on an audience's confidence that freaks are abnormal in their essence and thus distinct and separate from humanity per se. Adams particularly values the portrait work of Diane Arbus for its defiance of such stigmatization. Even in images where strong markers of difference in appearance or life style are present, Adams writes, an Arbus portrait subject "cannot be definitively segregated from an otherwise normal world, nor isolated within one part of the body."[40]

In revising the 1973 essay "Freak Show" into a chapter for *On Photography* Susan Sontag newly titled the piece "America, Seen Through Photographs, Darkly" and she tempered a few of the harsher moral judgments upon Arbus's character. The original finding of a "morbid sensibility" in Arbus,[41] for instance, is modified to a "dissociated way of seeing" (*On Photography*, 35). But the chapter does not alter Sontag's fundamental line of attack against the Arbus photographs and the social pathologies the critic finds reflected in them. Later in the decade Christopher Lasch's *The Culture of Narcissism* (1978), which assesses the contemporary American scene outside areas of photography and the art world, makes a similar general diagnosis of the culture and delivers a similar intellectual jeremiad.

Since Susan Sontag stands as one of our important modern public intellectuals and since, specifically, her judgments against Arbus have been widely persuasive, her critique warrants quotation and rebuttal at some length. The Sontag appraisal is based upon the 1972 Museum of Modern Art retrospective and the Aperture monograph published on that occasion. In Sontag's estimation the Arbus oeuvre is extremely narrow and specialized in social and visual range: it has "lined up assorted monsters and borderline cases—most of them ugly; wearing grotesque or unflattering clothing; in dismal or barren surroundings" (*On Photography*, 32). To judge from the monograph's actual depictions, however, the assertion is simply inadequate and untrue. By far the majority of the many individuals photographed in the streets and in parks, for example, share our common creatural lot in matters of personal appearance. Most of us dress according to a mass style of the day, our features are notably imperfect, we are not especially photogenic. How often does one among us find a photograph likeness particularly flattering or even appealing? Furthermore, in these two general settings the portraits typically minimize background and context and they thus negate environment as an observable determinant. The physical surroundings are not "dismal or barren" in any overtly visible way.

Two Arbus photographs involving the theme of patriotism—*Boy with a straw hat waiting to march in a pro-war parade, N.Y.C. 1967* and *Patriotic young man with a flag, N.Y.C. 1967*—are exemplary of her street portraiture, and they can serve to weigh Sontag's criticism. In them the grays of stone and concrete neutralize the background, and it does not serve up metaphor or commentary. The individuals are self-fashioned politically; they are not the dumb creatures of an external ideological determinism. The grotesque dimension to the images is presented as inherent to the subjects. It is a function of slight emphases in each individual's appearance, in the choice of patriotic insignia and their reiteration. In *Boy with a straw hat* there are the handheld flag and the flag lapel pin and redundancies such as the stars on the "God Bless America" button, the stripes on the bow tie, and the cinched shape of the bow tie and of the flag on the lapel pin. By comparison, Garry Winogrand's published photographs of a 1969 pro-war demonstration by construction workers in New York City present a compositional riot of American flags, hard-hats, and hostile gesticulations. In the Winogrand images patriotism is an exclamatory and outsized social expression; in the Arbus portraits it is a personalized determination.

None of these features in the two Arbus portraits make the individuals monstrous or deranged in physical appearance. At worst the first young man is marred by a poor choice of headwear, the second by a poor complexion. To be sure, both young men hold a political position that may be contrary to one's own and the call for a "Bomb Hanoi" strategy may be considered extremist. Yet even at their human extremes, as with the contortions to body and face from boyhood rage in *Child with a toy hand grenade in Central Park, N.Y.C. 1962,* Arbus images show nothing truly monstrous or borderline. Sontag's judgments resonate with her more general alarmist rhetoric of the time. In the summer of 1966 the editors of *Partisan Review* queried several writers and intellectuals on the topic "What's Happening in America" and published their replies in the winter 1967 issue. Sontag responded that conditions in American culture and politics are so severe as to "constitute a full-grown, firmly installed national psychosis." The populace inhabits a "Yahooland" where both "the barbarism and the innocence are lethal, outsized." And America looms as a monster on the geopolitical scene, as "the arch-imperium of the planet, holding man's biological as well as his historical future in its King Kong paws."[42]

In gauging American art audiences a decade later, Sontag determines that "the Arbus photographs convey the anti-humanist message which people of good will in the 1970s are eager to be troubled by" (*On Photography,* 32–33). Their vogue frisson is adjudged by Sontag to be sure evidence of an abandonment of social ideals and of the "Great American Cultural Revolution" envisioned by Walt Whitman, whose counterpart in contemporary world politics she identifies as the "great poet" leader Mao Tse-tung and his Red Guards (*On Photography,* 27). (While originally the ideological comparison may in the main reflect enthusiasms within the American Left of the early 1970s, to retain it in a publication of the late 1970s—when the repressive mass violence of the Chinese Cultural Revolution was disclosed to the West—seems politically irresponsible.) To Sontag's sensibility the Arbus work disserves audience and subjects alike in concentrating on "victims, on the unfortunate," on "people who are pathetic, pitiable, as well as repulsive" without an intention to "arouse any compassionate feelings" (*On Photography,* 33). It seems apparent that the critic here reifies her own strong emotional impressions into claims of substantive truth about the individuals photographed. Sontag presumes that the portrait subjects suffer profoundly for being who they are and appearing as they do. The photographer has committed an injustice by capturing them "in various degrees of unconscious or unaware relation to their pain, their ugliness" (*On Photography*, 36). Sontag is affronted that "few of the pictures actually show emotional distress. The photographs of deviates and real freaks do not accent their pain but, rather, their detachment and autonomy; [they] are mostly shown as cheerful, self-accepting, matter-of-fact" (*On Photography*, 36). For these reasons Sontag excludes the Arbus canon when she returns to the subject of photography in *Regarding the Pain of Others* (2003).

Within both *On Photography* and *Regarding the Pain of Others* Sontag posits that the definitive shortcoming of the medium is its essentially descriptive, nonnarrative nature: "Only that which narrates can make us understand. The limit of photographic knowledge of the world is that while it can goad conscience, it can, finally, never be ethical or political knowledge. The knowledge gained through still photographs will always be some kind of sentimentalism, whether cynical or humanist. It will be a knowledge at bargain prices—a semblance of knowledge, a semblance of wisdom" (*On Photography*, 23–24). *Regarding the Pain of Others* revises the formulation by a few degrees and allows that photographs do not in all cases lend to a general condition of miscomprehension. But any durable meaning they possess still remains dependent upon properties or contexts of narration, not on their descriptive capacities alone: "Harrowing photographs do not inevitably lose their power to shock. But they are not much help if the task is to understand. Narratives can make us understand. Photographs do something else: they haunt us."[43]

The critic presupposes that the milieu of many Arbus people is "an appalling underworld" filled with "the horror experienced by [its] denizens" (*On Photography*, 42). It is the very indifference to shock value in the Arbus portrait work, and the air of open familiarity and acceptance, that nettles Sontag. In response the critic condemns the situation as a serious human failing on the part of photographer and subject alike. While Sontag reproaches the photographer for practices that exploit and "colonize" individuals brought into the camera's view, the critic in her own right patronizes them through sentimentality and presumptions about their caste (*On Photography*, 42). In a display of moral rectitude, Sontag remonstrates that at least *she* is disquieted even while the portrait subjects appear unperturbed.

Arbus photograph portraits heed and accept differentia, degrees of abnormality, and discrepancies between intention and effect as the creatural norm for humanity. The work does not seek to mutate incongruity into stigma. Where stigma is already involved, her work declines to minstrelize. It accepts equably and without mockery, for instance, the elaborate artifices and aristocratic pretensions of "His Serene Highness, Prince Robert de Rohan Courtenay" and the tawdry female impersonation by the black man of *Transvestite at a drag ball, N.Y.C. 1970.* In published excerpts available from Arbus's diary, it is apparent that at times she allowed her thought patterns to become reversible to an extent that polarities are eclipsed, as in this musing:

> To think that I am not going
> To think of you anymore
> Is still thinking of you.
> Let me then try not to think
> That I am not going to think of you. (*Revelations,* 143)

Another formulation in the diary could stand as an envoi to much of her work: "For one who cannot distinguish the Beautiful from the Ugly from one who cannot distinguish the Ugly from the Beautiful" (*Revelations,* 143).

Arbus portraits tend not to stylize much further upon the individual, who by definition is already fully engaged in some kind of self-stylization. Individuals of extraordinary innate beauty and infants constitute something of an exception, and Arbus thought that they required a more intense approach. In a letter written around 1969 to suggest story ideas to an editor, Arbus remarks: "Think of this: That Beauty is itself an aberration, a burden, a mystery, even to itself. What if I were to photograph Great Beauties. (I don't know quite how they'd look but I think, like Babies, they can take the most remorseless scrutiny)" (*Magazine Work,* 168). The magazine assignment portraits published in 1968 and 1969 of Viva, the fashion model and Warhol-manufactured superstar, go to uncharacteristic lengths to deform a photographic genre (that of nude female beauty in this case) and to disfavor the subject's face and figure. Babies were a more frequent camera subject in Arbus's personal work, where they are typically presented in distress and marked by tears or slobber. While unflattering, these baby pictures are fully part of a creatural attitude since, after all, such situations are part of daily existence for the very young. Unsparingly close, even in the case of an infant in peaceful sleep like Anderson Hays Cooper, the baby pictures defy the easy sentimentalism of commercial and amateur photography on the subject of childhood.[44]

Recognition of the unfamiliar and the peculiar is the paradox that best describes the attitude of the grotesque communicated through Arbus's portrait work. Arbus has explained her sense of the incongruities involved at some length:

Everybody has that thing where they need to look one way but they come out looking another way and that's what people observe. You see someone on the street and essentially what you notice about them is the flaw. It's just extraordinary that we should have been given these peculiarities. And, not content with what we were given, we create a whole other set. Our whole guise is like giving a sign to the world to think of us in a certain way but there's a point between what you want people to know about you and what you can't help people knowing about you. And that has to do with what I've always called the gap between intention and effect. I mean if you scrutinize reality closely enough, if in some way you really, really get to it, it becomes fantastic. You know it really is totally fantastic that we look like this and you sometimes see that very clearly in a photograph. Something is ironic in the world and it has to do with the fact that what you intend never comes out like you intend it. (*Arbus*, 1–2)

Since these words have been held severely against Arbus's photography by some critics, a few explicit points should be reiterated right away. Peculiarities in the individual, both *born* and *made*, establish one's *propria persona* and they are the source for Arbus of a human's prepossessing qualities, though obviously not in any conventional sense of mass appeal. An eye for incongruity and a disinclination to portray an idealized image constructed either by the individual or by market culture are factors central to Arbus's attitude of the grotesque. It is inevitable that what a person considers to be individualizing traits are not the same qualities that individualize him or her for others. No faultfinding or character judgment is implicit in one's recognition of this situation. The flaw or gap Arbus finds is indicative of a profoundly mutual human predicament. Much the same holds true for the disjunctions between experience and expression embodied by the sympathetic grotesques of Sherwood Anderson's fiction.

The medium itself and her own performance as photographer are for Arbus part of the predicament: "I work from awkwardness.... The process of photography is itself a bit of a distortion."[45] Arbus's interest in the flaw or gap is often assessed by critics as proof of her antipathetic, exploitative aims. Judith Goldman, for one, considers it to be a sign of "compulsive cheating, made by someone who had the upper-hand." Arbus is moreover faulted by this critic for failing to provide with her images a narrative outlet or teleology for the portrait subject: "In reinforcing the surface, Arbus . . . stymied the narrative's movement. Her frontal compositions remain static in their symmetry and repeat the same story, forcing subject and viewer into a predetermined mental set of despair."[46] To be fair, it must be acknowledged that Arbus offers only a passing view of a person's existence: she does not pretend to reach into a person's life story or essence. But, where a photographer like Winogrand offers the momentary existential encounters of a *camera*, Arbus customarily has given the subject some personal time and space to dispose oneself for the photograph.

To better understand Arbus's attention to the flaw or gap we should turn to Freud's late, summary observations on the vicissitudes of mental life. Freudian ideas, of course, were broadly accepted in the New York milieu of artists and educated people around Arbus. Neuroses, Freud advises, "shade off by easy transitions into what is described as the normal; and, on the other hand, there is scarcely any state recognized as normal in which indications of neurotic traits could not be pointed out. Neurotics have approximately the same innate dispositions as other people, they have the same experiences and they have the same tasks to perform. Why is it, then, that they live so much worse and with so much greater difficulty and, in the process, suffer more feelings of unpleasure, anxiety and pain? . . . Quantitative *disharmonies* are what must be held responsible for the inadequacy and suffering of neurotics."[47] Healthy/ unhealthy and normal/abnormal, then, are a distinction not of kind but of quantity. Freud extends much further the range of vicissitudes in stating that the dreams of an average person possess "all the absurdities, delusions and illusions of a psychosis. A psychosis of short duration, no doubt, harmless, even entrusted with a useful function, introduced with the subject's consent and terminated by an act of his will. None the less it is a psychosis" (*SE* 23: 172). A normal or healthy ego, Freud cautions, is "like normality in general, an ideal fiction. The abnormal ego . . . is unfortunately no fiction. Every normal person, in fact, is only normal on the average. His ego approximates to that of the psychotic in some part or other and to a greater or lesser extent" (*SE* 23: 235). Freud thus advances, in effect, a radical theory of the equality of all persons, one we can term creatural at the psychological level.

Arbus's sense of photography as a process of deep recognition of the peculiar and the seemingly unfamiliar has much in common with the Freudian idea of the uncanny. As a psychological experience, Freud places the uncanny (*unheimlich*, literally "unhomely") within "that class of the frightening which leads back to what is known of old and long familiar" (*SE* 17: 220). Through a detailed survey of the etymology and semantics of *heimlich* Freud locates a set of fundamental double meanings that bind it to its antonym and he concludes that "*Unheimlich* is in some way or other a sub-species of *heimlich*" (*SE* 17: 226). (In this fundamental respect, the semantic relationship of *uncanny* to *canny* in English does not provide an adequate analogy.) The phenomenon, at both linguistic and psychological levels, is yet another instance of "the antithetical meaning of primal words" and it is replicated as well in the dreamwork's tendency "to disregard negation and to employ the same means of representation for expressing contraries" (*SE* 11: 155). The uncanny, Freud concludes, "is in reality nothing new or alien, but something which is familiar and old—established in the mind and which has become alienated from it. . . . The uncanny [is] something which ought to have remained hidden but has come to light" (*SE* 17: 241). The definition accords with the grotesque dynamic identified in its original sense as an unearthing of dark, recessed, and yet accommodating places.

Arbus photographs were exhibited to New York City audiences for the first time during October 1965 as a small part of a *Recent Acquisitions* show at the Museum of Modern Art. Two Arbus images were selected by the curator: *Retired man and his wife at home in a nudist camp one morning, N.J. 1963* (its title in *Arbus*) and *Female impersonators, N.Y.C. 1961*. Yuben Yee, a member of the Museum's Department of Photography, recalls that before reopening each day staff would have to wipe spit from the Arbus photographs.[48] What would possess a person to spit in the face of a portrait?

For one thing, most people would not be likely to spit directly in the face of someone. Perhaps because the target is only a photographed person there is a measure of license for this behavior. A complicating and implicating factor, however, intrudes for the viewer who spits. In combination, museum gallery lighting and the protective surface over the photograph can make the view vary in transparency and reflectivity, depending on one's angle. Put simply, the view can alternate between a window and a mirror in its effect. Though the mirror effect will be most often intermittent and secondary, still some aspects of the viewer's features are liable to become superimposed over the portrait image. To spit at a photograph on exhibition, obviously, is to ostracize its subject matter as an affront to one's own respectability. But such a show of disgust is complicated by the sheer optical possibility of the viewer's features becoming mirrored upon this Other. The situation can readily involve the kind of repressed familiarity evoked by the uncanny. An early modernist testament to such predicaments of the uncanny is Baudelaire's *The Flowers of Evil* (1857), whose opening, monitory verse is a catalogue of creatural realities and human failings itemized by the poet for each "Hypocrite reader,—my likeness,—my brother!" ("To the Reader").[49]

Grotesque to Monstrous

*T*HE GROTESQUE AS A LITERARY and a visual mode continues to be part of American cultural life to be sure, but its viability as an attitude toward history has largely given way to the monstrous. In the face of the organized extermination of humanity in unimaginable numbers under the official policy of dictators like Hitler, Stalin, and Pol Pot, and the annihilation of large civilian populations as a sanctioned act of war in cities like Nanjing, Dresden, Tokyo, Hiroshima, and Nagasaki, the grotesque has come to seem inadequate as a measure of human experience. Flannery O'Connor in "The Displaced Person" takes spiritual measure of the Holocaust in having a priest attempt to convey to the worldly, self-absorbed landowner Mrs. McIntyre the enormity of human suffering involved: "Think of the thousands of them, think of the ovens and the boxcars and the camps and the sick children and Christ Our Lord" (*Works,* 322). The death camps are concisely visualized for the reader in terms of a "room piled high with bodies of dead naked people all in a heap, their arms and legs tangled together, a head thrust in here, a head there, a foot, a knee, a part that should have been covered up sticking out, a hand raised clutching nothing" (*Works,* 287). This reality is beyond grotesque for O'Connor.[1] What *is* grotesque is Mrs. McIntyre's response to the priest's appeal: "I'm a logical practical woman and there are no ovens here and no camps and no Christ Our Lord" (*Works,* 322). As far as O'Connor herself is concerned, the grotesqueness of the woman's denials take us beyond politics and history into matters of Christian mystery. A humane reality of Christ persists for O'Connor in the face of mankind's own monstrous inhumanity.

When in the late 1950s O'Connor made an assessment of the American general public's notion of a "Southern School" of writers she supposed that "the term conjures up an image of Gothic monstrosities and the idea of everything deformed and grotesque. Most of us are considered, I believe, to be unhappy combinations of Poe and Erskine Caldwell" (*Mystery*, 28). What O'Connor begrudges is the reduction of the grotesque into gothic story content. While subject matter like physical malformation lends itself readily to grotesque treatment, for O'Connor the literary grotesque is created mainly through perspective and compositional rendering rather than through subject matter per se. And O'Connor had no patience for secular practitioners of the Southern grotesque and gothic like Caldwell or Carson McCullers. When she learned of the sale of foreign rights for *Wise Blood* to the publisher Gallimard in Paris, O'Connor quipped: "The French think Erskine Caldwell is the nuts so maybe they'll like me, provided the translation is bad enough" (*Letters*, 123). On several occasions in letters O'Connor expressed disdain for the fictional world imagined by Carson McCullers even while she could acknowledge that the first books "were at least respectable from the writing standpoint" (*Letters*, 446). At one point she grumbles that the very idea aired in the title of McCullers' stage play *The Square Root of Wonderful* (1958) "makes me cringe" (*Letters*, 246).

On behalf of McCullers it should be said that in her fiction the grotesque can be an effective means for compassionate recognition. Like those of Sherwood Anderson's fictional Winesburg, the grotesques in McCullers' first novel *The Heart is a Lonely Hunter* (1940) have come to feel that they occupy the most forlorn place on earth. The story revolves around an ill-sorted set of five people within a Southern town. Their lives closely intersect for a time but not in uniform harmony, and in the end no lasting bond among them is achieved. At the center of this temporary intimate circle is John Singer, a deaf-mute. Through sign language Singer's hands serve as a benevolent "voice." But, as in the cases of Wing Biddlebaum and Homer Simpson, they have also become a private hell: "His hands were a torment to him. They would not rest. They twitched in his sleep, and sometimes he awoke to find them shaping the words in his dreams before his face. . . . When he walked up and down the floor of his room he would crack the joints of his fingers and jerk at them until they ached."[2] Through its several political references to economic class, ethnicity, race, and the rise of fascism, *The Heart is a Lonely Hunter* signals that it has assembled these five misfits as a symbolic delegation on behalf of Western society's defenseless populations. The novel also develops a more specific response to the American racial grotesque in the character-ization of Doctor Copeland, a Negro physician tenaciously protective of his self-respect through the daily indignities aimed at black people.

CONTEMPORARY GROTESQUE

The one writer given to grotesque and gothic extremes with whom O'Connor remained in close personal contact was John Hawkes, even while she never believed herself to be truly in the same literary com-pany. Without reservation, though, O'Connor praised a quality that she thought Hawkes consistently achieved through his prose style: "The more fantastic the action the more precise the writing and this is the way it ought to be" (*Letters*, 292). In Hawkes' fiction the soulscape is that of the unconscious, about which the writer held some Jungian views, as in his declared "faith in the occult nature of minor coincidence."[3] Hawkes has spoken of his fiction in terms of the challenge for a writer to take taboo subject matter and to make it beautiful, to make it harmonize within a sense of the totality of life. He also has explained the affinities for pathology, crime, and pariahs in his writing as a process of reversed sympathy designed to make the reader aware of one's own potential for antisocial attitudes and behavior.[4]

The Lime Twig (1961) is the Hawkes novel to which O'Connor responded in the most personal terms. The fundamental dissimilarity of *The Lime Twig* from her fictional world can be suggested by the story's broad contours. Its events predominantly involve criminals and the race-track world, whose habitués include the vicious enforcer Thick and the drug-addicted war amputee Sparrow. The novel proceeds obliquely from an initial focus upon William Hencher, a man mentally scarred by the London Blitz ten years earlier. When a small-time scheme goes awry Hencher is trampled to death in a horse van, and from there matters unravel entirely in a phantasmagoria of drunkenness, drugs, betrayal, abduction, torture, rape, erotomania, brutality, and graphic murder. All human concerns are subsumed into this pitch-dark underworld, where the contrastive and differential methods of the grotesque are inoperative. Upon reading *The Lime Twig* the first time O'Connor conveyed at once her reactions to Hawkes by letter:

The action seems to take place at that point where dreams are lightest (and fastest?), just before you wake up.... I can't make any intelligent comments about this book any more than I could about the others; but I can register my sensations. You suffer this like a dream. It seems to be something that is happening to you, that you want to escape from but can't. It's quite remarkable. Your other books I could leave when I wanted to, but this one I might have been dreaming myself. The reader even has that slight feeling of suffocation that you have when you can't wake up and some evil is being worked on you. I don't know if you intended any of this, but it's the feeling I had when the book was happening to me. I want to read it again in a month or so and see if the second time I can take it as observer and not victim. (*Letters*, 412)

Notably, O'Connor discovers that her response is limited to immediate, dreamlike sensations since *The Lime Twig* does not foster a more conscious order of perception, to say nothing of reflection. Her genuine praise for the book's style is seriously qualified by her closing remark since for O'Connor the higher purpose of literature remains to elevate the reader into an acute witness of essential truth, not to reduce him or her to a mere victim. More generally, to O'Connor's mind Hawkes creates in his fiction a convenient stage devil for his thematic purposes in the presentation of evil, and she calculates that this devil is "co-equal to God, not his creature; this pride is his virtue, not his sin; and that his aim is not to destroy the Divine plan because there isn't any Divine plan to destroy" (*Letters*, 456). For her there is no basic objection to creating a figure of the Devil in fiction since "fallen spirits are of course still spirits and I suppose the Devil teaches most of the lessons that lead to self-knowledge" (*Letters*, 439). But she finds little beyond gothic romanticism in this novelist's approach to evil: "Jack Hawkes' view of the devil is not a theological one. His devil is an impeccable literary spirit whom he makes responsible for all good literature. Anything good he thinks must come from the devil" (*Letters*, 507). While O'Connor did not comment further on the trend, from the late 1950s on American literary propensities toward imagined experience born of criminality and violence were to become monstrously graphic in the fiction of writers like William Burroughs, Hubert Selby, Cormac McCarthy, Bret Easton Ellis, and Chuck Palahniuk.

Some American fiction has sought to achieve the grotesque mainly through a concentration on the milieux of the carnival and the freak show. A case in point is *Nightmare Alley* (1946) by William Lindsay

Gresham, a writer with whom Diane Arbus made contact in 1960. The novel's protagonist eventually becomes an alcoholic and a drifter and his last opportunity in life is to perform as a geek. The novel is forthrightly a morality tale and, with the exception of the geek show scene in which the performer appears to bite off the head of a live chicken, its prose declines to render the material as grotesque in any consistent sense of the term. In literary technique the book approaches the realism of Sinclair Lewis and John Dos Passos rather than the styles of the American modern masters of the grotesque Anderson, West, and O'Connor. The novel *The Gypsy's Curse* (1974) by Harry Crews takes for its inscription the Diane Arbus statement "My favorite thing is to go where I've never been." Its narrator and protagonist is a deaf mute with lifeless, atrophied legs who performs as a strongman and gymnast. Katherine Dunn's *Geek Love* (1989) is a story told by a bald albino hunchback dwarf born into the family that operates a traveling show that features home-bred freaks, the children that resulted from the parents' deliberate experimentations with street drugs, prescription medicines, insecticides, and radioisotopes during conception and pregnancy. The Crews and the Dunn novels are so dedicated to the milieux of "defectives" and so pitted against the social experience of "norms" that their prose lacks a descriptive purchase on the materials that would provide a revealing sense of incongruity and thus constitute an attitude of the grotesque in regard to the larger culture.

Bobbie Ann Mason provides a fuller social canvas in *Feather Crowns* (1993), a novel whose events, set mainly in 1900, involve the birth, short lives, and popular phenomenon of quintuplets. The book's experiential purview has at its center their mother, and it grounds the story in her domestic realities in the rural South, well before she gains a sideshow perspective on America. In terms of the political grotesque in American fiction, Kurt Vonnegut exemplifies several qualities established earlier by Nathanael West. Vonnegut's *Mother Night* (1966) offers a comparative case study in race hatred of the Third Reich and of the United States after World War II. Attributes of the political grotesque in Vonnegut's *Slaughterhouse-Five* (1969) are largely a product of the book's time-travel situations rather than one of immediate appearances. The protagonist Billy Pilgrim is a "spastic in time." From its comparative perspective on history *Slaughterhouse-Five* finds no war cause, neither Nazi expansion nor Allied self-defense, morally just or spiritually justified.[5]

Something of the grotesque persists in the short stories of A. M. Homes, George Saunders, and Rick Moody. Of these three Moody is the one most consciously responsive to ideas of the grotesque prized by Sherwood Anderson, particularly so in two stories published in Moody's collection

Demonology (2000). "Ineluctable Modality of the Vaginal" constitutes a postmodern riposte to the sentimentality exhibited in Anderson's "The Man Who Became a Woman." Moody engages the topic through the monologue of a young woman educated in the discourse of French psychoanalysis and poststructuralist feminism. Her predicament is that she shares life with a feckless intellectual who, because of his sophistication, is incapable of even conversing about something so mundane as commitment and marriage. He claims to understand completely "the second sex" on the basis of one minor incident of cross-dressing in his childhood. Her ultimate challenge to his pretentiousness is to make him watch as she conducts a full gynecological self-examination on the kitchen table in their apartment.

Moody's story "The Double Zero" is a closely refashioned version of Sherwood Anderson's "The Egg" (1921), as an author's note makes explicit. The Anderson story traces the efforts by a man, prompted by the ambitions of his wife, to succeed in a home enterprise. When his efforts at chicken farming fail he opens a restaurant, and facing failure once again the husband is overtaken with anxiety to satisfy his few customers, to offer them novelty and diversion with a meal. A deformed chicken hatchling proves to be his undoing. In desperation to please, one night the proprietor thrusts upon his sole customer a specimen from a collection of bottles containing "poultry monstrosities," one with seven legs and two heads.[6] Whereupon the customer retreats. At the end of the Anderson story the man breaks down in tearful humiliation before his wife and son.

In the Moody story a hapless small entrepreneur attempts to raise ostriches on his Rancho Double Zero. With the failure of that effort, he opens a restaurant and brings along his "ostrich freak exhibition," a collection of genetic abnormalities, many of them caused by local environmental hazards. At story's climax, the father experiences not only humiliation but "a shameful gastrointestinal problem" as well, "anal leakage."[7] The sheer vulgarity and gratuitousness of the last detail shows how much Moody fails to understand the workings of the grotesque in Anderson's fiction.

The photographer Ralph Eugene Meatyard pursued a direct link to an American literary tradition of the grotesque with his last series of images, published posthumously under the title *The Family Album of Lucybelle Crater* (1974). The name is a conscious variation upon that of a Flannery O'Connor character, two actually, an old woman and her daughter in "The Life You Save May Be Your Own" (1955). There the mother makes her introductions "Name Lucynell Crater and daughter Lucynell Crater" to a one-armed tramp who replies, "I can tell you my name is Tom T. Shiftlet and I come from Tarwater, Tennessee, but you never have seen me before: how you know I ain't lying?" (*Works*, 173–74). By this initial means O'Connor establishes themes of impersonation and authenticity in consideration of the profound spiritual question "what is a man?" (*Works*, 175).

The Lucybelle Crater image series features Meatyard's wife posed for each photograph in an oversized, full head mask with the exaggerated features of a crone—severely walleyed, gap-toothed, slack-jawed, jug-eared, with a nose shaped like a buzzard's beak, covered in warts, and gray hair drawn up into a topknot. For each image the Lucybelle figure is paired with another person who wears a thick transparent mask with deeply wrinkled surfaces that distort facial features to such a degree that it is impossible to discern an authentic facial likeness. In Meatyard's original set of captions for the series each companion in the pictures is named Lucybelle Crater as well. In the posthumous publication only the first and last photographs retain this feature: "Lucybelle Crater and her 46-year-old husband Lucybelle Crater" and "Lucybelle Crater and close friend Lucybelle Crater in the grape arbor." The book's editor has supplied the names of the family and friends who posed in all but one of these double portraits. A caption to the last image, however, indicates only "Mystery people." Elsewhere one learns that for this picture Meatyard himself wears the Lucybelle crone mask and the clothes of his wife and his wife wears the transparent mask and her husband's clothes.

For the Lucybelle Crater series, as in many earlier examples of his work, Meatyard operates as a frankly subjective photographer with fictional aims. The crone and transparent masks are worn by people posed in ordinary settings—standing by a tree, at a table, on a picnic bench, in front of a house or a car. Pictorial composition and framing are handled in a snapshot manner. Vagaries of sunlight and shadows are left unmastered. The portrait subjects wear ordinary clothing without much apparent thought to style or appearance's sake. Their body postures suggest that each individual is unaware of the mask and its grotesque features. Meatyard had already started photographing the series when in 1970 he was diagnosed with terminal cancer. He concentrated his efforts on the project over the two years of life that remained.[8] In late 1971 Meatyard wrote to a friend of the conscious principle underlying his current work: "the whole concept [is one] of minor nuances and shifts, and that there are only two people. I think I have been able to eliminate the idea of a third person: the Intruding Photographer. Natural in their own right, unlike so many portraits." The mystical root to such a conception of identity and being is apparent in another letter from this time where Meatyard, in further explanation of this principle, quotes from the spiritual meditations of art historian Max Picard in *The Human Face* (1931): "a face wanders about the world like a perpetual seal of God, stamping His image everywhere. So pictorial is the human face, even before God, that it is as if God did not create man at all, but only saw him in a dream-picture."[9]

The work of Diane Arbus has functioned for subsequent photographers as a benchmark of the medium's grotesque possibilities, with many of them striving to far exceed her precedent. For photographs of children with Down's syndrome published in 1975 Les Krims fashioned a sign for each of them to wear with the inscription "Diane Arbus Lives in Us."[10] The contrivance is symptomatic of how literal and limited in imagination and how remote from the Arbus precedent Krims is in his own photography. For a time Krims served as an official photographer for the Little People of America organization, and from personal work during that assignment he produced the limited edition folio, in small format, titled *The Little People of America* (1971). Many of these images are mildly satiric in their emphasis upon the diminutive size of individuals and their disproportions in comparison to the regular scale of the world around them. They lack the uncanny property of the mutual humanity within Arbus portraits of such people.

Photographer Mary Ellen Mark often concentrates on demimondes such as the brothel, the circus, transvestism, street children, gypsies, the homeless, and drug addicts. While most of her work utilizes the occasion of informal portraiture, social context remains for Mark equal to individuality in importance. In the service of social documentation the majority of her portraits present two or more persons within the frame, and her preferred form of publication is the extended photo essay. Her book *Twins* (2003) is more purely a collection of formal portraits, mostly of *identical* twins. Made with a huge format (20 × 24 inches) Polaroid view camera in sessions at the Twins Day Festival held in Twinsburg, Ohio, the photographs required a studio set up in a tent on the festival grounds, a crew of twelve people, and powerful lighting equipment. As part of the festivities many twins are exactly paired in outfit and grooming. The book remains unironic and respectful about all aspects of the social phenomenon of such a celebration and exhibition. The view camera's precise record of fine detail and Mark's strong emphasis on symmetry and doubling in the poses make the likeness between twins often appear nearly total, even after one's prolonged consideration of the image. All these factors strongly reinforce the phenomenon of identical twinship in the Mark book. By contrast, in Arbus's *Identical twins, Roselle, N. J. 1967* and

Triplets in their bedroom, N. J. 1963, where the portrait subjects are dressed alike but plainly, one's attention quickly shifts to difference and individuality, particularly in defining aspects of facial features like the eyes and mouth.

Since 1973 Shelby Lee Adams has photographed mountain people of Appalachia in eastern Kentucky, the home region of his family, and he often returns to the same households to make further portraits. Adams is conscious of the influence upon him of Depression-era photography sponsored by the Farm Security Administration, but his main interest is in a set of pictorial values, not in a tradition of the concerned documentarian. He conceives of this career project as an intense artistic quest. His first book, *Appalachian Portraits* (1993), bears as its epigraph a reflection by Flannery O'Connor on art and regionalism: "Art requires a delicate adjustment of the outer and inner worlds in such a way that, without changing their natures, they can be seen through each other. To know oneself is to know one's region. It is also to know the world, and it is also, paradoxically, a form of exile from that world."[11] O'Connor makes this statement, however, from a position of "Christian orthodoxy . . . centered in our Redemption by Christ and what I see in the world in its relation to that. I don't think that this is a position that can be taken halfway" (*Mystery,* 32).

What for O'Connor is a condition of spiritual exile is for Adams an opportunity for Romantic assertion: "These portraits are, in a way, self-portraits that represent a long autobiographical exploration of creativity, imagination, vision, repulsion, and salvation. My greatest fear as a photographer is to look into the eyes of a subject and not see my own reflection. My work has been an artist's search for a deeper understanding of my heritage and myself, using photography as a medium and the Appalachian people as collaborators."[12] Among these collaborations is *Hooterville Little Church, Hooterville* (1991), which portrays an old man who wears a chrome hubcap for headgear and a tee shirt emblazoned "Rude SURF GEAR" standing next to a younger man with an open Bible in his hands. Despite Adams' stated intentions, the photograph fits easily among national stereotypes of "The School of Southern Degeneracy" that O'Connor deplored in literature and the media (*Mystery,* 38).

Some outward features of Nan Goldin's photography—among them an interest in transvestites, the frequent choice of a bed as the portrait site, and attention to states of undress—have led commentators to liken her sensibility to that of Diane Arbus. In all instances, however, Goldin intensifies the displays of emotion and the confessional possibilities that Arbus generally avoided. Goldin's images offer a repertoire of the experiences of a group of lovers, close friends, and associates over the years that spans despondency, joy, isolation, celebration, sexual stimulation, physical suffering, and death. While Arbus pursued her mature work in the cultural capital of Pop Art during its height, she remained independent from its influences. Goldin, also based in New York City, found inspiration of sorts in the example of Andy Warhol and his Factory of self-designated "superstars": "One of the most important things about Warhol movies was their funkiness—the way they overthrew the whole craft ethos. . . . My support was [the example of] the Warhol films. I had a good eye for finding fabulous people and developing a community with them in a less passive way than Warhol."[13] Portrait and self-portrait work Goldin did over a long period makes up *The Ballad of Sexual Dependency*, a title perhaps intended as an echo of the Carson McCullers novella *The Ballad of the Sad Cafe* (1951). For several years Goldin re-edited her collection of photographs and exhibited them as a slide show in clubs, loft parties, galleries, and art festivals before a final selection was published in book form in 1986. The *Ballad* photographs are self-consciously autobiographical and narrative. By contrast, Arbus portraits are phenomenal and descriptive. The latter make no further promise than the occasion they offer an observer to consider a formal impression of another person come forward to the viewer's world through a photograph.

BEYOND GROTESQUE, THE MONSTROUS

At present we share a world where the headline "Man Confesses to Eating Internet Acquaintance" is not some sensational fabrication for a supermarket tabloid but the literal truth of an event reported in respectable metropolitan newspapers. The actual event was recounted in the courtroom confession of Armin Meiwes, a German computer expert who solicited through the Internet a young man for the purposes of "slaughter and consumption." Bernd Jurgen Brandes responded willingly to the proposal and Meiwes carried it out.[14] Under the banner "Cannibal's Video Reveals Mutilation and Slaughter," *The Times* of London reported in greater detail the actions recorded on videotape by Meiwes, who amputated the penis of Brandes, then cooked and tasted it while the victim was conscious and able to look on. Brandes remained alive and aware for ten hours until finally Meiwes, after first kissing his victim and saying a prayer, stabbed him to death.[15] A maximalism of the repulsive and the monstrous—and not the calculated contrasts, differentials, and disclosures of the grotesque—seems best suited to such matters, real or imagined.

In medical terminology, *monster* designates a fetus or newborn with malformities or anomalies usually so pronounced as to be incompatible with prolonged life expectancy. A similar meaning is present in *Paradise Lost* (1667) when Milton renders the "Universe of death, . . . /Where all life dies, death lives, and Nature breeds, / Perverse, all monstrous" (2:22–25). In *The Origin of Species* (1859) Darwin isolates "monstrous forms" of life as a "considerable deviation of structure generally injurious or not useful to the species."[16] In the field of medicine, the New York physician George Jackson Fisher published a series of articles from 1865 to 1868 on "Diploteratology" (the study of double or compound monsters) illustrated with photographs taken by him and by others. Fisher declared his intention to overturn a "history of monsters [that] consisted chiefly of marvelous tales, inaccurate descriptions, and absurd and superstitious prejudices." And pictorial documentation would help greatly to correct "the defective manner in which cases of monstrosities are usually reported."[17] The clinical term *monster* was in common usage well into the 1980s, but it has now been generally replaced in the lexicon by the scientistic word *teras*.

In the cultural study of the monstrous, which has expanded significantly since 1990, few have followed the earlier, narrowly Freudian lead of Bruno Bettelheim, who considered monsters to be equivalent to "the dark forces of the id."[18] One current perspective treats the category instead as foundational in the cultural and political construction of social order, and it has been applied, variously, to the Renaissance, the Enlightenment, and the present.[19] Another approach finds the monstrous to be symptomatic of the traditional cultural status of females who, since the time of Aristotle, were thought to be the specific generative cause of bodily deformity.[20] A third contemporary approach accounts monsters to be an agent of endless division and indeterminacy, and they thus exemplify deconstructive processes.[21]

The grotesque, which may well contain figures of monsters, is not finally monstrous in the senses of the liminal conditions and the extremes to culture that are emphasized in much present-day commentary on the subject of monsters. Like other traditional cultural attitudes toward history, the grotesque has been susceptible to the trivialization, negations, parody, and totalization of *différance* conducted by postmodern thought and art. We do well to recall that Goya, a master of the grotesque, populates his famous etching *El sueño de la rázon produce monstruos* in *Los Caprichos* (1799) not with monsters at all but with common animals whose emblematic significance is broadly familiar (see fig. 5.1). The bats and owls, as creatures of the night, represent ignorance. The beaks of several owls in the scene are parted; the cry of an owl is commonly taken to be an omen of disaster and death. The black cat is an obviously sinister presence. The lynx, a traditional emblem of keen-sightedness, counterposes these themes. As Robert Hughes has explained, the lynx was believed to have the power to "see through the thickest darkness and immediately tell truth from error."[22] In his own commentary on the image, Goya explicated: "Imagination abandoned by reason produces impossible monsters: united with reason, she is the mother of the arts and the source of their wonders."[23] In other works Goya does imagine monsters, witches, and devils, but often he renders them as human figures imbruted and made demonic by war, persecution, and the other scourges mankind has devised.

Within postmodernism, ideas on the grotesque in the visual arts have redefined the term radically. One prominent instance is the exhibition *Repulsion: Aesthetics of the Grotesque* held at the Alternative Museum in New York in 1986. Allan Ludwig, its organizer, advances a univocal understanding of the attributes involved: "We often characterize certain works of art as grotesque and by this we mean something particularly hideous, frightful, revolting, monstrous or bone chilling in its atavistic ability to evoke feelings of naked terror or repugnance within us. . . . Nothing in these extraordinary works of art conforms to the ways in which our culture has structured the world, even when the images contain a familiar religious or social code."[24] Ludwig's statement thus excludes from the grotesque an attitude of incongruity toward dominant cultural structures, among them a tradition of the grotesque itself. Further on Ludwig asserts that "the true grotesque" stems from a "dimension of pure horror or revulsion" and that it inspires art works "gruesome and incomprehensible in their excessive morbidity" (*Repulsion*, 5, 4). What are described here are not truly grotesques but rather monstrosities, excesses beyond art, designed to elicit terror but not pathos.

Ludwig's claims advocate an absolute condition, beyond boundaries of familiar social codes and the knowable, whereas an attitude of the grotesque operates through differential renderings and meanings., Commenting on the Arbus photograph *A Jewish giant at home with his parents in the Bronx, N.Y. 1970,* Ludwig projects onto the image a scenario ending in repulsion: "His tiny and shocked parents look on in utter horror, astonishment and finally stupification [*sic*]. One can almost hear them cry out from the depths of their once comfortable and orderly middle class world" (*Repulsion*, 9). But his interpretation denies the obvious phenomenal content of the picture. All three family members are home, together in a life they have shared for decades. Obviously, the parents did not wake suddenly from a terrifying nightmare to discover their adult son turned into a giant.

Critic Mark Dery terms the aesthetic trend toward medical and morgue photography "the New Grotesque" and he thinks that its impersonal air reflects "a collective body loathing in the age of AIDS, flesh-eating bacteria, and Ebola viruses. Then, too, it constitutes a deliberation on the growing irrelevance of the body in an ever more virtual world, where terminally-wired technophiles regard the 'meat' with open contempt, as an evolutionary vestige."[25] Irrespective of postmodern rhetoric, however, for the foreseeable future where all of us are concerned we continue to exist among "the thousand natural shocks that flesh is heir to," in Hamlet's phrase. The grotesque in its core sense entails an element of refuge and delight, if only in the insights it affords and even while the pleasure may be to a degree guilty or perverse. In this the grotesque remains distinct from monstrosity, whose powers to horrify eclipse other responses.

Stephen Crane's *The Monster* holds true to this idea of monstrosity in the total exclusion of the disfigured black stableman Henry Johnson from the town's social life, white and black, with the near exception of Dr. Trescott's family, which finds itself ostracized. In *The Day of the Locust* Nathanael West maintains a distinction between the grotesque and the monstrous on somewhat different grounds: "It is hard to laugh at the need for beauty and romance, no matter how tasteless, even horrible, the results of that need are. But it is easy to sigh. Few things are sadder than the truly monstrous" (*Novels,* 243). Many people and situations that Tod encounters appear at first to be monstrous, such as the truculent adult dwarf "Honest" Abe Kusich, whose most prominent feature is a "slightly hydrocephalic head" (*Novels,* 245). But Kusich's pugnacity, as it turns out, was "often a joke" and "despite the sincere indignation that Abe's grotesque depravity aroused in [Tod], he welcomed his company" (*Novels,* 249, 245). No, Abe Kusich is not monstrous in West's novel, mass society is in its betrayals of the common person's needs of imagination and spirit.

The postmodern redefinition of the grotesque as the monstrous is conspicuous in the aesthetic of postmortem photography practiced by Jeffrey Silverthorne, Andres Serrano, and Joel-Peter Witkin and the "morbid history" school of photography criticism.[26] Roland Barthes did not contemplate such a literal fascination with the dead among photographers when he remarked: "All those young photographers who are at work in the world, determined upon the capture of actuality, do not know that they are agents of Death. This is the way in which our time assumes Death: with the denying alibi of the distractedly 'alive,' of which the Photographer is in a sense the professional" (*Camera Lucida,* 92). Weegee's press photo *Joy of Living*, with its rich ironies over the dead and the living, fully registers the paradoxes Barthes finds in the alibi of *actuality*, the word itself a synonym for news and documented fact. No equivalent alibi is made in the postmortem work of Silverthorne, Serrano, and Witkin, in most of which the living are nowhere to be seen. Their death photography is concerned with an exceptional condition of actuality—a state devoid of any further human action or agency on the part of the photographed subject. Their death imagery requires a bona fide of corpses.

Joel-Peter Witkin has judged the grotesques portrayed by Arbus to lack spiritual authenticity: "Because my subjects are kind of agreed-to victims, they have their own reasons for being in the photograph. Arbus' images are of social and medical outcasts who parade the small, tin banners of the perverse. I seem to incorporate these tendencies, but my initial interest has always been to show the lostness within us. I am an aesthetic priest."[27] By means of a seemingly deliberate reformulation of Arbus's famous statement "My favorite thing is to go where I've never been," Witkin has expressed his own otherworldly concerns: "My life wish is to be connected with a place we can't know, hope to go, or hope to be."[28] Witkin does claim an affinity with the sensibility of Weegee, whom he considers to be a man of "sadistic benevolence, driven from paradise, like me."[29] In technique and subject matter, however, Witkin takes measures well beyond photojournalism as Weegee and others have practiced it.

Witkin freely intrudes into the photographic process at all levels, starting often from an elaborately preplanned and staged scenario as the camera's subject matter. His obvious interventions continue through development and enlargement to printing, with a final encaustic surface added to some images in special edition. With the film negative, which according to Witkin is initially sharp in focus and standard in tonality in most cases, he scratches and draws on both the emulsion side (thus giving black lines on the final print) and the base side (giving white lines). In enlarging and printing the negative he inserts over the photographic paper a layer of tissue, onto which water and chemicals are sprinkled in places. By these means, and by varying the pressure on the tissue or by distressing or tearing it, the substance, focus, and texture of the printed image are altered and variegated. Further modifications to the final print are made through the use of special toners. To explain his intention in employing such techniques, Witkin has said: "I wanted a surface that was tough and granular, very much like a very quickly processed photograph of a battlefield or a war, or a photograph of Nagasaki or Hiroshima."[30] Tellingly, the aura of actuality Witkin seeks has as factual counterpart only events of extreme devastation.

As a corollary to the absolute assertion of his own sense of reality over any other consideration, the models in Witkin images typically wear masks. When not explicitly masked, their faces are otherwise obscured or defaced from the picture to eliminate personalizing features. Early in his career, Witkin had the following realization: "To me people were only masks. My interests would not be to reveal what the individual subject chose to hide, but instead to make the qualities of the hidden more meaningful. This is why I could engage the world on my own terms. I could deal with people by superimposing my own mask on theirs. . . . My work would have the impact of my irreality."[31]

By comparison, the individuals in Diane Arbus photographs who bear masks are not thereby deprived of their separable reality. The masks typically present in her portraits are occasioned by unexceptional social events such as a costume party, charity ball, or Halloween. The masks themselves tend toward the ordinary, from store-bought scary faces and homemade designs to a minimal covering for the area around the eyes, with decorative touches added in some cases. In most cases, the masks present in Arbus portraits are only partial guises, they do not cover up other expressive features of the face such as the forehead, cheeks, or mouth. For Arbus the masked or costumed figure is thinly disguised. He or she continues to exist *in propria persona* in an existential sense. This quality is most poignantly true in the Arbus photographs of asylum Halloween participants seen in the 1972 exhibition and in the later collection *Untitled* (1995).

Witkin, in contrast, is concerned to portray a "condition of being" rather than the individual models he selects. The portrait encounter is an *occasion* primarily for himself, not for the portrait subject. It is his opportunity to costume, stage, and pose a live mannequin according to the wishes of his daemon. It is clear from photographs such as *Las Meniñas* (1987), which reimagines the Velázquez canvas, *Studio of the Painter (Courbet)* (1990), *Studio de Winter* (1994), and *Poussin in Hell* (1999) that Witkin conceives of the photographer in his studio on a grand artistic scale. There the photographer engages in a transformative process to devise a scene in the image of its creator's inner truths. When required by circumstances to be on location Witkin continues to work in much the same manner.

The differences between the work of Arbus and that of Witkin are further clarified through a consideration of the ideas of Emmanuel Levinas on the matter of "ethics and the face." One primary objective for Levinas is to endow contemporary phenomenology with the principle of transcendence, and in doing so he identifies it as the ground for ethics, the fundamental responsibility of self with others and thus the basis for selfhood in the first place: "The idea of infinity, the infinitely more contained in the less, is concretely produced in the form of a relation with the face" of another person.[32] This concept of infinity leads directly into personal ethics: "The face opens the primordial discourse whose first word is obligation, which no 'interiority' permits avoiding" ("Ethics," 520). The face, thus perceived, is not a fixed entity nor an appearance that can be fully or finally comprehended: "Inasmuch as the access to beings concerns vision, it dominates those beings, exercises a power over them. . . . [Yet] the face is present in its refusal to be contained" ("Ethics," 515). One thus regards not only another person but a fundamental of being: "The relation between the Other and me . . . draws forth in his expression" and "in expression the being that imposes itself does not limit but promotes my freedom" ("Ethics," 515, 519).

Such possibilities, I believe, can remain true in the photograph, even while the expression it contains is produced through the stop-action, fixed impression of a camera. Arbus—like Sander, Strand, Evans, and other great portraitists before her—provides a remarkable vantage upon the faces of others. Many facial expressions in Arbus's *Untitled*, even where the face is partially masked, are available to our regard. Such portraiture is ethical in Levinas' sense of the term, and it refuses the mystifications that Witkin promotes. "The face to face," Levinas explains, "cuts across every relation one could call mystical, where events other than that of the presentation of the original being come to overwhelm or sublimate the pure sincerity of this presentation. . . . Here resides the rational character of the ethical relation and of language. No fear, no trembling could alter the straightforwardness of relationship" ("Ethics," 521).

Witkin obviously holds mystical views on the bodily fact of death, as exemplified in his statement "Knowledge goes beyond the physical. At the moment of death there's bodyweight loss, and that supposedly can mean the ascension of the spirit."[33] Witkin believes himself to be an emissary on behalf of such transformation: "I have consecrated my life to changing matter into spirit with the hope of someday seeing it all. Seeing its total form, while wearing the mask, from the distance of death."[34] With many of his images of the dead it is impossible to comprehend how even Witkin could imagine that a transmutation of flesh into spirit takes place through photography. *The Kiss* (1982), to take just one example, was a result of an unexpected discovery Witkin made while posing the severed head of an old man. An anatomist at the medical school that provided the specimen had completely bisected the head so that Witkin could place one side of the face mouth to mouth with the other side. Far from any spiritual mystery and apart from its shock value, the whole composition basically offers a crude art history joke on the famous sculptures created by Auguste Rodin and Constantin Brancusi.

The first decade of our twenty-first century is marked by a proliferation of "reality" shows that are entirely the product of a television mentality and whose content and format are intentionally grotesque, but only in the most limited senses of the term. Much of this reality TV is an exercise in grossness and humiliation performed by more than willing participants. *The Osbournes* is a video "diary," recorded by a full camera and sound crew, of the family and professional life of an aged heavy metal rock star whose mind and physical affect are addled by decades of drug use. The MTV production *Jackass* for three seasons received some of the cable network's highest ratings. Hosted by the daredevil Johnny Knoxville, the series offered mindless feats such as driving blind, butt piercing, hurling a person from a giant slingshot, being tarred and feathered, devising a beard of leeches and a bikini of bees, and farting on a goat. The inspiration for *Jackass* came from Knoxville's original notion to have himself shot with pepper spray, a taser, a stun gun, and a .38 revolver and then to report on the experiences for a magazine piece. Another variant of reality television is the physical challenge competitions where amateurs engage in activities—to take examples from *Fear Factor*—such as being dragged by a horse; lying in a pit full of rats, a coffin full of worms, a hole with snakes; and eating sheep's eyes, buffalo testicles, cockroaches, and horse rectum. When Nathanael West has his pilgrim hero in *The Dream Life of Balso Snell* enter through the rectum into the lower intestine of the Trojan Horse the incident serves as the inception of a grotesque odyssey through American culture, not as a stunt merely in the hope of prize money. Instead of the grotesque in its traditional senses, a current reader and observer is much more likely to encounter the gratuitous and the utterly ridiculous and on occasion the monstrous as the signs now of our times.

CHAPTER 1

1. Flannery O'Connor, *Mystery and Manners: Occasional Prose,* ed. Sally and Robert Fitzgerald (New York: Farrar, Straus, and Giroux, 1969), 33. Subsequent references to this source are indicated by the title *Mystery.*

2. Kenneth Burke, *Attitudes toward History* (1937), 3rd ed. (Berkeley: University of California Press, 1984), 34. Subsequent references to this source are indicated by the title *Attitudes.*

3. Vitruvius, *On Architecture,* 2 vols., trans. Frank Granger, 1934 (Cambridge: Harvard University Press, 1970), 2:105.

4. For an invaluable account of the palace decor, see Nicole Dacos, *La découverte de la Domus Aurea et la formation des grotesques à la Renaissance* (London: Warburg Institute, 1969).

5. E. H. Gombrich, *The Sense of Order: A Study in the Psychology of Decorative Art* (Ithaca, NY: Cornell University Press, 1979), 263, 251. Subsequent references to this source are indicated by the title *Sense of Order.*

6. Naomi Miller, *Heavenly Caves: Reflections on the Garden Grotto* (New York: Braziller, 1982), 11. Miller reserves *grotesque* to designate the irrational side of imagination, "the dark forces of nature as yet uncontrolled by art" (68). Barbara Jones's *Follies and Grottoes* (London: Constable, 1974) is a detailed history and illustrated survey of such structures throughout the British Isles, where they had great vogue among the leisure class in the eighteenth and nineteenth centuries. A folly is a sham ruin, labyrinth, prospect tower, hermitage, pagoda, pyramid, teahouse, or some other architectural eye-catcher added to a gentleman's estate.

7. Mark Dorrian, "On the Monstrous and the Grotesque," *Word & Image* 16, no. 3 (July–September 2000): 312.

8. Michel de Montaigne, *Selected Essays,* ed. Walter Kaiser, trans. John Florio (Boston: Houghton Mifflin, 1964), 57.

9. Sir Thomas Browne, *The Major Works,* ed. C. A. Patrides (New York: Penguin, 1977), 77.

10. W. J. T. Mitchell, *Iconology: Image, Text, Ideology* (Chicago: University of Chicago Press, 1986); and Mitchell, *Picture Theory: Essays on Verbal and Visual Representation* (Chicago: University of Chicago Press, 1994).

11. Frederick Burwick, *The Haunted Eye: Perception and the Grotesque in English and*

German Romanticism (Heidelberg: Carl Winter Universitätsverlag, 1987), 60.

12. Wolfgang Kayser, *The Grotesque in Art and Literature* (1957), trans. Ulrich Weisstein (Bloomington: Indiana University Press, 1963), 186. Kayser's consideration of the grotesque in twentieth-century culture excludes American contexts altogether. The early study in English by Thomas Wright, *A History of Caricature and Grotesque in Literature and Art* (London: Virtue Brothers, 1865), focuses on the evolution of comic and satiric modes of expression in the West from classical antiquity to 1800 without really explaining the specificity of the grotesque. Howard Daniel, *Devils, Monsters, and Nightmares: An Introduction to the Grotesque and Fantastic in Art* (New York: Abelard-Schuman, 1964) is a pictorial survey of world art and artifacts with only surface commentary about the cultural dynamics of its nearly three hundred examples. Daniel traces the origins of the grotesque primarily to "the murky depths of the unconscious and the irrational" and he gives pride of place to the Devil in the discussion (19). A few other relevant studies merit citation here. Philip Thomson's *The Grotesque* (London: Methuen, 1972) offers a brief survey of the mode in literature, explains its motivations as the product of unconscious sadism, and associates it with realism rather than with the fantastic or the uncanny. *The Grotesque in English Literature* (Oxford: Clarendon, 1965), by Arthur Clayborough, limits most of its attention to three authors before the twentieth century (Swift, Coleridge, Dickens) in working out the thesis that the grotesque is a product of polar interaction between the practical, rational side of the human mind and a fantastic or mystical sense of experience. Bernard McElroy, *Fiction of the Modern Grotesque* (London: Macmillan, 1989), which includes American examples, situates the mode largely in the realms of fantasy, dream, and hallucination. Further literary examples are treated in Michael J. Meyer, ed., *Literature and the Grotesque* (Atlanta: Rodopi, 1995). In her introduction to *Modern Art and the Grotesque* (New York: Cambridge University Press, 2003) Frances S. Connelly defines the mode in terms of dissimilarity, deformity, and metamorphosis.

13. Geoffrey Galt Harpham, *On the Grotesque: Strategies of Contradiction in Art and Literature* (Princeton, NJ: Princeton University Press, 1982), 3. Subsequent references to this work are indicated by the author's name. Mary Russo, *The Female Grotesque: Risk, Excess and Modernity* (New York: Routledge, 1995) poses the grotesque as a mode of liminality and the uncanny that at once marginalizes and fascinates. Russo asserts a feminist reading of the concept and mode as, in its origins, a misogynistic literalization of the female anatomy and an abjection of classical body ideals.

14. John Ruskin, *The Stones of Venice*, 3 vols. (London: Dent, 1907), 3:110. Subsequent references to this source are indicated by the title *Venice*.

15. John Ruskin, *Modern Painters*, ed. David Barrie (New York: Knopf, 1987), 320–21.

16. Ernst Kris and E. H. Gombrich, "The Principles of Caricature," in Kris, *Psychoanalytic Explorations in Art*, 1952 (New York: Schocken, 1964), 198.

17. Charles Baudelaire, *Selected Writings on Art and Artists*, trans. P. E. Charvet (Baltimore: Penguin, 1972), 152. Subsequent references to this source are indicated by the title *Art and Artists*.

18. See Oliver W. Larkin, *Daumier: Man of His Time* (Boston: Beacon, 1968), 26–28; and Howard P. Vincent, *Daumier and His World* (Evanston, IL: Northwestern University Press, 1968), 57–60.

19. Henry James, *French Poets and Novelists*, ed. Leon Edel (New York: Grosset and Dunlap, 1964), 60.

20. Henry James, *Picture and Text* (New York: Harper, 1893), 135, 123, 122, 135.

CHAPTER 2

1. Charles Brockden Brown, *Ormond,* ed. Mary Chapman (Orchard Park, NY: Broadview, 1999), 145.

2. Edgar Allan Poe, *Poetry and Tales,* ed. Patrick F. Quinn (New York: Library of America, 1984), 129. Subsequent references to this volume are indicated by the title *Poetry and Tales.*

3. On the subject of Poe's choice of terms for the title of the 1840 *Tales,* Daniel Hoffman in *Poe Poe Poe . . .* (Garden City, NY: Doubleday, 1972), 205–11, generalizes that they designate two imaginative categories of his fiction as a whole: the grotesque serves the function of satire and pertains mainly to social milieu, while the arabesque is the prose equivalent of a pure expression of the soul's terrors and fixations.

4. Frederick Burwick, "Edgar Allan Poe: The Sublime, the Picturesque, the Grotesque, and the Arabesque," *Amerikastudien/American Studies* 43, no. 3 (1998): 433.

5. Poe's relationship to various aspects of print culture, both in his literary career and in imagination, is the subject of Kevin J. Hayes, *Poe and the Printed Word* (New York: Cambridge University Press, 2000). While the Hayes study considers the significance of the printed page to interpretation of some Poe writings, it does not do so in terms of the tales collected in the 1840 volumes.

6. Edgar Allan Poe, "The Daguerreotype" (1840), in *Literature and Photography: Interactions, 1840–1990,* ed. Jane M. Rabb (Albuquerque: University of New Mexico Press, 1995), 5.

7. The first two phrases are used in Poe's 1846 essays on "The Literati of New York City," the third in his review of the second edition of *Twice-Told Tales* (1842). The citations are taken from Poe, *Essays and Reviews,* ed. G. R. Thompson (New York: Library of America, 1984), 1119, 577.

8. Nathaniel Hawthorne, *Nathaniel Hawthorne's Tales,* ed. James McIntosh (New York: Norton, 1987), 137. Subsequent references to this source are indicated by the title *Hawthorne's Tales.*

9. Nathaniel Hawthorne, *The House of the Seven Gables* (New York: Oxford University Press, 1991), 91.

10. Nathaniel Hawthorne, *Mosses from an Old Manse* (Boston: Houghton, Mifflin, 1882), 21. Subsequent references to this source are indicated by the title *Mosses.*

11. Herman Melville, *Redburn* (New York: Penguin, 1977), 335.

12. Herman Melville, *Moby-Dick* (Berkeley: University of California Press, 1979), 197.

13. Herman Melville, *Pierre; or, The Ambiguities* (New York: Grove, 1957), 231, 93, 114.

14. Herman Melville, *The Confidence-Man: His Masquerade,* ed. Hershel Parker (New York: Norton, 1971), 65. Subsequent references to this source are indicated by the title *Confidence-Man.*

15. Harry Levin, *The Power of Blackness: Hawthorne, Poe, Melville,* 1958 (New York: Knopf, 1976), xi.

16. Of much valuable commentary on race in American literature, I particularly recommend Toni Morrison, *Playing in the Dark: Whiteness and the Literary Imagination* (Cambridge: Harvard University Press, 1992) and Eric J. Sundquist, *To Wake the Nations: Race in the Making of American Literature* (Cambridge: Harvard University Press, 1993).

17. Leonard Cassuto, *The Inhuman Race: The Racial Grotesque in American Literature and Culture* (New York: Columbia University Press, 1997).

18. Ralph Ellison, *Invisible Man* (New York: Vintage, 1980), 217, 218. Subsequent references to this source are indicated by the title *Invisible Man*. This paradoxical dynamic is the subject of insightful discussion in Harryette Mullen, "Optic White: Blackness and the Production of Whiteness," *Diacritics* 24, nos. 2–3 (Summer–Fall 1994): 71–89, whose principal thesis is that "passing [for white] on an individual level models the cultural production of whiteness as a means of nation building and as a key to national identity" (72).

19. Mikhail Bakhtin, *Rabelais and His World* (1965), trans. Hélène Iswolsky (Cambridge: MIT Press, 1968), 19. Subsequent references to this source are indicated by the title *Rabelais*.

20. See Michael Mitchell, *Monsters of the Gilded Age: The Photographs of Charles Eisenmann* (Toronto: Gage, 1979).

21. From a statement published in the *Philadelphia Times*, 2 August 1885; the quotation is taken from Anita Ventura Mozley's "Introduction" to Eadweard Muybridge, *Complete Human and Animal Locomotion: All 781 Plates from the 1887 "Animal Locomotion,"* 3 vols. (New York: Dover, 1979), 1:xxi. Subsequent references to this source are indicated by the title *Locomotion*. Robert Bartlett Haas, *Muybridge: Man in Motion* (Berkeley: University of California Press, 1976), provides a useful account of the photographer's life and career. Most attention in the important study by Rebecca Solnit, *River of Shadows: Eadweard Muybridge and the Technological Wild West* (New York: Viking, 2003), is devoted to his life and work in California; a brief section (220–27) considers the motion studies he made in Philadelphia. Phillip Prodger in *Muybridge and the Instantaneous Photography Movement* (New York: Oxford University Press, 2003) provides a history of the technical innovations that enabled Muybridge to record a great variety of movements, some of them irregular and nonlinear.

22. See Jayne Morgan, "Eadweard Muybridge and W. S. Playfair: An Aesthetics of Neurasthenia," *History of Photography* 23, no. 3 (Autumn 1999): 225–31.

23. A. D. Coleman, *The Grotesque in Photography* (New York: Summit Books, 1977), 12.

24. Ibid., 7n, 72, 148. Some ideas of Coleman as well ones from Kayser, Harpham, and Bakhtin are adopted by contributors to the special issue "Essays on the Photographic Grotesque," *Exposure*, 31, no. 3–4 (1998). Brooks Adams, "Grotesque Photography," *Print Collector's Newsletter* 21, no. 6 (January–February 1991): 205–11, provides a survey of the mode during the 1980s.

25. For further discussion of this photographic style see Jonathan Green, ed., *The Snap-Shot* (Millerton, NY: Aperture, 1974), and Colin Westerbeck and Joel Meyerowitz, *Bystander: A History of Street Photography* (Boston: Little, Brown, 1994).

26. Henri Bergson, *Laughter* (1900), no trans., in *Comedy*, ed. Wylie Sypher (Garden City, NY: Doubleday, 1956), 67. Subsequent references to this source are indicated by the title *Laughter*. For the purposes of Martha Banta in *Barbaric Intercourse: Caricature and the Culture of Conduct, 1841–1936* (Chicago: University of Chicago Press, 2003) Bergson's definitions prove inadequate (60–61) since cultural politics in the arts of caricature and cartoon involve "the barbaric set over against the civilized" (37).

27. The accounts of the project and examples from the files, along with essays by Lawrence W. Levine and Alan Trachtenberg, in Carl Fleischhauer and Beverly W. Brannan, eds., *Documenting America, 1935–1943* (Berkeley: University of California Press, 1988) are indispensable.

28. A brief discussion of the assignment is available in Susan Harris Edwards, "Ben Shahn: A New Deal Photographer in the Old South," Ph.D. dissertation, City University of New York, 1996 (Ann Arbor, MI: UMI, 1996), 106–10. Examples of the photographer's work from the period, including two images from this assignment,

are included in Margaret R. Weiss, *Ben Shahn, Photographer: An Album from the Thirties* (New York: De Capo, 1973).

29. On the subject of race and American photographs, two very different books must be mentioned. Deborah Willis, ed., *Picturing Us: African American Identity in Photography* (New York: New Press, 1994) is a collection of reflections, often deeply personal, about the depiction through black-and-white photography of African American experience. James Allen et al., *Without Sanctuary: Lynching Photography in America* (Santa Fe, NM: Twin Palms, 2000), which includes an essay by Leon F. Litwack, examines the visual record of this crime against humanity. Many images reproduced in the book originally were postcards printed and sold by local photographers.

CHAPTER 3

1. The statement is made in a speech by Party member Karl Radek, "Contemporary World Literature and the Tasks of Proletarian Art," and it appears in A. Zhdanov et al., *Problems of Soviet Literature: Reports and Speeches at the First Soviet Writers' Conference,* ed. H. G. Scott (New York: International, 1935), 153.

2. Georg Lukács, *The Meaning of Contemporary Realism,* 1957, trans. John and Necke Mander (London: Merlin, 1963), 25–26.

3. From "Narrate or Describe?" (1936), in Georg Lukács, *Writer and Critic, and Other Essays,* ed. and trans. Arthur D. Kahn (New York: Grosset and Dunlap, 1971), 127.

4. Ibid., 190–91.

5. For an affirmative evaluation of the contributions of still photography and motion pictures to literary modernism, see Michael North, *Camera Works: Photography and the Twentieth-Century Word* (New York: Oxford University Press, 2005).

6. Based upon the citation in Walter Benjamin, "A Short History of Photography" (1931), trans. Stanley Mitchell, *Screen* 13, no. 1 (Spring 1972): 24.

7. Ibid., 25.

8. Walter Benjamin, *Illuminations,* ed. Hannah Arendt, trans. Harry Zohn (New York: Schocken, 1969), 226. An alignment of history and photography has been undertaken by Eduardo Cadava with his suggestive book *Words of Light: Theses on the Photography of History* (Princeton, NJ: Princeton University Press, 1997), which proceeds from the premise that "the state of emergency, the perpetual alarm that for Benjamin characterizes all history, corresponds with the photographic event" (3).

9. Roman Jakobson "Two Aspects of Language and Two Types of Aphasic Disturbance" (1956), in Jakobson and Morris Halle, *Fundamentals of Language,* 2d ed., rev. (The Hague: Mouton, 1980), 91, 72.

10. Roland Barthes, "The Reality Effect" (1968), in Barthes, *The Rustle of Language,* trans. Richard Howard (New York: Hill and Wang, 1986), 142, 143.

11. Susan Sontag, *On Photography* (New York: Farrar, Straus and Giroux, 1977), 22–23. Subsequent references to this source are indicated by the title *On Photography.*

12. John Berger and Jean Mohr, *Another Way of Telling* (New York: Pantheon, 1982), 89. Subsequent references to this source are indicated by the title *Telling.*

13. John Berger, *About Looking* (New York: Pantheon, 1980), 48, 29, 43.

14. The point is also made in Marx Wartofsky, "Cameras Can't See: Representation, Photography, and Human Vision," *Afterimage* 7, no. 9 (April 1980): 8–9.

15. James J. Gibson, *The Ecological Approach to Visual Perception* (Boston: Houghton, Mifflin, 1979), 220.

16. Oliver Wendell Holmes, "Sun-Painting and Sun-Sculpture," *Atlantic Monthly*, July 1861: 14. The other Holmes articles, "The Stereoscope and the Stereograph" (1859) and "Doings of the Sunbeam" (1863), are reprinted in Beaumont Newhall, ed., *Photography: Essays and Images* (New York: Museum of Modern Art, 1980), 53–77.

17. Arthur C. Danto, *Playing with the Edge: The Photographic Achievement of Robert Mapplethorpe* (Berkeley: University of California Press, 1996), 46.

18. Though they are not always in agreement over every aspect of the faculty of human vision, the principal sources for my discussion here are Gibson, *Ecological Approach*, which aims in part to rectify "the deep errors of the snapshot theory of vision" (205); Richard L. Gregory, *Eye and Brain: The Psychology of Seeing*, 3rd ed. (London: Weidenfeld and Nicolson, 1977); Richard L. Gregory et al., *The Artful Eye* (New York: Oxford University Press, 1995); and Donald D. Hoffman, *Visual Intelligence: How We Create What We See* (New York: Norton, 1998). For discussion of essential differences between the photograph image and the human experience of seeing, I recommend Maurice H. Pirenne, *Optics, Painting, and Photography* (Cambridge: Cambridge University Press, 1970); Joel Snyder and Neil Walsh Allen, "Photography, Vision, and Representation," *Critical Inquiry* 2, no. 1 (Autumn 1975): 143–69; and Joel Snyder, "Picturing Vision," *Critical Inquiry* 6, no. 3 (Spring 1980): 499–526, which is reprinted in W. J. T. Mitchell, ed., *The Language of Images* (Chicago: University of Chicago Press, 1980), 219–46.

19. Pirenne, *Optics,* 9.

20. E. H. Gombrich, "The Mask and the Face: The Perception of Physiognomic Likeness in Life and in Art," in Gombrich, Julian Hochberg, and Max Black, *Art, Perception, and Reality* (Baltimore: Johns Hopkins University Press, 1972), 32, 16. See also E. H. Gombrich, *Art and Illusion: A Study in the Psychology of Pictorial Representation* (New York: Pantheon, 1960), part 3, "The Beholder's Share," 179–287; and Gombrich, "Standards of Truth: The Arrested Image and the Moving Eye," in Mitchell, *The Language of Images*, 181–217.

21. Oscar Wilde, *The Picture of Dorian Gray and Other Selected Stories* (New York: New American Library, 1962), 39.

22. Patrick Maynard, *The Engine of Visualization: Thinking through Photography* (Ithaca, NY: Cornell University Press, 1997), 114.

23. Quoted in Suzanne Muchnic, "A Window on the World," *Los Angeles Times Calendar,* 12 January 1997: 92.

24. Clifford Geertz, "Thick Description: Toward an Interpretive Theory of Culture" (1973), in his book *The Interpretation of Cultures* (New York: Basic Books, 1973), 7, 21, 23, 6.

25. Quoted in Brooks Johnson, ed., *Photography Speaks: 66 Photographers on their Art* (New York: Aperture, 1989), 96.

26. Quoted in Green, *Snap-Shot,* 84.

27. Quoted in *Documentary Photography* (New York: Time-Life, 1972), 190.

28. Quoted in Green, *Snap-Shot,* 27.

29. André Bazin, *What Is Cinema?*, trans. Hugh Gray, vol. 1 (Berkeley: University of California Press, 1967), 14–15. In response to such claims of equivalence Kendall Walton has argued for the necessity of a distinction between the situation specific to looking at a photograph and ordinary kinds of seeing in his article "Transparent Pictures: On the Nature of Photographic Realism," *Critical Inquiry* 11, no. 2 (December 1984): 246–77.

30. Stanley Cavell, *The World Viewed: Reflections on the Ontology of Film*, enl. ed. (Cambridge: Harvard University Press, 1979), 16, 24.

31. Siegfried Kracauer, *Theory of Film: The Redemption of Physical Reality* (New

York: Oxford University Press, 1960), 3–23.

32. Siegfried Kracauer, "Photography" (1927), trans. Thomas Y. Levin, *Critical Inquiry* 19, no. 3 (Spring 1993): 427. Dagmar Barnouw provides valuable commentary on these issues in *Critical Realism: History, Photography, and the Work of Siegfried Kracauer* (Baltimore: Johns Hopkins University Press, 1994).

33. See Michael Hammond, Jane Howarth, and Russell Keat, *Understanding Phenomenology* (Oxford: Blackwell, 1991), 44–49.

34. Norton Batkin, *Photography and Philosophy* (New York: Garland, 1990), 82, 144.

35. Roland Barthes, *Camera Lucida: Reflections on Photography,* trans. Richard Howard (New York: Hill and Wang, 1981), 20. Subsequent references to this source are indicated by the title *Camera Lucida.*

36. John-Paul Sartre, *The Psychology of Imagination,* trans. not identified (New York: Citadel Press, 1948), 172. Subsequent references to this source are indicated by the title *Imagination.*

37. Barthes, *The Grain of the Voice: Interviews 1962–1980,* trans. Linda Coverdale (New York: Hill and Wang, 1985), 356.

38. Such an approach has come under strong ideological critique in recent decades by commentators on photography. Instead of the freely directed intentionality of perception that phenomenology proposes, Victor Burgin finds deep psychological determinism. See Burgin, "Photography, Phantasy, Function," in *Thinking Photography,* ed. Burgin (London: Macmillan, 1982); "Looking at Photographs," in the same collection; and "Seeing Sense," in *Language, Image, and Media,* ed. Howard Davis and Paul Walton (Oxford: Blackwell, 1983), 226–44. In *The Burden of Representation: Essays on Photographies and Histories* (Minneapolis: University of Minnesota Press, 1988), John Tagg maintains that the technical and cultural adhesions of photography mean that any given image cannot "be reduced to a phenomenological guarantee" (3). Jacques Derrida deems the claim in phenomenology of immediate contact between a perceived world and consciousness to be a fallacy since for him there is always preemption of "the eye and the world within speech," in *Speech and Phenomena, and Other Essays on Husserl's Theory of Signs,* trans. David B. Allison (Evanston, IL: Northwestern University Press, 1973), 86.

39. Maurice Merleau-Ponty, *Phenomenology of Perception* (1945), trans. Colin Smith (London: Routledge, 1962), vii. Subsequent references to this source are indicated by the title *Phenomenology.*

40. Maurice Merleau-Ponty, *Sense and Non-Sense* (1948), trans. Hubert L. Dreyfus and Patricia Allen Dreyfus (Evanston, IL: Northwestern University Press, 1964), 59, 58.

41. Edmund Husserl, "Phenomenology," *Encyclopedia Britannica,* 14th ed. (New York: Britannica, 1929), 17: 700.

42. Eugenio Donato, "Language, Vision, and Phenomenology: Merleau-Ponty as a Test Case" (1970), in Richard Macksey, ed., *Velocities of Change: Critical Essays from "MLN"* (Baltimore: Johns Hopkins University Press, 1974), 292–303, detects an absolute primacy of vision over language in Merleau-Ponty's later writings.

43. Maurice Merleau-Ponty, *The Prose of the World* (left unfinished in 1952), ed. Claude Lefort, trans. John O'Neill (Evanston, IL: Northwestern University Press, 1973), 89, 90.

44. Maurice Merleau-Ponty, *The Visible and the Invisible,* ed. Claude Lefort, trans. Alphonso Lingis (Evanston, IL: Northwestern University Press, 1968), 151. Among visual media Merleau-Ponty values painting far above all other forms for it alone can achieve a sense of "movement without displacement, a movement by vibration or

radiation." Painting can "offer to my eyes almost the same thing offered them by real movements: a series of appropriately mixed, instantaneous glimpses." The instantaneous medium of the photograph, on the other hand, provides only a solitary glimpse in which movement and time have been stopped cold. The photograph "destroys the overtaking, the overlapping, the 'metamorphosis' of time. But this is what painting, in contrast, makes visible." These statements are made in "Eye and Mind" (1961), the last publication before his death, trans. Carleton Dallery in Merleau-Ponty, *The Primacy of Perception,* ed. James M. Edie (Evanston, IL: Northwestern University Press, 1964), 184, 186.

45. In "Phenomenology of Reading," *New Literary History* 1, no. 1 (October 1969): 53–64, Georges Poulet characterizes the experience for a reader of a powerful work of literature as an encounter with "the consciousness of another . . . open to me" (54). Though it bears some resemblance to Merleau-Ponty's idea of the invisible operations of language, Poulet's conception of the role of a reader is one finally of compliant receptivity rather than active agency: "I myself, although conscious of whatever [the literary work] may be conscious of, I play a much more humble role, content to record passively" (59). There are a host of reader-response theories that utilize phenomenology in various degrees and permutations; a useful introductory anthology is Jane Tompkins, ed., *Reader-Response Criticism: from Formalism to Post-Structuralism* (Baltimore: Johns Hopkins University Press, 1980). Adopting a different course in *The Erotic Bird: Phenomenology in Literature* (Princeton, NJ: Princeton University Press, 1998) Maurice Natanson is attentive to a phenomenology *in* as distinct from *of* literature: "My interest lies in the manner in which a literary work . . . may reveal a phenomenological structure which has been formed or shaped by the literary work in which it has been confined or in which it has lain immanent" (8). Paul Ricoeur adapts phenomenology in his development of a hermeneutics, or interpretation theory, for literature. For Ricoeur issues of semantics, metaphor, and symbolism are of necessity at the center of any worthwhile practice of interpretation. A useful introduction to his work is Paul Ricoeur, *A Ricoeur Reader: Reflection and Imagination,* ed. Mario J. Valdés (Toronto: University of Toronto Press, 1991).

46. The poem is included in Wallace Stevens, *Collected Poems* (New York: Knopf, 1961).

47. Joseph Conrad, preface to *The Nigger of the "Narcissus,"* published in 1897, and reprinted as "The Condition of Art," in *The Portable Conrad,* ed. Morton Dauwen Zabel (New York: Viking, 1947), 705–710; all the quotations here are from this source.

CHAPTER 4

1. Both poems are available in William Carlos Williams, *The Collected Poems,* vol. 1 (New York: New Directions, 1986).

2. Williams, "The American Background," in *America and Alfred Stieglitz: A Collective Portrait,* ed. Waldo Frank et al. (New York: Literary Guild, 1934), 32, 18, 30. Though Williams makes no mention of specific pictures, when he credits Stieglitz with the creative achievement of "local realization," one "well understood in defined detail," he obviously has in mind the early city views and candid portraits rather than later, abstract images in the "Equivalent" series (31, 32).

3. See William L. Phillips, "How Sherwood Anderson Wrote *Winesburg, Ohio*" (1951), reprinted in Walter B. Rideout, ed., *Sherwood Anderson: A Collection of Critical Essays* (Englewood Cliffs, NJ: Prentice-Hall, 1974), 18–38; Kim Townsend, *Sherwood Anderson* (Boston: Houghton Mifflin, 1987), 107–110, 156; and Walter B. Rideout, *Sher-*

wood Anderson: A Writer in America (Madison: University of Wisconsin Press, 2006), 1:206–211. Among commentaries on *Winesburg, Ohio* opinions on the grotesque vary widely. Irving Howe in *Sherwood Anderson* (New York: William Sloane, 1951) associates the atmosphere of the book to "a buried ruin of a once vigorous society" (99) but he does not examine more specific textual and graphic practices of the grotesque. In his appraisal "Sherwood Anderson" (1941), collected in *The Liberal Imagination: Essays on Literature and Society*, 1950 (New York: Anchor, 1953), 20–31, Lionel Trilling considers the mode to have impaired severely the book's capacity to gain human insight. Edwin Fussell in his piece "*Winesburg, Ohio*: Art and Isolation" (1960), reprinted in the Rideout collection (39–48), thinks that more important to the book than the grotesque is the theme of George Willard's maturation and of the development within him of artistic intelligence and independence. A study by David Stouck on "Anderson's Expressionist Art," in *New Essays on "Winesburg, Ohio,"* ed. John W. Crowley (New York: Cambridge University Press, 1990), 27–51, correlates the grotesque mode of the stories to the work of Expressionist painters and dramatists of the period.

4. Constance Rourke, *American Humor: A Study of the National Character* (1931) (Tallahassee: Florida State University Press, 1986), 182.

5. Sherwood Anderson, *Winesburg, Ohio* (New York: Signet, 1993), 4. Subsequent references to this edition are indicated by the title *Winesburg*.

6. In the chapter "Sherwood Anderson's Little Things" to *The Reign of Wonder: Naivety and Reality in American Literature* (New York: Cambridge University Press, 1965), 205–27, Tony Tanner determines Anderson's story method to consist in the "sudden concentration on an all but static instant" and "the trapped and arrested fragment" (210, 219). Thomas Yingling's "*Winesburg, Ohio* and the End of Collective Experience," in *New Essays on "Winesburg, Ohio,"* 99–128 discusses Anderson's reactions to the passing of oral traditions of the storyteller. In the essay "Dreams of Manhood: Narrative, Gender, and History in *Winesburg, Ohio*," *Studies in American Literature* 30:2 (Autumn 2002): 229–48, Mark Whalan understands the failures of narrative totalization in the book as evidence of the impact of World War I on Anderson's views.

7. See Robert Bogdan, *Freak Show: Presenting Human Oddities for Amusement and Profit* (Chicago: University of Chicago Press, 1988), 17–20, 26–27.

8. Walt Whitman, "Song of Myself," section 14, line 6, from *Complete Poetry and Collected Prose* (New York: Library of America, 1982).

9. Thomas Mann, "Conrad's *The Secret Agent*" (1927), in Mann, *Past Masters and Other Papers*, trans. H. T. Lowe-Porter (New York: Knopf, 1933), 240–41.

10. Howard Mumford Jones and Walter B. Rideout, eds., *Letters of Sherwood Anderson* (Boston: Little, Brown, 1953), 50. Subsequent references to this source are indicated by the title *Letters*.

11. Sherwood Anderson, *Early Writings*, ed. Ray Lewis White (Kent, OH: Kent State University Press, 1989), 59. Subsequent references to this source are indicated by the title *Early Writings*. Rideout, in his biography (1:106–110), identifies some positive influences on Anderson's mature imagination from the work in advertising.

12. Sherwood Anderson, "An Apology for Crudity," *The Dial*, 8 November 1917: 437–38.

13. Sherwood Anderson, *Memoirs*, ed. Ray Lewis White (Chapel Hill: University of North Carolina Press, 1969), 353. Subsequent references to this source are indicated by the title *Memoirs*.

14. Sherwood Anderson, *A Story Teller's Story: Memoirs of Youth and Middle Age* (New York: Viking, 1969), 356. Subsequent references to this source are indicated by the title *Story Teller*.

15. William Faulkner, "Sherwood Anderson: An Appreciation" (1953), in Rideout, *Sherwood Anderson*, 167.

16. Henry Miller, "Anderson the Storyteller," *Story*, September–October 1941: 72.

17. Ben Hecht, "Go, Scholar-Gypsy!" *Story*, September–October 194: 92.

18. Gertrude Stein, *Selected Writings*, ed. Carl Van Vechten (New York: Vintage, 1972, 198. Subsequent references to this source are indicated by the title *Selected Writings*).

19. Citations from the story are based upon *The Portable Sherwood Anderson*, rev. ed., ed. Horace Gregory (New York: Penguin, 1972), 365. Subsequent references to this source are indicated by the title "The Man."

20. Sherwood Anderson, *Dark Laughter* (New York: Boni and Liveright, 1925), 62.

21. Ibid., 106.

CHAPTER 5

1. Nathanael West, "Miss Lonelyhearts and the Lamb," *Contact* 1, no. 1 (February 1932; New York: Kraus Reprint, 1967): 80–85. The relationship of this material to the novel is examined in Carter A. Daniel, "West's Revisions of *Miss Lonelyhearts*" (1963), in *Nathanael West: A Collection of Critical Essays*, ed. Jay Martin (Englewood Cliffs, NJ: Prentice-Hall, 1971), 52–65.

2. Nathanael West, *Novels and Other Writings*, ed. Sacvan Bercovitch (New York: Library of America, 1997), 59. Subsequent references to this source are indicated by the title *Novels*.

3. Jay Martin, *Nathanael West: The Art of His Life* (New York: Hayden, 1970), 64–65.

4. John Bunyan, *The Pilgrim's Progress*, rev. ed., ed. James Blanton Wharey and Roger Sharrock (New York: Oxford University Press, 1960), 15–16.

5. Included in a "Symposium on *Miss Lonelyhearts*" published in *Contempo* 3, no. 11 (25 July 1933); in Martin, *West: Essays*, 72, 73.

6. Rita Barnard, "'When You Wish Upon a Star': Fantasy, Experience, and Mass Culture in Nathanael West," *American Literature* 66, no. 2 (June 1994): 331.

7. Jonathan Veitch, *American Superrealism: Nathanael West and the Politics of Representation in the 1930s* (Madison: University of Wisconsin Press, 1997).

8. Mark Fearnow, *The American Stage and the Great Depression: A Cultural History of the Grotesque* (New York: Cambridge University Press, 1997).

9. Roland Barthes, *Mythologies*, trans. Annette Lavers (New York: Hill and Wang, 1972), 128, 159.

10. Don DeLillo, *The Body Artist* (New York: Scribner, 2001), 19, 18.

11. Hugh Sykes Davies, "American Periodicals," *The Criterion* 11, no. 45 (July 1932): 772.

12. W. H. Auden, "West's Disease" (1957), in Martin, *West: Essays*, 147, 149.

13. Martin, *Nathanael West*, 129; the source for this quotation is left undocumented.

14. Jay Martin, "Introduction," in *West: Essays*, 7; and in his biography *Nathanael West*, 231.

15. Kenneth Burke, "The Rhetoric of Hitler's 'Battle,'" *The Southern Review* 5, no. 1 (Summer 1939): 1–21; reprinted in Burke, *The Philosophy of Literary Form: Studies in Symbolic Action*, 2nd ed. (Baton Rouge: Louisiana State University Press, 1967), 192, 194.

16. The poem is included in Williams, *Collected Poems*, vol. 1.

17. Franklin D. Roosevelt, *Looking Forward* (New York: John Day, 1933), 262.

18. See J. Patrice Marandel, *François de Nomé: Mysteries of a Seventeenth-Century Neapolitan Painter* (Austin: University of Texas Press, 1991).

19. Martin, *Nathanael West*, 156. Connections with German Expressionism and specifically with Grosz are noted in Ralph Ciancio, "Laughing in Pain with Nathanael West," in Meyer, *Literature and the Grotesque*.

20. See M. Kay Flavell, *George Grosz: A Biography* (New Haven: Yale University Press, 1988), 64, 72–105.

21. George Grosz, "Self Portrait of the Artist," *Americana*, n.s. 1, no. 1 (November 1932): 22.

22. George Grosz, *A Little Yes and a Big No: The Autobiography of George Grosz*, trans. Lola Sachs Dorin (New York: Dial, 1946), 301.

23. See Martin, *Nathanael West*, 220–23, 342–53.

24. From Faulkner's letter to Bennett Cerf, in Joseph Blotner, ed., *Selected Letters of William Faulkner* (New York: Random, 1977), 69.

25. The quotation is taken from Joseph Blotner, *Faulkner: A Biography*, 2 vols. (New York: Random, 1974), 1357.

26. Quoted in Martin, *Nathanael West*, 177.

27. Fearnow, *The American Stage and the Great Depression*, 105–26.

28. Kenneth Burke, "Caldwell: Maker of Grotesques," first published in *The New Republic*, 10 April 1935; reprinted in Burke, *The Philosophy of Literary Form*, 350–60.

CHAPTER 6

1. Rosemary M. Magee, ed., *Conversations with Flannery O'Connor* (Jackson: University of Mississippi Press, 1987), 30. Subsequent references to this source are indicated by the title *Conversations*.

2. Flannery O'Connor, *Collected Works*, ed. Sally Fitzgerald (New York: Library of America, 1988), 1215. Subsequent references to this source are indicated by the title *Works*.

3. Flannery O'Connor, *The Habit of Being: Letters*, ed. Sally Fitzgerald (New York: Farrar, Straus and Giroux, 1979), 365. Subsequent references to this source are indicated by the title *Letters*.

4. As one would expect, the grotesque has been a central topic in the study of her fiction. While their emphases differ from the discussion here, worth mention are Gilbert Muller, *Nightmares and Visions: Flannery O'Connor and the Catholic Grotesque* (Athens: University of Georgia Press, 1972), which considers the mode to be her "antidote" against modern alienation and absurdity (18); Marshall Gentry in *Flannery O'Connor's Religion of the Grotesque* (Jackson: University Press of Mississippi, 1986) associates her fiction with a medieval, redemptive tradition that regards the grotesque to be a "result of the degradation of an ideal" (11); Anthony DiRenzo, *American Gargoyles: Flannery O'Connor and the Medieval Grotesque* (Carbondale: Southern Illinois University Press, 1993) sees the greatest influence of that tradition on her in a constant, paradoxical interplay of the sacred and the profane; Jon Lance Bacon, *Flannery O'Connor and Cold War Culture* (New York: Cambridge University Press, 1993), pursues political dimensions contemporary to her literary career and, specifically, her expressions of dissent from consensus views of American values and national purpose. Jean W. Cash in *Flannery O'Connor: A Life* (Knoxville: University of Tennessee Press, 2002) gives an account of O'Connor's cartoons and illustrations for student

publications (52–53, 60–62, 64, 69–72).

5. In "Understanding Iowa: Flannery O'Connor, B.A., M.F.A.," *American Literary History* 19, no. 2 (Summer 2007): 527–45, Mark McGurl considers her work as exemplary of new institutional conditions of high literature in postwar America.

6. Erich Auerbach, "'Figura'" (1944), trans. Ralph Manheim, in Auerbach, *Scenes from the Drama of European Literature* (New York: Meridian, 1959), 30. These ideas are reiterated in Auerbach, *Mimesis: The Representation of Reality in Western Literature,* trans. Willard R. Trask (Princeton, NJ: Princeton University Press, 1953), 16, 48–49, 73–76, 156–62.

7. "God-Intoxicated Hillbillies," *Time,* 29 February 1960: 118, 121.

8. Harold Bloom in the "Introduction" to his collection of criticism, *Flannery O'Connor* (New York: Chelsea House, 1986), 1–8, contends that the writer's Catholic moralism shielded her from a vital truth about her actual aesthetic practice of the grotesque, which possesses elements of Gnostic mysticism, creates a "grandeur or sublimity that shines through ruined creation, [and provides] a kind of abyss-radiance" (5). Against such claims Richard K. Cross examines the "salvation history" provided by O'Connor as a Catholic writer in his essay "Flannery O'Connor and the History behind History," in *Re-Visioning the Past: Historical Self-Reflexivity in American Short Fiction,* ed. Bernd Engler and Oliver Scheiding (Trier, Germany: Wissenschaftlicher Verlag Trier, 1998), 231–47.

9. John Hawkes, "Flannery O'Connor's Devil," *Sewanee Review* 70, no. 3 (Summer 1962): 396, 403.

10. See O'Connor, *Letters,* 455–57, 470–71.

11. Ralph C. Wood, "From Fashionable Tolerance to Unfashionable Redemption," in Bloom, *O'Connor,* 60. Also see Wood, *Flannery O'Connor and the Christ-Haunted South* (Grand Rapids, MI: Eerdmans, 2004), 93–119, 121–53.

12. Robert Coles, *Flannery O'Connor's South* (Baton Rouge: Louisiana State University Press, 1980), 44.

13. Alice Walker, *In Search of Our Mothers' Gardens* (New York: Harcourt Brace Jovanovich, 1983), 53.

14. Frederick Crews, "The Power of Flannery O'Connor," *New York Review of Books,* 26 April 1990: 54, 55. Biographer Jean Cash concludes that "O'Connor's public pronouncements on the race issue and her treatment of both black characters and themes in her fiction present a much more liberal and intellectual view than her facetiously rendered private comments" (152).

15. "Huck, Continued: Five American Writers Reflect on Twain's Novel," *New Yorker,* 26 June and 3 July 1995: 133.

CHAPTER 7

1. Weegee, *Weegee by Weegee: An Autobiography* (New York: Ziff-Davis, 1961), 15. Subsequent references to this source are indicated by the title *Weegee.*

2. The carefully researched biographical profile and chronology in Miles Barth, ed., *Weegee's World* (Boston: Bullfinch, 1997), 15–16 and 252, date the employment 1921 and identify a position that Fellig held briefly with the New York *Times* and its syndicate Wide World Photos. The Barth book places the initial year of his employment with Acme Newspictures sometime in the period 1924–1927.

3. Samuel Fuller, *A Third Face: My Tale of Writing, Fighting, and Filmmaking* (New York: Knopf, 2002), 25; the account of his New York newspaper experiences is contained on 21–65.

4. In *The New York School: Photographs 1936–1963* (New York: Stewart, Tabori, and Chang, 1992) Jane Livingston identifies a movement within photography based in the city that consisted of sixteen photographers at its core, including Weegee, Lisette Model, Louis Faurer, Helen Levitt, Diane Arbus, Robert Frank, and William Klein. Several of these photographers have an eye for the grotesque in their work, but for Livingston the defining, shared features of this photography are found elsewhere.

5. Federal Writers' Project, *New York Panorama* (New York: Random, 1938), 13, 80, 81. Subsequent references to this volume are indicated by the title *Panorama*.

6. Federal Writers' Project, *New York City Guide* (New York: Random, 1939), 167, 472, 120.

7. The phrases are taken from "On Some Motifs in Baudelaire" (1939) and "The Work of Art in the Age of Mechanical Reproduction" in Benjamin, *Illuminations*, 175, 240. Within Benjamin's consideration of photography and historiography, catastrophe and ruptures to continuity mark a zone of meaning indispensable for historical materialism.

8. Weegee, *Naked City*, 1945 (New York: Da Capo, 1985), 206.

9. Benjamin, *Illuminations*, 175.

10. Jodi Hauptman, "Flash! The Speed Graphic Camera," *The Yale Journal of Criticism* 11, no. 1 (Spring 1998): 129–37, discusses camera technology and the tabloid style of Weegee's work. This essay also likens the role of flash illumination in that style to properties of shock and the photographic in Benjamin's theses on history.

11. See J. Hoberman, "American Abstract Sensationalism," *Artforum* 19, no. 6 (February 1981): 42–49.

12. Westerbeck and Meyerowitz, *Bystander*, 335.

13. Luc Sante, *Evidence* (New York: Farrar, Straus and Giroux, 1992). The exhibition and catalogue *Police Pictures: The Photograph as Evidence* (San Francisco: San Francisco Museum of Modern Art, 1997), organized by Sandra S. Phillips, Mark Haworth-Booth, and Carol Squiers, presents a broad social and historical range of materials, reaching well beyond American metropolitan police files to incorporate lynching, execution, and assassination images and episodes such as the Paris Commune and Khmer Rouge death camps. The exhibition, which includes a few Weegee photographs, consists largely of physiognomic studies, mug shots, portraits for identity papers, wanted posters, evidence photographs, surveillance images, and postmortem photographs from coroner examinations.

14. Where Miles Orvell in "Weegee's Voyeurism and the Mastery of Urban Disorder," *American Art* 6, no. 1 (Winter 1992): 18–41, finds similarities to Nathanael West's fiction, I observe underlying differences.

15. Ellen Handy, "Picturing New York, the Naked City: Weegee and Urban Photography," in Barth, *Weegee's World*, 150, 148.

16. Alain Bergala, "Weegee and Film Noir," in Barth, *Weegee's World*, 72.

17. Beaumont Newhall, *The History of Photography from 1839 to the Present Day* (New York: Museum of Modern Art, 1949), 194–95. The sole Weegee photograph reprinted, *Tenement Fire, Brooklyn, 1939*, which shows two grief-stricken victims beside a fire truck, does not display these stated attributes nor does it receive any specific commentary where it appears, in a separate chapter (231). The book's 1964 edition retains the same evaluation (157–58) but substitutes Weegee's *The Critic*, 1943 (183), a satiric depiction of opening night at the opera.

18. Louis Stettner, ed., *Weegee* (New York: Knopf, 1977), 13.

19. Ibid., 7.

20. Earl Wilson, "Weegee," *The Saturday Evening Post*, 22 May 1943: 37.

21. From the interview "Naked Weegee," *Photograph* 1, no. 1 (Summer 1976): 24,

26, 4. Contextual indications make it apparent that the interview was conducted in the mid-1960s, though a specific date is not given.

22. David Hopkins, "Weegee and Warhol: Voyeurism, Shock and the Discourse on Criminality," *History of Photography* 25, no. 4 (Winter 2001): 358.

23. André Laude, *Weegee*, trans. Marianne Tinnell Faure (New York: Pantheon, 1986), np.

24. Margit, Zuckriegl, ed., *Weegee's Story: From the Berinson Collection* (Oxford, England: Museum of Modern Art, 1999), 6–7.

25. Colin L. Westerbeck, Jr., "Night Light: Brassaï and Weegee," *Artforum* 15, no. 4 (December 1976): 42, 41.

26. Ibid., 44.

27. John Coplans, "Weegee the Famous," *Art in America* 65, no. 5 (September–October 1977): 41.

28. Max Kozloff, "Mass Hysteria: The Photography of Weegee," *Artforum* 36, no. 7 (March 1998): 77.

29. Max Kozloff, *New York: Capital of Photography* (New Haven: Yale University Press, 2002), 45, 33.

30. Ibid., 76.

31. Hopkins, "Weegee and Warhol," 361.

32. Aaron Siskind, *Harlem Document: Photographs 1932–1940* (Providence, RI: Matrix, 1981).

33. *Time*, 23 July 1945: 71; as cited in Barth, *Weegee*, 29.

34. Weegee, *Weegee's People* (New York: Duell, Sloan and Pearce, 1946), np.

35. Weegee and Mel Harris, *Naked Hollywood* (New York: Pellegrini and Cudahy, 1953).

36. Weegee, "Here's Fun from My Bag of Camera Tricks," *Popular Mechanics Magazine*, April 1956: 127.

37. Weegee, with Roy Ald, *Weegee's Creative Camera* (Garden City, NY: Hanover House, 1959), 8.

38. Stettner, *Weegee*, 16.

39. William Klein, *In and Out of Fashion* (London: Cape, 1994), 6–7.

40. From a 1992 interview included in Livingston, *New York School*, 314.

41. William Klein, *Life is Good and Good for You in New York: Trance Witness Revels* (Paris: Seuil, 1956).

42. Livingston, *New York School*, 315.

CHAPTER 8

1. The principal sources for information on Arbus's career are Diane Arbus, *Diane Arbus: Revelations* (New York: Random, 2003), with the detailed chronology prepared by Elisabeth Sussman and Doon Arbus; Thomas W. Southall, "The Magazine Years, 1960–1971," in Arbus, *Magazine Work* (New York: Aperture, 1984), 152–71; and Partricia Bosworth, *Diane Arbus: A Biography* (New York: Avon, 1984). The Bosworth source is used with caution since it contains many undocumented factual claims and questionable characterizations of Arbus's emotional states and thought processes. One reaction to the biography by Bosworth considers it "hagiography gone berserk"; see Catherine Lord, "What Becomes a Legend Most: The Short, Sad Career of Diane Arbus" (1985), in *The Contest of Meaning: Critical Histories of Photography*, ed. Richard Bolton (Cambridge: MIT Press, 1989), 115. Another cautions that "a pall of smut hangs over the book"; see Jonathan Lieberson, "Snapshots of the Photographer," *New York*

Review of Books, 16 August 1984: 9.

2. My main sources for information on Model's life, career, and the relationship with Arbus are Ann Thomas, *Lisette Model* (Ottawa: National Gallery of Canada, 1990), and *Revelations.*

3. The quotation is taken from Livingston, *New York School,* 297.

4. I have transcribed the statement, without editorial correction, from the interview with Model in the video program, part of the Masters of Photography series, *Going Where I've Never Been: The Photography of Diane Arbus* (New York: Camera Three Productions, 1989).

5. The article is included in *Magazine Work,* 8–13, but this reprinting reverses the original order in which *Esquire* presented the Dickinson and Ratoucheff portraits. No Arbus photographs are available for reproduction in the present study due to restrictions on them; it is my hope that readers have access to the available book publications of her work.

6. Edith Sitwell, *English Eccentrics* (New York: Vanguard, 1957), 17–18, 20; the quotation Arbus cites in her letter appears on 22.

7. John Stuart Mill, *On Liberty* (1859), ed. Alburey Castell (New York: Appleton-Century-Crofts, 1947), 67.

8. See Sean Callahan, "American Photography's Greatest Primitive Has Left Us a Message," *Village Voice,* 3 November 1975: 132–33.

9. The exhibition catalog by John Szarkowski, *From the Picture Press* (New York: Museum of Modern Art, 1973) includes this acknowledgment: "A major portion of the preliminary picture research was done by the late Diane Arbus and by Carole Kismaric. The quality of the pictures reproduced here is in large measure a tribute to their eyes and understanding" (2).

10. Joseph Mitchell, *McSorley's Wonderful Saloon* (New York: Duell, Sloan and Pearce, 1943), 87–103. Subsequent references to this source are indicated by the title *Saloon.*

11. The auction catalogue Diane Arbus, *Hubert's Museum Work 1958–1963* (New York: Phillips de Pury, 2008), makes available some of this work. Gregory Gibson, *Hubert's Freaks: The Rare-Book Dealer, the Times Square Talker, and the Lost Photos of Diane Arbus* (New York: Harcourt, 2008), recreates the scene at the Museum in the 1960s and imagines Arbus's relationship to it.

12. From an interview cited in James Rogers and Norman Sims, "Joseph Mitchell," *Dictionary of Literary Biography* 185 (Detroit: Gale, 1998), 203.

13. Diane Arbus, "The Full Circle," *Infinity* 11, no. 2 (February 1962): 13.

14. Mailer's comment is recollected by Harold Hayes in his "Editor's Notes," *Esquire,* November 1971: 216.

15. Walker Evans, "Photography," in *Quality: Its Image in the Arts,* ed. Louis Kronenberger (New York: Atheneum, 1969), 172.

16. Adam Gopnick, "The Light Writer," in *Richard Avedon: Evidence 1944–1994,* ed. Mary Shanahan (New York: Random, 1994), 113.

17. Richard Avedon, *In the American West* (New York: Abrams, 1985), np.

18. Avedon's comment is included in the unsigned review "Telling It As It Is," *Newsweek,* 20 March 1967: 110.

19. Westerbeck and Meyerowitz, *Bystander,* 385.

20. The statement appears in "Diane Arbus," *Infinity* 19, no. 9 (September 1970): 16.

21. Gombrich, *Art, Perception, and Reality,* 36.

22. From an interview with Studs Terkel in December 1969, cited in Bosworth, *Arbus,* 324.

23. The gallery publication *Diane Arbus: The Libraries* (San Francisco: Fraenkel Gallery, 2004) pictures and lists books in her personal collection.

24. Erving Goffman, *The Presentation of Self in Everyday Life* (Garden City, NY: Doubleday, 1959), 22, 237. Another treatment of this connection is contained in Nigel Warburton, "Diane Arbus and Erving Goffman: The Presentation of Self," *History of Photography* 16, no. 4 (Winter 1992): 401–404.

25. Shelley Rice, "Essential Differences: A Comparison of the Portraits of Lisette Model and Diane Arbus," *Artforum* 18, no. 9 (May 1980): 68, 70, 69.

26. See, for example, Carol Shloss, "Off the (W)rack: Fashion and Pain in the Work of Diane Arbus," in *On Fashion,* ed. Shari Benstock and Suzanne Ferriss (New Brunswick, NJ: Rutgers University Press, 1994); and Ariella Budick, "Factory Seconds: Diane Arbus and the Imperfections in Mass Culture," *Art Criticism* 12, no. 2 (1997): 50–70.

27. See Jane Allen, "Charade of Losers in the Arbus World," *Chicago Tribune,* 8 April 1973: 6: 8, 10; Sean Callahan, "American Photography's Greatest Primitive Has Left Us a Message"; David Sylvester, "Flaw Show," *The Sunday Times Magazine* (London), 17 March 1974: 68–75; Mike Steele, "Visions of a Crazy World," *The Minneapolis Tribune Picture Magazine,* 6 January 1974: 20–23; Lou Stettner, "Speaking Out: Politics of Despair," *Camera 35* 17, no. 2 (March 1973): 9, 12; and Calvin Bedient, "The Hostile Camera: Diane Arbus," *Art in America* 73, no. 1 (January 1985): 11–12.

28. Ian Jeffrey, "Diane Arbus and the American Grotesque," *The Photographic Journal* 114 (May 1974): 224.

29. Heather McPherson, "Diane Arbus's Grotesque 'Human Comedy,'" *History of Photography* 19, no. 2 (Summer 1995): 118.

30. Diana Emery Hulick, "Diane Arbus's Women and Transvestites: Separate Selves," *History of Photography* 16, no. 1 (Spring 1992): 34–39; the article reaches the conclusion that "images in which the sense of the grotesque is paramount are not chosen" (38).

31. Robert Doty, *Human Concern/Personal Torment: The Grotesque in American Art* (New York: Whitney Museum of American Art, 1969).

32. Max Kozloff, "The Uncanny Portrait: Sander, Arbus, Samaras," *Artforum* 11, no. 10 (June 1973): 63, 61.

33. Max Kozloff, *The Privileged Eye: Essays on Photography* (Albuquerque: University of New Mexico Press, 1987), 99.

34. Ibid., 87.

35. Stettner, "Speaking Out: Politics of Despair," 9.

36. Jed Perl, "Not-So-Simple Simplicity," *New Republic,* 27 October 2003: 32.

37. Erving Goffman, *Stigma: Notes on the Management of Spoiled Identity* (Englewood Cliffs, NJ: Prentice-Hall, 1963), 5, 109–110. The epigraph to *Stigma* reproduces in its entirety the letter signed "Desperate" from Nathanael West's *Miss Lonelyhearts.*

38. The statements are taken from "Composition as Explanation" (1926), in Stein, *Selected Writings,* 515, 513, 514. Stein's idea of "the refused," it must be acknowledged, is mainly an aesthetic category, while it is a social one for Arbus.

39. Leslie Fiedler, *Freaks: Myths and Images of the Secret Self* (New York: Simon and Schuster, 1978), 19, 262.

40. Rachel Adams, *Sideshow U.S.A.: Freaks and the American Cultural Imagination* (Chicago: University of Chicago Press, 2001), 126.

41. Susan Sontag, "Freak Show," *New York Review of Books,* 15 November 1973: 14.

42. The *Partisan Review* article is reprinted in Susan Sontag, *Styles of Radical Will* (New York: Dell, 1978), 193–204.

43. Susan Sontag, *Regarding the Pain of Others* (New York: Farrar, Straus and Giroux, 2003), 89.

44. The Cooper portrait is included in *Magazine Work,* 92–93.

45. The statements are taken from the full interview for the 1967 "Telling It As It Is" *Newsweek* article; they are provided in Bosworth, *Arbus,* 290, 291.

46. Judith Goldman, "Diane Arbus: The Gap Between Intention and Effect," *Art Journal* 34, no. 1 (Fall 1974): 35, 33. Carol Armstrong in "Biology, Destiny, Photography: Difference According to Diane Arbus," *October,* no. 66 (Fall 1993): 29–54, approaches the matter in the interests of deconstruction and a critique of gender.

47. From "An Outline of Psycho-Analysis" (1940), in *The Standard Edition of the Complete Psychological Works of Sigmund Freud,* 24 vols., ed. James Strachey (London: Hogarth, 1953), 23: 183. Subsequent references to this source are indicated by the abbreviation *SE.*

48. As reported in an interview with Yee; Bosworth, *Arbus,* 274.

49. "*Hypocrite lecture,—mon semblable,—mon frère!.*"

CONCLUSION

1. In a letter dated 14 September 1963 O'Connor reflects: "I am reading *Eichmann in Jerusalem.* . . . Anything is credible after such a period of history. I've always been haunted by the boxcars, but they were actually the least of it" (*Letters,* 539).

2. Carson McCullers, *The Heart is a Lonely Hunter* (New York: Bantam, 1968), 175.

3. Hawkes, "O'Connor's Devil," 397.

4. See Patrick O'Donnell, "Life and Art: An Interview with John Hawkes," *The Review of Contemporary Fiction* 3, no. 3 (Fall 1983): 107–26.

5. Kurt Vonnegut, *Slaughterhouse-Five* (New York: Delacorte, 1969), 20.

6. Anderson, *Portable Anderson,* 347.

7. Rick Moody, *Demonology* (New York: Little, Brown, 2000), 72, 80.

8. Biographical information is provided in Barbara Tannebaum, "Fiction as a Higher Truth," in *Ralph Eugene Meatyard: An American Visionary,* ed. Tannebaum (New York: Rizzoli, 1991), 13–51.

9. Ralph Eugene Meatyard, *The Family Album of Lucybelle Crater* (Millerton, NY: The Jargon Society, 1974), 73, 76. The original quotation is to be found in Max Picard, *The Human Face,* trans. Guy Endore (London: Cassell, 1931), 10.

10. As reported in Jonathan Green, *American Photography: A Critical History, 1945 to the Present* (New York: Abrams, 1984), 124.

11. The original statement is found in O'Connor, *Mystery,* 34–35.

12. Shelby Lee Adams, *Appalachian Portraits* (Jackson: University of Mississippi Press, 1993), 11.

13. Nan Goldin, *I'll Be Your Mirror* (New York: Scalo, 1996), 137.

14. "Man Confesses to Eating Internet Acquaintance," *Los Angeles Times,* 4 December 2003· 1, 13.

15. Roger Boyes, "Cannibal's Video Reveals Mutilation and Slaughter," *The Times* (London), 9 December 2003: 13.

16. Charles Darwin, *The Origin of Species* (New York: Modern Library, 1936), 39, 38.

17. As cited in Stanley B. Burns, *Early Medical Photography in America (1839–1883)* (New York: Burns Archive, 1983), 1934; the book reprints seven articles by Burns first published in the *New York State Journal of Medicine* in 1979–1981.

18. Bruno Bettelheim, *The Uses of Enchantment: The Meaning and Importance of Fairy Tales* (New York: Knopf, 1976), 121.

19. Representative of this approach are Barbara M. Benedict, *Curiosity: A Cultural History of Early Modern Inquiry* (Chicago: University of Chicago Press, 2001); Barbara Maria Stafford, *Body Criticism: Imaging the Unseen in Enlightenment Art and Medicine* (Cambridge: MIT Press, 1991); Julia V. Douthwaite, *The Wild Girl, Natural Man, and the Monster: Dangerous Experiments in the Age of Enlightenment* (Chicago: University of Chicago Press, 2002); Marina Warner, *Managing Monsters: Six Myths of Our Time* (London: Vintage, 1994); and Edward J. Ingebretsen, *At Stake: Monsters and the Rhetoric of Fear in Public Culture* (Chicago: University of Chicago Press, 2001).

20. Marie-Hélène Huet, *Monstrous Imagination* (Cambridge: Harvard University Press, 1993), advances this thesis.

21. Exemplary of this approach are Jeffrey Jerome Cohen, ed., *Monster Theory: Reading Culture* (Minneapolis: University of Minnesota Press, 1996); and Judith Halberstam, *Skin Shows: Gothic Horror and the Technology of Monsters* (Durham: Duke University Press, 1995). Helen Deutsch in *Resemblance and Disgrace: Alexander Pope and the Deformation of Culture* (Cambridge: Harvard University Press, 1996) makes judicious use of deconstruction in reaching an understanding of Pope's neoclassicism and satire.

22. Robert Hughes, *Goya* (New York: Knopf, 2003), 171.

23. My translation from Goya's commentary, included in F. J. Sanchez Canton, *Los Caprichos de Goya* (Barcelona: Instituto Amatller de Arte Hispanico, 1949), 87.

24. Allan I. Ludwig, *Repulsion: Aesthetics of the Grotesque* (New York: Alternative Museum, 1986), 4. Subsequent references to this source are indicated by the title *Repulsion.*

25. Mark Dery, "Lost in the Funhouse," *World Art*, no. 2 (1995): 51. Hal Foster in "Obscene, Abject, Traumatic," *October*, no. 78 (Fall 1996): 107–24, finds in contemporary art and theory a general shift in the conception of reality, *"from the real understood as an effect of representation to the real understood as an event of trauma,"* which he also attributes partly to "the persistent AIDS crisis, invasive disease and death" (107, 122; his emphasis). But Foster ultimately questions the effectiveness of concepts like trauma and the abject in understanding the cultural and political infrastructures of that reality.

26. Erin O'Connor, "Camera Medica: Towards a Morbid History of Photography," *History of Photography* 23, no. 3 (Autumn 1999): 238. See also Bret Wood, "Photo Mortis: Resurrecting Photographs of Crime and Death," *Art Papers* 24, no. 2 (March–April 2000): 18–23.

27. Quoted in Hal Fischer, "Joel-Peter Witkin: The Dark End of the Spectrum," *Fotografie*, no. 32/33 (1984): 32.

28. *Arbus*, 1; Fischer, "Witkin," 34.

29. Joel-Peter Witkin, *Joel-Peter Witkin, disciple et maître* (Paris: Marval, 2000), 19; my translation from the French.

30. Witkin, "Joel-Peter Witkin," *Transcript* 1, no. 3 (1995): 49.

31. Taken from statements published under the title "Revolt" in Germano Celant, *Witkin*, trans. Stephen Sartarelli (New York: Scalo, 1995), 51.

32. Emmanuel Levinas, "Ethics and the Face" (1961), in *The Phenomenology Reader*, ed. Dermot Moran and Timothy Mooney (New York: Routledge, 2002), 516. Subsequent references to this source are indicated by the title "Ethics."

33. Fischer, "Witkin," 32.

34. Witkin, *Joel-Peter Witkin* (Pasadena, CA: Twelvetrees Press, 1985), np.

WORKS CITED

Adams, Brooks. "Grotesque Photography." *Print Collector's Newsletter* 21, no. 6 (January–February 1991): 205–211.

Adams, Rachel. *Sideshow U.S.A.: Freaks and the American Cultural Imagination.* Chicago: University of Chicago Press, 2001.

Adams, Shelby Lee. *Appalachian Legacy.* Jackson: University of Mississippi Press, 1998.

———. *Appalachian Lives.* Jackson: University of Mississippi Press, 2003.

———. *Appalachian Portraits.* Jackson: University of Mississippi Press, 1993.

Allen, James et al. *Without Sanctuary: Lynching Photography in America.* Santa Fe, NM: Twin Palms, 2000.

Allen, Jane. "Charade of Losers in the Arbus World." *Chicago Tribune,* 8 April 1973: section 6: 8, 10.

Anderson, Sherwood. "An Apology for Crudity." *The Dial* 8 (November 1917): 437–38.

———. *Dark Laughter.* New York: Boni and Liveright, 1925.

———. *Early Writings.* Edited by Ray Lewis White. Kent, OH: Kent State University Press, 1989.

———. *Memoirs,* Edited by Ray Lewis White. Chapel Hill: University of North Carolina Press, 1969.

———. *The Portable Sherwood Anderson.* Rev. ed. Edited by Horace Gregory. New York: Penguin, 1972.

———. *A Story Teller's Story: Memoirs of Youth and Middle Age.* New York: Viking, 1969.

———. *Winesburg, Ohio.* New York: Signet, 1993.

Arbus, Diane. "Diane Arbus." *Infinity* 19, no. 9 (September 1970): 16–17.

———. *Diane Arbus.* New York: Aperture, 1972.

———. *Diane Arbus: Revelations.* New York: Random, 2003.

———. *Diane Arbus: The Libraries.* San Francisco. Fraenkel Gallery, 2004.

———. "The Full Circle." *Infinity* 11, no. 2 (February 1962): 4–13, 19, 21.

———. *Hubert's Museum Work 1958–1963.* New York: Phillips de Pury, 2008.

———. *Magazine Work.* New York: Aperture, 1984.

———. *Untitled.* New York: Aperture, 1995.

Armstrong, Carol. "Biology, Destiny, Photography: Difference According to Diane Arbus." *October,* no. 66 (Fall 1993): 29–54.

Auerbach, Erich. *Mimesis: The Representation of Reality in Western Literature.* Translated by Willard R. Trask. Princeton, NJ: Princeton University Press, 1953.

———. *Scenes from the Drama of European Literature.* New York: Meridian, 1959.

Avedon, Richard. *In the American West.* New York: Abrams, 1985.

Bacon, Jon Lance. *Flannery O'Connor and Cold War Culture.* New York: Cambridge University Press, 1993.

Bakhtin, Mikhail. *Rabelais and His World.* Translated by Hélène Iswolsky. Cambridge: MIT Press, 1968.

Banta, Martha. *Barbaric Intercourse: Caricature and the Culture of Conduct, 1841–1936.* Chicago: University of Chicago Press, 2003.

Barnard, Rita. "'When You Wish upon a Star': Fantasy, Experience, and Mass Culture in Nathanael West." *American Literature* 66, no. 2 (June 1994): 325–51.

Barnouw, Dagmar. *Critical Realism: History, Photography, and the Work of Siegfried Kracauer.* Baltimore: Johns Hopkins University Press, 1994.

Barth, Miles, ed. *Weegee's World.* Boston: Bullfinch, 1997.

Barthes, Roland. *Camera Lucida: Reflections on Photography.* Translated by Richard Howard. New York: Hill and Wang, 1981.

———. *The Grain of the Voice: Interviews 1962–1980.* Translated by Linda Coverdale. New York: Hill and Wang, 1985.

———. *Mythologies.* Translated by Annette Lavers. New York: Hill and Wang, 1972.

———. *The Rustle of Language.* Translated by Richard Howard. New York: Hill and Wang, 1986.

Batkin, Norton. *Photography and Philosophy.* New York: Garland, 1990.

Baudelaire, Charles. *Selected Writings on Art and Artists.* Translated by P. E. Charvet. Baltimore: Penguin, 1972.

Bazin, André. *What Is Cinema?* Vol. 1. Translated by Hugh Gray. Berkeley: University of California Press, 1967.

Bedient, Calvin. "The Hostile Camera: Diane Arbus." *Art in America* 73, no. 1 (January 1985): 11–12.

Benedict, Barbara M. *Curiosity: A Cultural History of Early Modern Inquiry.* Chicago: University of Chicago Press, 2001.

Benjamin, Walter. *Illuminations.* Edited by Hannah Arendt. Translated by Harry Zohn. New York: Schocken, 1969.

———. "A Short History of Photography." Translated by Stanley Mitchell. *Screen* 13, no. 1 (Spring 1972): 5–26.

Benstock, Shari, and Suzanne Ferriss, eds. *On Fashion.* New Brunswick, NJ: Rutgers University Press, 1994.

Berger, John. *About Looking.* New York: Pantheon, 1980.

Berger, John, and Jean Mohr. *Another Way of Telling.* New York: Pantheon, 1982.

Bergson, Henri. *Laughter.* In *Comedy.* Edited by Wylie Sypher. Garden City, NY: Doubleday, 1956.

Bettelheim, Bruno. *The Uses of Enchantment: The Meaning and Importance of Fairy Tales.* New York: Knopf, 1976.

Bloom, Harold, ed. *Flannery O'Connor.* New York: Chelsea House, 1986.

Blotner, Joseph. *Faulkner: A Biography.* 2 vols. New York: Random, 1974.

———, ed. *Selected Letters of William Faulkner.* New York: Random, 1977.

Bogdan, Robert. *Freak Show: Presenting Human Oddities for Amusement and Profit.* Chicago: University of Chicago Press, 1988.

Bolton, Richard, ed. *The Contest of Meaning: Critical Histories of Photography.* Cambridge: MIT Press, 1989.

Bosworth, Partricia. *Diane Arbus: A Biography*. New York: Avon, 1984.

Boyes, Roger. "Cannibal's Video Reveals Mutilation and Slaughter." *The Times* (London), 9 December 2003: 13.

Brown, Charles Brockden. *Ormond*. Edited by Mary Chapman. Orchard Park, NY: Broadview, 1999.

Browne, Sir Thomas. *The Major Works*. Edited by C. A. Patrides. New York: Penguin, 1977.

Budick, Ariella. "Factory Seconds: Diane Arbus and the Imperfections in Mass Culture." *Art Criticism* 12, no. 2 (1997): 50–70.

Bunyan, John. *The Pilgrim's Progress*. Rev. ed. Edited by James Blanton Wharey and Roger Sharrock. New York: Oxford University Press, 1960.

Burgin, Victor, ed. *Thinking Photography*. London: Macmillan, 1982.

Burke, Kenneth. *Attitudes toward History*. 3rd ed. Berkeley: University of California Press, 1984.

———. *The Philosophy of Literary Form: Studies in Symbolic Action*. 2nd ed. Baton Rouge: Louisiana State University Press, 1967.

Burns, Stanley B. *Early Medical Photography in America (1839–1883)*. New York: Burns Archive, 1983.

Burwick, Frederick. "Edgar Allan Poe: The Sublime, the Picturesque, the Grotesque, and the Arabesque." *Amerikastudien/American Studies* 43, no. 3 (1998): 423–36.

———. *The Haunted Eye: Perception and the Grotesque in English and German Romanticism*. Heidelberg: Carl Winter Universitätsverlag, 1987.

Cadava, Eduardo. *Words of Light: Theses on the Photography of History*. Princeton, NJ: Princeton University Press, 1997.

Callahan, Sean. "American Photography's Greatest Primitive Has Left Us a Message." *Village Voice*, 3 November 1975: 132–33.

Canton, Sanchez F. J. *Los Caprichos de Goya*. Barcelona: Instituto Amatller de Arte Hispanico, 1949.

Cash, Jean W. *Flannery O'Connor: A Life*. Knoxville: University of Tennessee Press, 2002.

Cassuto, Leonard. *The Inhuman Race: The Racial Grotesque in American Literature and Culture*. New York: Columbia University Press, 1997.

Cavell, Stanley. *The World Viewed: Reflections on the Ontology of Film*. Enl. ed. Cambridge: Harvard University Press, 1979.

Celant, Germano. *Witkin*. Translated by Stephen Sartarelli. New York: Scalo, 1995.

Clayborough, Arthur. *The Grotesque in English Literature*. Oxford: Clarendon, 1965.

Cohen, Jeffrey Jerome, ed. *Monster Theory: Reading Culture*. Minneapolis: University of Minnesota Press, 1996.

Coleman, A. D. *The Grotesque in Photography*. New York: Summit Books, 1977.

Coles, Robert. *Flannery O'Connor's South*. Baton Rouge: Louisiana State University Press, 1980.

Connelly, Frances S., ed. *Modern Art and the Grotesque*. New York: Cambridge University Press, 2003.

Conrad, Joseph. *The Portable Conrad*. Edited by Morton Dauwen Zabel. New York: Viking, 1947.

Coplans, John. "Weegee the Famous." *Art in America* 65, no. 5 (September–October 1977): 37–41.

Crews, Frederick. "The Power of Flannery O'Connor." *New York Review of Books*, 26 April 1990: 49–55.

Crews, Harry. *The Gypsy's Curse*. New York: Knopf, 1974.

Crowley, John W., ed. *New Essays on "Winesburg, Ohio."* New York: Cambridge University Press, 1990.

Dacos, Nicole. *La découverte de la Domus Aurea et la formation des grotesques à la Renaissance.* London: Warburg Institute, 1969.

Daniel, Howard. *Devils, Monsters, and Nightmares: An Introduction to the Grotesque and Fantastic in Art.* New York: Abelard-Schuman, 1964.

Danto, Arthur C. *Playing with the Edge: The Photographic Achievement of Robert Mapplethorpe.* Berkeley: University of California Press, 1996.

Darwin, Charles. *The Origin of Species.* New York: Modern Library, 1936.

Davies, Hugh Sykes. "American Periodicals." *The Criterion* 11, no. 45 (July 1932): 772.

Davis, Howard, and Paul Walton, eds. *Language, Image, and Media.* Oxford: Blackwell, 1983.

DeLillo, Don. *The Body Artist.* New York: Scribner, 2001.

Derrida, Jacques. *Speech and Phenomena, and Other Essays on Husserl's Theory of Signs.* Translated by David B. Allison. Evanston, IL: Northwestern University Press, 1973.

Dery, Mark. "Lost in the Funhouse." *World Art,* no. 2 (1995): 46–51.

Deutsch, Helen. *Resemblance and Disgrace: Alexander Pope and the Deformation of Culture.* Cambridge: Harvard University Press, 1996.

DiRenzo, Anthony. *American Gargoyles: Flannery O'Connor and the Medieval Grotesque.* Carbondale: Southern Illinois University Press, 1993.

Documentary Photography. New York: Time-Life, 1972.

Dorrian, Mark. "On the Monstrous and the Grotesque." *Word & Image* 16, no. 3 (July–September 2000): 310–17.

Doty, Robert. *Human Concern/Personal Torment: The Grotesque in American Art.* New York: Whitney Museum of American Art, 1969.

Douthwaite, Julia V. *The Wild Girl, Natural Man, and the Monster: Dangerous Experiments in the Age of Enlightenment.* Chicago: University of Chicago Press, 2002.

Dunn, Katherine. *Geek Love.* New York: Knopf, 1989.

Edwards, Susan Harris. "Ben Shahn: A New Deal Photographer in the Old South." Ph.D. diss., City University of New York, 1996. Ann Arbor, MI: University Microfilms, 1996.

Ellison, Ralph. *Invisible Man.* New York: Vintage, 1980.

Engler, Bernd, and Oliver Scheiding, eds. *Re-Visioning the Past: Historical Self-Reflexivity in American Short Fiction.* Trier, Germany: Wissenschaftlicher Verlag Trier, 1998.

"Essays on the Photographic Grotesque." *Exposure* 31, no. 3–4 (1998).

Evans, Walker. "Photography." In *Quality: Its Image in the Arts.* Edited by Louis Kronenberger. New York: Atheneum, 1969.

Fearnow, Mark. *The American Stage and the Great Depression: A Cultural History of the Grotesque.* New York: Cambridge University Press, 1997.

Federal Writers' Project. *New York City Guide.* New York: Random, 1939.

———. *New York Panorama.* New York: Random, 1938.

Fiedler, Leslie. *Freaks: Myths and Images of the Secret Self.* New York: Simon and Schuster, 1978.

Fischer, Hal. "Joel-Peter Witkin: The Dark End of the Spectrum." *Fotografie,* no. 32/33 (1984): 30–37.

Flavell, M. Kay. *George Grosz: A Biography.* New Haven: Yale University Press, 1988.

Fleischhauer, Carl, and Beverly W. Brannan, eds. *Documenting America, 1935–1943.* Berkeley: University of California Press, 1988.

Foster, Hal. "Obscene, Abject, Traumatic." *October,* no. 78 (Fall 1996): 107–24.

Frank, Waldo et al., eds. *America and Alfred Stieglitz: A Collective Portrait.* New York: Literary Guild, 1934.

Freud, Sigmund. *The Standard Edition of the Complete Psychological Works of Sigmund Freud.* 24 vols. Edited by James Strachey. London: Hogarth, 1953.

Fuller, Samuel. *A Third Face: My Tale of Writing, Fighting, and Filmmaking.* New York: Knopf, 2002.

Geertz, Clifford. *The Interpretation of Cultures.* New York: Basic Books, 1973.

Gentry, Marshall. *Flannery O'Connor's Religion of the Grotesque.* Jackson: University Press of Mississippi, 1986.

Gibson, Gregory. *Hubert's Freaks: The Rare-Book Dealer, the Times Square Talker, and the Lost Photos of Diane Arbus.* New York: Harcourt, 2008.

Gibson, James J. *The Ecological Approach to Visual Perception.* Boston: Houghton, Mifflin, 1979.

"God-Intoxicated Hillbillies." *Time,* 29 February 1960: 118, 121.

Goffman, Erving. *The Presentation of Self in Everyday Life.* Garden City, NY: Doubleday, 1959.

———. *Stigma: Notes on the Management of Spoiled Identity.* Englewood Cliffs, NJ: Prentice-Hall, 1963.

Goldin, Nan. *The Ballad of Sexual Dependency.* New York: Aperture, 1986.

———. *I'll Be Your Mirror.* New York: Scalo, 1996.

Goldman, Judith. "Diane Arbus: The Gap Between Intention and Effect." *Art Journal* 34, no. 1 (Fall 1974): 30–35.

Gombrich, E. H. *Art and Illusion: A Study in the Psychology of Pictorial Representation.* New York: Pantheon, 1960.

———. *The Sense of Order: A Study in the Psychology of Decorative Art.* Ithaca, NY: Cornell University Press, 1979.

Gombrich, E. H., Julian Hochberg, and Max Black. *Art, Perception, and Reality.* Baltimore: Johns Hopkins University Press, 1972.

Green, Jonathan. *American Photography: A Critical History, 1945 to the Present.* New York: Abrams, 1984.

———, ed. *The Snap-Shot.* Millerton, NY: Aperture, 1974.

Gregory, Richard L. *Eye and Brain: The Psychology of Seeing.* 3rd ed. London: Weidenfeld and Nicolson, 1977.

——— et al. *The Artful Eye.* New York: Oxford University Press, 1995.

Gresham, William Lindsay. *Nightmare Alley.* New York: Rinehart, 1946.

Grosz, George. *A Little Yes and a Big No: The Autobiography of George Grosz.* Translated by Lola Sachs Dorin. New York: Dial, 1946.

———. "Self Portrait of the Artist." *Americana,* n.s. 1, no. 1 (November 1932): 22.

Haas, Robert Bartlett. *Muybridge: Man in Motion.* Berkeley: University of California Press, 1976.

Halberstam, Judith. *Skin Shows: Gothic Horror and the Technology of Monsters.* Durham, NC: Duke University Press, 1995.

Hammond, Michael, Jane Howarth, and Russell Keat. *Understanding Phenomenology.* Oxford: Blackwell, 1991.

Harpham, Geoffrey Galt. *On the Grotesque: Strategies of Contradiction in Art and Literature.* Princeton, NJ: Princeton University Press, 1982.

Hauptman, Jodi. "Flash! The Speed Graphic Camera." *The Yale Journal of Criticism* 11, no. 1 (Spring 1998): 129–37.

Hawkes, John. "Flannery O'Connor's Devil." *Sewanee Review* 70, no. 3 (Summer 1962): 395–407.

————. *The Lime Twig.* New York: New Directions, 1961.

Hawthorne, Nathaniel. *The House of the Seven Gables.* New York: Oxford University Press, 1991.

————. *Mosses from an Old Manse.* Boston: Houghton, Mifflin, 1882.

————. *Nathaniel Hawthorne's Tales.* Edited by James McIntosh. New York: Norton, 1987.

Hayes, Harold. "Editor's Notes." *Esquire,* November 1971: 8, 216.

Hayes, Kevin J. *Poe and the Printed Word.* New York: Cambridge University Press, 2000.

Hecht, Ben. "Go, Scholar-Gypsy!" *Story,* September–October 1941: 92–93.

Hoberman, J. "American Abstract Sensationalism." *Artforum* 19, no. 6 (February 1981): 42–49.

Hoffman, Daniel. *Poe Poe Poe* . . . Garden City, NY: Doubleday, 1972.

Hoffman, Donald D. *Visual Intelligence: How We Create What We See.* New York: Norton, 1998.

Holmes, Oliver Wendell. "Sun-Painting and Sun-Sculpture." *Atlantic Monthly,* July 1861, 14.

Hopkins, David. "Weegee and Warhol: Voyeurism, Shock and the Discourse on Criminality." *History of Photography* 25, no. 4 (Winter 2001): 357–67.

Howe, Irving. *Sherwood Anderson.* New York: William Sloane, 1951.

"Huck, Continued: Five American Writers Reflect on Twain's Novel." *New Yorker,* 26 June and 3 July 1995: 130–33.

Huet, Marie-Hélène. *Monstrous Imagination.* Cambridge: Harvard University Press, 1993.

Hughes, Robert. *Goya.* New York: Knopf, 2003.

————. "To Hades with Lens." *Time,* 13 November 1972: 83–84.

Hulick, Diana Emery. "Diane Arbus's Women and Transvestites: Separate Selves." *History of Photography* 16, no. 1 (Spring 1992): 34–39.

Husserl, Edmund. "Phenomenology." In *Encyclopedia Britannica.* 14th ed. New York: Britannica, 1929.

Ingebretsen, Edward J. *At Stake: Monsters and the Rhetoric of Fear in Public Culture.* Chicago: University of Chicago Press, 2001.

Jakobson, Roman, and Morris Halle. *Fundamentals of Language.* 2nd ed. The Hague: Mouton, 1980.

James, Henry. *French Poets and Novelists.* Edited by Leon Edel. New York: Grosset and Dunlap, 1964.

————. *Picture and Text.* New York: Harper, 1893.

Jeffrey, Ian. "Diane Arbus and the American Grotesque." *The Photographic Journal* 114 (May 1974): 224–29.

Johnson, Brooks, ed. *Photography Speaks: 66 Photographers on their Art.* New York: Aperture, 1989.

Jones, Barbara. *Follies and Grottoes.* London: Constable, 1974.

Jones, Howard Mumford, and Walter B. Rideout, eds. *Letters of Sherwood Anderson.* Boston: Little, Brown, 1953.

Kayser, Wolfgang. *The Grotesque in Art and Literature.* Translated by Ulrich Weisstein. Bloomington: Indiana University Press, 1963.

Klein, William. *In and Out of Fashion.* London: Cape, 1994.

————. *Life is Good and Good for You in New York: Trance Witness Revels.* Paris: Seuil, 1956.

Kozloff, Max. "Mass Hysteria: The Photography of Weegee." *Artforum* 36, no. 7 (March 1998): 76–81.

———. *New York: Capital of Photography*. New Haven: Yale University Press, 2002.

———. *The Privileged Eye: Essays on Photography*. Albuquerque: University of New Mexico Press, 1987.

———. "The Uncanny Portrait: Sander, Arbus, Samaras." *Artforum* 11, no. 10 (June 1973): 58–66.

Kracauer, Siegfried. "Photography." Translated by Thomas Y. Levin. *Critical Inquiry* 19, no. 3 (Spring 1993): 421–36.

———. *Theory of Film: The Redemption of Physical Reality*. New York: Oxford University Press, 1960.

Krims, Les. *The Little People of America*. Artist's limited edition, 1971.

Kris, Ernst. *Psychoanalytic Explorations in Art*. New York: Schocken, 1964.

Larkin, Oliver W. *Daumier: Man of His Time*. Boston: Beacon, 1968.

Laude, André. *Weegee*. Translated by Marianne Tinnell Faure. New York: Pantheon, 1986.

Levin, Harry. *The Power of Blackness: Hawthorne, Poe, Melville*. New York: Knopf, 1976.

Levinas, Emmanuel. "Ethics and the Face." In *The Phenomenology Reader*. Edited by Dermot Moran and Timothy Mooney. New York: Routledge, 2002.

Lieberson, Jonathan. "Snapshots of the Photographer." *New York Review of Books*, 16 August 1984: 9–12.

Livingston, Jane. *The New York School: Photographs 1936–1963*. New York: Stewart, Tabori, and Chang, 1992.

Ludwig, Allan I. *Repulsion: Aesthetics of the Grotesque*. New York: Alternative Museum, 1986.

Lukács, Georg. *The Meaning of Contemporary Realism*. Translated by John and Necke Mander. London: Merlin, 1963.

———. *Writer and Critic, and Other Essays*. Edited and translated by Arthur D. Kahn. New York: Grosset and Dunlap, 1971.

Macksey, Richard, ed. *Velocities of Change: Critical Essays from "MLN."* Baltimore: Johns Hopkins University Press, 1974.

Magee, Rosemary M., ed. *Conversations with Flannery O'Connor*. Jackson: University of Mississippi Press, 1987.

"Man Confesses to Eating Internet Acquaintance." *Los Angeles Times*, 4 December 2003: section 1: 13.

Mann, Thomas. *Past Masters and Other Papers*. Translated by H. T. Lowe-Porter. New York: Knopf, 1933.

Marandel, J. Patrice. *François de Nomé: Mysteries of a Seventeenth-Century Neapolitan Painter*. Austin: University of Texas Press, 1991.

Mark, Mary Ellen. *Twins*. New York: Aperture, 2003.

Martin, Jay. *Nathanael West: The Art of His Life*. New York: Hayden, 1970.

———, ed. *Nathanael West: A Collection of Critical Essays*. Englewood Cliffs, NJ: Prentice-Hall, 1971.

Mason, Bobbie Ann. *Feather Crowns*. New York: HarperCollins, 1993.

Masters of Photography. *Going Where I've Never Been: The Photography of Diane Arbus*. New York: Camera Three Productions, 1989.

Maynard, Patrick. *The Engine of Visualization: Thinking through Photography*. Ithaca, NY: Cornell University Press, 1997.

McCullers, Carson. *The Heart is a Lonely Hunter*. New York: Bantam, 1968.

McElroy, Bernard. *Fiction of the Modern Grotesque*. London: Macmillan, 1989.

McGurl, Mark. "Understanding Iowa: Flannery O'Connor, B.A., M.F.A." *American Literary History* 19, no. 2 (Summer 2007): 527–45.

McPherson, Heather. "Diane Arbus's Grotesque 'Human Comedy.'" *History of Photography* 19, no. 2 (Summer 1995): 117–20.

Meatyard, Ralph Eugene. *The Family Album of Lucybelle Crater.* Millerton, NY: The Jargon Society, 1974.

Melville, Herman. *The Confidence-Man: His Masquerade.* Edited by Hershel Parker. New York: Norton, 1971.

———. *Moby-Dick.* Berkeley: University of California Press, 1979.

———. *Pierre; or, The Ambiguities.* New York: Grove, 1957.

———. *Redburn.* New York: Penguin, 1977.

Merleau-Ponty, Maurice. *Phenomenology of Perception.* Translated by Colin Smith. London: Routledge, 1962.

———. *The Primacy of Perception.* Edited by James M. Edie. Evanston, IL: Northwestern University Press, 1964.

———. *The Prose of the World.* Edited by Claude Lefort. Translated by John O'Neill. Evanston, IL: Northwestern University Press, 1973.

———. *Sense and Non-Sense.* Translated by Hubert L. Dreyfus and Patricia Allen Dreyfus. Evanston, IL: Northwestern University Press, 1964.

———. *The Visible and the Invisible.* Edited by Claude Lefort. Translated by Alphonso Lingis. Evanston, IL: Northwestern University Press, 1968.

Meyer, Michael J., ed. *Literature and the Grotesque.* Atlanta: Rodopi, 1995.

Mill, John Stuart. *On Liberty.* Edited by Alburey Castell. New York: Appleton-Century-Crofts, 1947.

Miller, Henry. "Anderson the Storyteller." *Story,* September–October 1941: 70–74.

Miller, Naomi. *Heavenly Caves: Reflections on the Garden Grotto.* New York: Braziller, 1982.

Mitchell, Joseph. *McSorley's Wonderful Saloon.* New York: Duell, Sloan and Pearce, 1943.

Mitchell, Michael. *Monsters of the Gilded Age: The Photographs of Charles Eisenmann.* Toronto: Gage, 1979.

Mitchell, W. J. T. *Iconology: Image, Text, Ideology.* Chicago: University of Chicago Press, 1986.

———. *Picture Theory: Essays on Verbal and Visual Representation.* Chicago: University of Chicago Press, 1994.

———, ed. *The Language of Images.* Chicago: University of Chicago Press, 1980.

Montaigne. *Selected Essays.* Edited by Walter Kaiser. Translated by John Florio. Boston: Houghton Mifflin, 1964.

Moody, Rick. *Demonology.* New York: Little, Brown, 2000.

Morgan, Jayne. "Eadweard Muybridge and W. S. Playfair: An Aesthetics of Neurasthenia." *History of Photography* 23, no. 3 (Autumn 1999): 225–31.

Morrison, Toni. *Playing in the Dark: Whiteness and the Literary Imagination.* Cambridge: Harvard University Press, 1992.

Muchnic, Suzanne. "A Window on the World." *Los Angeles Times,* 12 January 1997: Calendar section: 7, 92.

Mullen, Harryette. "Optic White: Blackness and the Production of Whiteness." *Diacritics* 24, no. 2–3 (Summer–Fall 1994): 71–89.

Muller, Gilbert. *Nightmares and Visions: Flannery O'Connor and the Catholic Grotesque.* Athens: University of Georgia Press, 1972.

Muybridge, Eadweard. *Complete Human and Animal Locomotion: All 781 Plates from the 1887 "Animal Locomotion."* 3 vols. New York: Dover, 1979.

———. *The Human Figure in Motion: An Electro-Photographic Investigation of Consecutive Phases of Muscular Actions.* London: Chapman and Hall, 1901.

Natanson, Maurice. *The Erotic Bird: Phenomenology in Literature.* Princeton, NJ: Princeton University Press, 1998.

Newhall, Beaumont. *The History of Photography from 1839 to the Present Day.* New York: Museum of Modern Art, 1949.

———, ed. *Photography: Essays and Images.* New York: Museum of Modern Art, 1980.

North, Michael. *Camera Works: Photography and the Twentieth-Century Word.* New York: Oxford University Press, 2005.

O'Connor, Erin. "Camera Medica: Towards a Morbid History of Photography." *History of Photography* 23, no. 3 (Autumn 1999): 232–44.

O'Connor, Flannery. *Collected Works.* Edited by Sally Fitzgerald. New York: Library of America, 1988.

———. *The Habit of Being: Letters.* Edited by Sally Fitzgerald. New York: Farrar, Straus and Giroux, 1979.

———. *Mystery and Manners: Occasional Prose.* Edited by Sally and Robert Fitzgerald. New York: Farrar, Straus, and Giroux, 1969.

O'Donnell, Patrick. "Life and Art: An Interview with John Hawkes." *The Review of Contemporary Fiction* 3, no. 3 (Fall 1983): 107–26.

Orvell, Miles. "Weegee's Voyeurism and the Mastery of Urban Disorder." *American Art* 6, no. 1 (Winter 1992): 18–41.

Perl, Jed. "Not-So-Simple Simplicity." *New Republic,* 27 October 2003: 30–34.

Philips, Sandra S., Mark Haworth-Booth, and Carol Squiers. *Police Pictures: The Photograph as Evidence.* San Francisco: San Francisco Museum of Modern Art, 1997.

Picard, Max. *The Human Face.* Translated by Guy Endore. London: Cassell, 1931.

Pirenne, Maurice H. *Optics, Painting, and Photography.* Cambridge: Cambridge University Press, 1970.

Poe, Edgar Allan. "The Daguerreotype." In *Literature and Photography: Interactions, 1840–1990.* Edited by Jane M. Rabb. Albuquerque: University of New Mexico Press, 1995.

———. *Essays and Reviews.* Edited by G. R. Thompson. New York: Library of America, 1984.

———. *Poetry and Tales.* Edited by Patrick F. Quinn. New York: Library of America, 1984.

Poulet, Georges. "Phenomenology of Reading." *New Literary History* 1, no. 1 (October 1969): 53–68.

Prodger, Phillip. *Muybridge and the Instantaneous Photography Movement.* New York: Oxford University Press, 2003.

Rice, Shelley. "Essential Differences: A Comparison of the Portraits of Lisette Model and Diane Arbus." *Artforum* 18, no. 9 (May 1980): 66–71.

Ricoeur, Paul. *A Ricoeur Reader: Reflection and Imagination.* Edited by Mario J. Valdés. Toronto: University of Toronto Press, 1991.

Rideout, Walter B. *Sherwood Anderson: A Writer in America.* 2 vols. Madison: University of Wisconsin Press, 2006.

———, ed. *Sherwood Anderson: A Collection of Critical Essays.* Englewood Cliffs, NJ: Prentice-Hall, 1974.

Rogers, James, and Norman Sims. "Joseph Mitchell." *Dictionary of Literary Biography.* Vol. 185. Detroit: Gale, 1998.

Roosevelt, Franklin D. *Looking Forward.* New York: John Day, 1933.

Rourke, Constance. *American Humor: A Study of the National Character.* Tallahassee: Florida State University Press, 1986.

Ruskin, John. *Modern Painters.* Edited by David Barrie. New York: Knopf, 1987.

———. *The Stones of Venice*. 3 vols. London: Dent, 1907.

Russo, Mary. *The Female Grotesque: Risk, Excess and Modernity*. New York: Routledge, 1995.

Sante, Luc. *Evidence*. New York: Farrar, Straus and Giroux, 1992.

Sartre, Jean-Paul. *The Psychology of Imagination*. New York: Citadel Press, 1948.

Serrano, Andres. *The Morgue*. Paris: Galerie Yvon Lambert, 1993.

———. *Works 1983–1993*. Philadelphia: Institute of Contemporary Art, 1994.

Shanahan, Mary, ed. *Richard Avedon: Evidence 1944–1994*. New York: Random, 1994.

Siskind, Aaron. *Harlem Document: Photographs 1932–1940*. Providence, RI: Matrix, 1981.

Sitwell, Edith. *English Eccentrics*. New York: Vanguard, 1957.

Snyder, Joel. "Picturing Vision." *Critical Inquiry* 6, no. 3 (Spring 1980): 499–526.

Snyder, Joel, and Neil Walsh Allen. "Photography, Vision, and Representation." *Critical Inquiry* 2, no. 1 (Autumn 1975): 143–69.

Solnit, Rebecca. *River of Shadows: Eadweard Muybridge and the Technological Wild West*. New York: Viking, 2003.

Sontag, Susan. "Freak Show." *New York Review of Books*, 15 November 1973: 13–19.

———. *On Photography*. New York: Farrar, Straus and Giroux, 1977.

———. *Regarding the Pain of Others*. New York: Farrar, Straus and Giroux, 2003.

———. *Styles of Radical Will*. New York: Dell, 1978.

Stafford, Barbara Maria. *Body Criticism: Imaging the Unseen in Enlightenment Art and Medicine*. Cambridge: MIT Press, 1991.

Steele, Mike. "Visions of a Crazy World." *Minneapolis Tribune Picture Magazine*, 6 January 1974: 20–23.

Stein, Gertrude. *Selected Writings of Gertrude Stein*. Edited by Carl Van Vechten. New York: Vintage, 1972.

Stettner, Louis. "Speaking Out: Politics of Despair." *Camera 35* 17, no. 2 (March 1973): 9, 12.

———, ed. *Weegee*. New York: Knopf, 1977.

Stevens, Wallace. *Collected Poems*. New York: Knopf, 1961.

Sundquist, Eric J. *To Wake the Nations: Race in the Making of American Literature*. Cambridge: Harvard University Press, 1993.

Sylvester, David. "Flaw Show." *The Sunday Times Magazine* (London), 17 March 1974: 68–75.

Szarkowski, John. *From the Picture Press*. New York: Museum of Modern Art, 1973.

Tagg, John. *The Burden of Representation: Essays on Photographies and Histories*. Minneapolis: University of Minnesota Press, 1988.

Tannebaum, Barbara. *Ralph Eugene Meatyard: An American Visionary*. New York: Rizzoli, 1991.

Tanner, Tony. *The Reign of Wonder: Naivety and Reality in American Literature*. New York: Cambridge University Press, 1965.

"Telling It As It Is." *Newsweek*, 20 March 1967: 110.

Thomas, Ann. *Lisette Model*. Ottawa: National Gallery of Canada, 1990.

Thomson, Philip. *The Grotesque*. London: Methuen, 1972.

Tompkins, Jane, ed. *Reader-Response Criticism: From Formalism to Post-Structuralism*. Baltimore: Johns Hopkins University Press, 1980.

Townsend, Kim. *Sherwood Anderson*. Boston: Houghton Mifflin, 1987.

Trilling, Lionel. *The Liberal Imagination: Essays on Literature and Society*. New York: Anchor, 1953.

Veitch, Jonathan. *American Superrealism: Nathanael West and the Politics of Representation in the 1930s*. Madison: University of Wisconsin Press, 1997.

Vincent, Howard P. *Daumier and His World*. Evanston, IL: Northwestern University Press, 1968.

Vitruvius. *On Architecture*. Translated by Frank Granger. 2 vols. Cambridge: Harvard University Press, 1970.

Vonnegut, Kurt. *Mother Night*. New York: Harper and Row, 1966.

———. *Slaughterhouse-Five*. New York: Delacorte, 1969.

Walker, Alice. *In Search of Our Mothers' Gardens*. New York: Harcourt Brace Jovanovich, 1983.

Walton, Kendall. "Transparent Pictures: On the Nature of Photographic Realism." *Critical Inquiry* 11, no. 2 (December 1984): 246–77.

Warburton, Nigel. "Diane Arbus and Erving Goffman: The Presentation of Self." *History of Photography* 16, no. 4 (Winter 1992): 401–404.

Warner, Marina. *Managing Monsters: Six Myths of Our Time*. London: Vintage, 1994.

Wartofsky, Marx. "Cameras Can't See: Representation, Photography, and Human Vision." *Afterimage* 7, no. 9 (April 1980): 8–9.

Weegee. "Here's Fun from My Bag of Camera Tricks." *Popular Mechanics Magazine*, April 1956: 126–31, 228–36.

———. *Naked City*. New York: Da Capo, 1985.

———. "Naked Weegee." *Photograph* 1, no. 1 (Summer 1976): 2–4, 24, 26.

———. *Weegee by Weegee: An Autobiography*. New York: Ziff-Davis, 1961.

———. *Weegee's People*. New York: Duell, Sloan and Pearce, 1946.

Weegee, and Roy Ald. *Weegee's Creative Camera*. Garden City, NY: Hanover House, 1959.

Weegee, and Mel Harris. *Naked Hollywood*. New York: Pellegrini and Cudahy, 1953.

Weiss, Margaret R., ed. *Ben Shahn, Photographer: An Album from the Thirties*. New York: De Capo, 1973.

West, Nathanael. "Miss Lonelyhearts and the Lamb." *Contact* 1, no. 1 (February 1932): 80–85. New York: Kraus Reprint, 1967.

———. *Novels and Other Writings*. Edited by Sacvan Bercovitch. New York: Library of America, 1997.

Westerbeck, Colin. "Night Light: Brassaï and Weegee." *Artforum* 15, no. 4 (December 1976): 34–45.

Westerbeck, Colin, and Joel Meyerowitz. *Bystander: A History of Street Photography*. Boston: Little, Brown, 1994.

Whalan, Mark. "Dreams of Manhood: Narrative, Gender, and History in *Winesburg, Ohio*." *Studies in American Literature* 30:2 (Autumn 2002): 229–48.

Whitman, Walt. *Complete Poetry and Collected Prose*. New York: Library of America, 1982.

Wilde, Oscar. *The Picture of Dorian Gray and Other Selected Stories*. New York: New American Library, 1962.

Williams, William Carlos. *The Collected Poems*. Vol. 1. New York: New Directions, 1986.

Willis, Deborah, ed. *Picturing Us: African American Identity in Photography*. New York: New Press, 1994.

Wilson, Earl. "Weegee." *The Saturday Evening Post*, 22 May 1943: 37.

Witkin, Joel-Peter. *The Bone House*. Santa Fe, NM: Twin Palms, 1998.

———. *Forty Photographs*. San Francisco: San Francisco Museum of Modern Art, 1985.

———. *Gods of Earth and Heaven*. Altadena, CA: Twelvetrees Press, 1989.

———. *Joel-Peter Witkin*. Pasadena, CA: Twelvetrees Press, 1985.

———. "Joel-Peter Witkin," *Transcript* 1, no. 3 (1995): 43–59.

———. *Joel-Peter Witkin, disciple et maître*. Paris: Marval, 2000.

———, ed. *Harms Way: Lust and Madness, Murder and Mayhem*. Santa Fe, NM: Twin Palms Publishers, 1994.

WORKS CITED

Witkin, Joel-Peter, and Stanley B. Burns. *Masterpieces of Medical Photography: Selections from the Burns Archive.* Pasadena, CA: Twelvetrees Press, 1987.

Wood, Bret. "Photo Mortis: Resurrecting Photographs of Crime and Death." *Art Papers* 24, no. 2 (March–April 2000): 18–23.

Wood, Ralph C. *Flannery O'Connor and the Christ-Haunted South.* Grand Rapids, MI: Eerdmans, 2004.

Wright, Thomas. *A History of Caricature and Grotesque in Literature and Art.* London: Virtue Brothers, 1865.

Zhdanov, A. et al. *Problems of Soviet Literature: Reports and Speeches at the First Soviet Writers' Conference.* Edited by H. G. Scott. New York: International, 1935.

Zuckriegl, Margit, ed. *Weegee's Story: From the Berinson Collection.* Oxford, England: Museum of Modern Art, 1999.

INDEX

Washington, George, 77–78
Weegee, 2, 36, 145, 151, 154, 158, 185;
 Auto Accident Victim, 130, *131;*
 autobiography, 143; early life,
 119–20; early press work, 120–21;
 freelance work, 122–23, 125, 141;
 *Gunman Killed by Off Duty Cop
 at 344 Broome St., 126,* 126–27;
 "Here is the actual birth of a riot
 in Harlem," 138, *139,* 140; *Joy
 of Living,* 127, *128,* 129, 184–85;
 Murder at the Feast of San Gennaro,
 131–32; *Naked City,* 122–23, 124,
 132, 135, 138, 139–40, 141; *Naked
 Hollywood,* 142; *Their First Murder,*
 135, *136; Weegee's Creative Camera,*
 142; *Weegee's People,* 141–42
West, Nathanael, 76, 102, 112, 118, 145,
 176; "The Adventurer," 82–83; *A
 Cool Million,* 83–84; *The Day of the
 Locust,* 2, 85–92, 94, 129, 132, 135,
 154, 162, 184; *The Dream Life of
 Balso Snell,* 76, 82, 188; "Makers of
 Mass Neuroses," 129; *Miss Lonely-
 hearts,* 74–75, 77–78, 79–81, 95, 97;
 "Some Notes on Miss L.," 75–76;
 "Some Notes on Violence," 80–81
Westerbeck, Colin L., 135

Whitman, Walt, 166; "Song of Myself,"
 63
Wilde, Oscar, 45, 54
Williams, William Carlos, 57, 74,
 76; "At the Ball Game," 84–85;
 "Grotesque," 57, on photography,
 57–58; "Sordid? Good God!," 78;
 "Sub Terra," 57
Wilson, Earl, 134
Winogrand, Garry, 30, 47, 158, 165–66,
 170
Winters, Yvor, 76
Witkin, Joel-Peter, 184–88; *The Kiss,*
 186–87; *Las Meniñas,* 186; *Poussin
 in Hell,* 186; *Studio of the Painter
 (Courbet),* 186; *Studio de Winter,* 186
Wolcott, Marion Post, 32, 33; "Dolly
 Dimples: Personality Fat Girl,"
 33, *34*
Wood, Edward: *Glen or Glenda?,* 163
Wood, Ralph, 113

Yee, Yuben, 171

Zukofsky, Louis, 76